W9-CHI-450

A Union of Professionals

Labor Relations and Educational Reform

Charles Taylor Kerchner
Julia E. Koppich

in association with
William Ayers
Krista D. Caufman
Anthony M. Cresswell
James J. Gallagher
Byron King
Perry Lanier
LeRae Phillips
Mark A. Smylie

Teachers College, Columbia University
New York and London

Published by Teachers College Press, 1234 Amsterdam Avenue, New York, NY 10027

Library of Congress Cataloging-in-Publication Data

A Union of professionals : labor relations and educational reform /
   Charles Taylor Kerchner and Julia E. Koppich with William Ayers . . .
   [et al.].
        p.   cm. — (Professional development and practice series)
     Includes bibliographical references and index.
     ISBN 0-8077-3266-4. — ISBN 0-8077-3265-6 (pbk.)
     1. Teachers' unions — United States — Case studies.   2. Collective
   bargaining — Teachers — United States — Case studies.   3. School
   personnel management — United States — Case studies.   4. Educational
   change — United States — Case studies.   I. Kerchner, Charles T.
   II. Koppich, Julia.   III. Series.
   LB2844.53.U6U65   1993
   331.88′113711′00973 — dc20

                                                    92–43304
                                                    CIP

Printed on acid-free paper
Manufactured in the United States of America

00 99 98 97 96 95 94 93   1 2 3 4 5 6 7 8

Charles Kerchner dedicates this book to Leanne B. Kerchner . . .
teacher, wife, mother, friend.

Contents

From the Series Editor

The central task of the current reform movement in education is nothing less than building and transforming schools that are struggling to achieve democratic ideals. The purpose of the Professional Development and Practice series is to contribute to this historic transformation by presenting a variety of descriptions of practice-oriented research — narratives, stories, cases of innovative work — that can lead to a deeper understanding of educational practice and how to improve it. At this time of important educational change, we need to be informed by the special knowledge of university- and school-based educators who are working in and with the schools to illuminate how and in what ways positive change can take place.

As new organizational arrangements and collaborative relationships are being forged and studied, old enduring problems are being looked at in new ways that are leading us to fresh insights. For example, the connections between teaching, learning, and assessment are being re-examined, and views of how teachers and students develop and learn are changing toward more actively engaging them in their own constructions of knowledge. The writers in this series are attempting to involve us in a dialogue about action, participation, and change based on the best evidence. They are educators who have undertaken to struggle with the problems of practice and the challenge of rethinking the future of our nation's schools.

In this book, Charles Kerchner and Julia Koppich, with their clarity of expression and insightful discussion of the issues, involve us from the first paragraph in the changing role of the two national teacher unions in the reform movement. Presenting an unromantic, yet clearly empathic, view of the importance of unionism, Kerchner and Koppich have created what they call the "beginning text" for understanding the necessary conditions that must exist if the unions are to play a new and powerful role in helping to transform schools.

The search for the meaning of "professional unionism" is pursued in the nine contributed case studies written about unions from all over the country that are forging new collaborative, rather than adversarial, relationships with management. As they shift from the older attitudes of industrial unions, which focused solely on a win/lose mentality, to a new mode of thinking, we see how working collectively, although a seemingly simple prescription for change, is really a radical idea that affects every part of a teacher's life. The changes are *structural*: committees of all kinds involve teachers in decisions that have heretofore been solely that of management; they are *process oriented*: teachers learn to take authority and responsibility for areas as disparate as budgets, peer review, and conflict management, as well as for new approaches to teaching and instruction; and they are *personal and interpersonal*: teachers and administrators are blurring the lines of previously clearly defined management and labor positions.

Shifting bases of authority, legitimation of intellectual leadership, and a radical shift in the very meaning of collective bargaining are explored in these fascinating cases. We see the struggle, the conflict and tension, that is an inevitable part of the changing union stance, as it moves from the simpler idea of protection of due process to the more complex one of "representing teachers and representing teaching."

ANN LIEBERMAN

Acknowledgments

One acquires many debts in the course of a research project. This book would not have come to light without the extraordinary openness and hospitality of hundreds of educators — teachers, principals, unionists, and superintendents — who shared their work places and their life stories with us. We were the beneficiaries of their candor and their humor, and scores of acts of human kindness, making time for us within impossible schedules, welcoming weary travelers with fresh fruit, and recharging us with chocolate chip cookies.

This research would not have been possible without the generous support of the Carnegie Corporation of New York and the United States Department of Labor. Alden Dunham, Mary Kiely, and Karin Egan supported the grant and followed its progress at Carnegie. At the Labor Department we are particularly grateful for the assistance of H. Charles Spring, Ronald Glass, and J. Douglas Marchant in leaping tall bureaucratic hurdles. The Stuart Foundations, and particularly their president Theodore Lobman and educational officer Ellen Hershey, provided support for the Educational Policy Trust Agreement project that was the precursor to this research.

We are also grateful to those who encouraged us to take on this venture, and who encouraged others to help us: Albert Shanker, Bella Rosenberg, and Marilyn Rauth at the AFT, and Sharon Robinson at the NEA. They opened many doors for us.

A number of academic colleagues made intellectual contributions to this book, particularly Joseph Weeres (Claremont Graduate School), Susan Moore Johnson (Harvard), Michael Kirst (Stanford), Miles Myers (National Council of Teachers of English), Douglas Mitchell (University of California, Riverside), and James Guthrie (University of California, Berkeley).

While some of the collaborators in this book are visible in the text as authors of chapters or as the primary actors within those pages, others worked behind the scenes. Several Claremont Graduate School students read and commented on cases, provided analysis of the data, and helped pull together information and literature. Particularly, we recognize the contributions of Lyn Ledbetter, Linder O'Rourke, Michael Kwaitkowski, and David Quinn. Teresa Wilborn processed the text, files, and correspondence with style and grace, and CGS education faculty executive secretary Ethel Parker both read the text and programmed the schedule of the department so this work could be brought to a conclusion. Carol Gamble, Lisa Loop, and Eleanor Soulam made sure people were paid and helped us with the mountain of paper work and accounting.

Finally, Marjorie Dokken, who has been a CGS secretary and receptionist for 15 years, has announced her retirement as this book goes to press. In acknowledging her contribution to the book as well as her manifold services over the years, we disobey her strict prohibition against retirement sentiments. Thank you and keep dancing.

CTK/JEK

A Union of Professionals

Labor Relations and Educational Reform

Building The Airplane While It's Rolling Down the Runway

Charles Taylor Kerchner
Krista D. Caufman

Within these pages we view reform in public education through the lens of labor relations. The labor relations perspective is important for two reasons: Unions are powerful influences on teachers' work lives and school operations, and labor relations provide a particularly revealing outlook on educational change. Unions affect both the written contract under which teachers and administrators interact and the psychological contract through which they define themselves as workers. Widespread teacher unionism ranks among the most powerful educational policy interventions in the last half century. We expect that the emergence of the new union ideology we are now witnessing will be equally important. We call this emerging ideology *professional unionism*.

The story we tell is unfinished. The changes in labor-management relationships we describe exist in no more than a few hundred of the nation's 16,000 school districts. Despite the headlines about breakthrough contracts and the academic interest in new labor-management arrangements, the *institution* of labor relations has changed little in the past decade. Most unions and school districts still negotiate over a relatively narrow package of items. Most act as if the consequences of collective bargaining are somehow divorced from the problems of school operation and student achievement. Most simply follow patterns established by state union organizations on the one hand and management associations on the other, both of which largely support the old order. The old order is being threatened by heretics, but its resistance slows the momentum of change. So when we describe professional unionism, we engage in social forecasting. As we sketch these pioneering districts, we are creating a portrait of what can be, of how unions

and schools can operate to create workplaces of both dignity and pro-
ductiveness.

Teacher unions as we know them materialized within complex
bureaucracies that have characterized public education for the last century. Constructed from a mix of industrial-style scientific management
and Progressive Era governmental reforms, U.S. public schools have
become a maze of rules and hierarchies. Labor law and practice add
to this rule-bound atmosphere. Unions take their form and function
from the school districts where their members work. Even though they
are adversaries, unions are utterly dependent on school districts for
meaning and purpose. At their worst, unions and school districts are
two prisoners manacled together slugging it out with their free hands.
At their most productive, they are self-interested partners in a joint
civic venture.

Neither schools nor unions can change without the other changing
too. Unions are utterly incapable of empowering teachers to reorganize
schools, to impose and monitor professional standards, or to increase
student achievement except by working through the school districts.
Likewise, managements are incapable of reorganizing schools, changing their schedules, or altering the duties of employees without also
changing the labor relations contracts and work-role definitions of
teachers and administrators. Because of our industrial mind-sets and
industrial-era labor laws and ideology, we legitimated unions around a
very narrowly conceived collective bargaining system associated almost
wholly with economic advancement and procedural due process protections for employees. Because unionism has been accepted as a protection for employees, unions have been more successful in preventing
things from happening than in getting things done.

The cases in this book reveal the tandemness of labor relations
when directed toward educational reform. Unions and managements
learn to work differently, and working on reform together consequently
changes both union and management beliefs and operations.

WHAT WE DID

This book contains nine case studies taken from a larger set of 14
undertaken by Claremont Project V•I•S•I•O•N. The project began
on a stifling July day in Washington, D.C. Four thousand teachers at
an American Federation of Teachers (AFT) conference had spent three
days in animated conversation talking about how union-sponsored projects were creating educational reform. (Later that year we witnessed
similarly engrossed teachers at a National Education Association (NEA)

meeting.) With an offhand remark that someone ought to chronicle these changes and a little encouragement, the project was born.

A cab ride away at the Department of Labor, we found an appreciative but impoverished audience who took pains to explain that although the department was supposed to study cooperative labor relations, there were no funds for research — maybe next year. Inquiries to the Carnegie Corporation of New York yielded a similar response.

A two-year search for funds followed, but the wait turned out to be rewarding. Both the Department of Labor and Carnegie pledged to support the project, and the delay allowed us to gain greater perspective on the work.

During those two years, many of the reforms gained notoriety in the public press and in educational journals. There was a rosy glow about the reforms happening in places such as Rochester and Miami, and expectations for fast and painless changes started to grow. Phrases such as "turning around a school district" were heard at academic conferences, and the word "renaissance" was used unabashedly. For a while, we even believed it ourselves.

But political and social reality intervened, and we learned that there were no quick and easy fixes. The stories of change became more difficult and convoluted. "The first thing you have to realize about change," said one superintendent, "is that not everyone is crazy about it." Teachers, principals, and the public — commonly pictured as tripping the yellow brick road of reform together — were more frequently divided, confused, and angry. Reform was messy. No one had sure answers. By the end of our research process, Rochester's teacher association president, Adam Urbanski — whose reform contract initially captured the front pages — was making speeches titled "Real Reform Is Real Hard."

Doing field research as the warts and difficulties of reform appeared proved to be valuable. Through the processes of coping with these difficulties, the schools showed more of their own history and revealed a greater capacity for problem solving. They also showed the extent to which institutional change is slow, grinding, exhausting work.

Research Methods

Space in this volume does not allow us a long section on research methods. We have issued a technical report on the methods used, and it, along with the other research reports, can be ordered directly from Claremont Project V•I•S•I•O•N (ordering information at the end of the book). Here, a shorter description must suffice.

For two years, we engaged in intensive case studies of 12 school districts, ranging in size from Miami-Dade County, Florida, with more than 297,000 students, to Glenview, Illinois, with just over 3,000 students. Investigators worked with a common set of questions and data elements, but each was encouraged to follow any unique or unusual aspects of the district's story.

We set out to capture each school district and union reform experience within its own political and organizational context. We created a case outline that borrowed elements from several research traditions. Robert Yin's (1984) case study methods were used. Harry Levinson's (1972) concept of organizational diagnosis influenced our decisions about what information to collect. Lee Bolman and Terry Deal's (1991) concept of problem framing became a part of our analytic development of the cases.

In addition to allowing each of the localities to tell its own story, we wanted the authors' special skills and different backgrounds to show through. Julia Koppich and Charles Kerchner visited several cities to gain a comparative perspective on the changes. Each of the other authors brought his or her own interpretative framework — Bill Ayers's activist interpretation of the Chicago school reforms, for example — and each was encouraged to use it.

Raw material for the cases came from documents, interviews, and tours of schools. We had no standard interview schedule or invariant list of persons to talk with. The primary actors in each district were encouraged to tell their stories. Putting the cases in context demanded that we approach them from the perspective of governance and politics, organizational change, and changes in teacher and administrator work lives. Doing so involved visiting classrooms, principals' offices, school district offices, union headquarters, corporate boardrooms, and sometimes city halls and state capitols.

Document gathering was similarly situational. We gathered the information necessary to fit the framework. In addition to certain standard items, such as the labor contract, each reform generated its own stream of reports, position papers, newspaper articles, speeches, and internal district and union documents. Writing and analysis proceeded both individually and collectively. Several of the authors met at academic conferences and corresponded and worked with the principal authors.

Case Selection

Each of the cases tells the story of a locale and was chosen because it illustrates a different aspect of professional unionism, the reform process, or the varying context in which reforms take place.

- Jefferson County (Louisville), Kentucky, shows the use of intensive training and staff development as a precursor to organizational decentralization and the contractual agreements supporting it. It also illustrates the creation of a civic elite and the use of its support to undergird reform.
- Pittsburgh, Pennsylvania, illustrates a somewhat different approach to training and development and a much more centralized and highly structured set of interactions between labor and management. However, we again see the conscious development and protection of the civic coalition by both labor and management. We also see the union's explicit attempt to define professionalism and link it to teacher responsibility for quality assurance.
- Cincinnati, Ohio, shows a situation in which the union rather than the administration first raised the issues of school inadequacy, particularly inner-city failings, and activated corporate and civic participation. It shows the teachers' union in a much more volatile and at times adversarial relationship with the administration, but one aimed at reform. The Cincinnati case also illustrates the use of agreements outside the contract and the creative use of joint committees, particularly one that allocates teacher positions and other resources to schools whose enrollments change during the school year.
- Greece, New York, illustrates a continuity of change even though the union officers who created the initial breakthroughs were retired from office by the members. Surprisingly, their successors have continued and strengthened the reforms.
- Glenview, Illinois, exchanged its labor contract for a joint labor-management constitution. Still a legally binding agreement that includes wages and benefits, the new constitution restructures operations of the school district into a series of committees and incorporates the teacher union as a full operating partner.
- Dade County (Miami), Florida, started a whirlwind of reform in the midst of economic and social turbulence. Its site decision-making plan allocates substantive authority to the schools, and the Saturn Schools program encourages radical breaks with the conventional wisdom. The program in Miami has persisted despite substantial administrative turnover and deep fiscal crisis.
- Rochester, New York, has likewise entered the hard implementation phase of reform in which soaring initial expectations meet the realities of organizational change. Our view of Rochester concentrates on the political dynamics surrounding change and the difficulty of resolving issues of teacher incentives, accountability, and quality assurance.
- Toledo, Ohio, and Poway, California, illustrate the use of peer

review and assessment for teachers. Forming workable ways for unions to represent the rights and interests of their members and still advance the quality of teaching is a keystone of professional unionism.

• Chicago, Illinois, represents a situation in which the school administration and the teacher union were the objects of reform rather than its agents. The Chicago reforms of 1987 represent a radical departure from the traditional organization of public bureaucracies, and they cut across the grain of both administrative authority and union power.

WHAT WE SAW

We saw change that was simultaneously radical and conservative, incremental and pattern breaking. New schools were being built, but old schools continued to operate.

In several different cities, educators used the same words to describe what they were doing. "It's like building the plane as it's rolling down the runway," they said. At first, we were struck by the sentence's repetition in different cities. It was a wry way of putting things. Then we began to see the sentence as an apt metaphor for the reform process, including its importance and its limitations.

Like a plane taxiing down the runway, these schools were expected to take off with a full load of students and carry them to a predetermined location. But they were expected to provide a different type of flight with fewer bumps, better movies, and first-class service throughout. The schools we visited were expected to be "new and improved" in the commercial argot. Yet all the daily functions and conventional operations continued. Classes were held, bells sounded for successive periods, fights broke out in hallways, grade cards were issued, students were subjected to discipline and suspension — all the rituals and folkways associated with school continued to be acted out.

Almost all the existing structures remained in place. School boards, superintendents, central offices, state departments of education, and thousands of laws, rules, compliance mandates, court precedents, civil-rights expectations, and political realities continued. In each of the cases, schools started with existing teachers, students, and buildings. New labor relations agreements relaxed the structures, opened up the search for alternatives, and redirected resources, but the legal and structural contexts were familiar.

These schools are testing the proposition that it is possible to make systemic change gradually. Educational reform in the 1980s started with a bold rhetorical stroke, with comparisons to invasions by foreign powers and calls to arms. The National Commission on Excellence in Education, in its report *A Nation at Risk* (1983), clearly started something. Bold strokes were repeated locally in district declarations and in labor contracts heralded as breakthroughs. But the march toward changing organizational structures, politics, interpersonal behavior, and cultures is a long one that is not over yet.

Comparisons have been drawn between what is happening in schools and the development of General Motors' Saturn automobile— advertised as "a different kind of car; a different kind of car company." Indeed, the Miami-Dade schools have invoked the name Saturn Schools to describe their most radical changes.

Comparisons with the Saturn automobile venture are instructive. Like the car company, the schools we visited changed basic assumptions about how work was to be done and how quality was to be measured. And, also like the car company, public schools came up with a relatively conventional product. The Saturn is a better car, not an alternative mode of transportation. Teachers and administrators in the places we visited came up with arguably better schools, not an alternative mode of education.

The radical nature of the changes we have seen is in their capacity building, not in the immediate product. What General Motors and the United Auto Workers are learning at Saturn is a different mode of production. This mode of production may or may not have the capacity to solve the country's environmental and transportation problems. It is part of the solution to making the company competitive, but not all of it. It is developing a different ethos among production workers and a different relationship between the car company and its customers. And so it is with the schools we visited.

These schools have not changed their form and function so much as they have established processes for continual improvement. Almost uniformly, they have become more conscious of their own data. Teachers in Pittsburgh receive timely reports on student achievement in ways that are directly linked to the curriculum. In Louisville, teachers use student achievement scores or other evaluative artifacts as clues that tell them where to design new student programs. Teachers have also expanded their conception of their work, taking responsibility for school improvement. Of equal importance is the administration's recognition that joint custody of reforms is a legitimate role for teachers.

Although not immediately dramatic, the capacity for continued self-analysis and improvement constitutes radical change for public schools. Moving the ability to analyze, design, and evaluate into the schools and into the hands of people who actually see children every day represents a fundamental shift in the control and operation of American schools. Teachers are quite literally redesigning their jobs. It is impossible to visit the Eggers Middle School in Hammond, Indiana, the Martin Luther King Elementary School in Miami, or the West Ridge Elementary School in Greece, New York, without seeing teaching being redefined. Moreover, teachers are redefining the meaning of good teaching and good teachers. To watch and listen to the teachers on the peer review governing board in Poway, California, is to recognize that discussing one's craft articulately requires strong and persuasive ideas about what constitutes teaching. Only by working together with other teachers, and only by possessing responsibility for the quality of teaching, can an image of quality be spread.

Besides good work, we also saw hard work. One December morning before the sun was up, Charles Kerchner slip-slided up a hill in Pittsburgh to the Margaret Milliones Middle School. Teachers and principal were already assembled as the school's instructional cabinet. Mercifully, they had made coffee. The teachers' contract, negotiated to foster reform, included provision for common meeting and planning times, but there was never enough time. So at this school, like at scores of others, teachers and administrators extended their days. Despite general salary increases through much of the 1980s, the fact is that school reforms were largely paid for by the freewill offerings of teachers and school administrators. Teachers regularly put in hours beyond their contractual "duty days" to make reform work. They were willing to do so as long as their participation appeared to be valued and to be making a difference.

We saw a combination of enactment and definition. Professional unionism is being made up as it goes along. Embracing this idea of unionism is unlike adopting collective bargaining. Collective bargaining, and the structures of industrial unionism, were present in labor law and union practice long before they were adapted to public school settings. Professional unionism has no text. Indeed, one of the purposes of studies like this one is to establish the basis for description and policy, leading to a text of professional unionism.

What is perhaps most radical in these schools is the developing sense of freedom to try, risk, and *fail*. These teachers and principals are becoming analytic about what works and what does not. They are willing to invent and to reflect on their inventions. As Rochester's Adam Urbanski put it, "we are becoming increasingly blunt in our self-criticism." Paraphrasing Churchill, he notes that success "is moving from failure to failure with undiminished enthusiasm."

It is, of course, important to distill from the experiences of these teachers those ideas and techniques that hold promise for wider distribution. We believe that there is a growing craft knowledge around how to implement tandem union and school reforms. But the important underlying change is in the working relationship, establishing the capacity for continuing renewal.

PROFESSIONAL UNIONISM

By the time teachers entered into collective bargaining in the 1960s and 1970s, the word *unionism* largely meant industrial unionism. Older forms of worker organizations, guilds, artisan associations, and craft unions had largely been supplanted by a form of unionism designed and fitted to large hierarchies with an atomistic division of labor. It was the worker's counterpart to scientific management. Beliefs, laws, and labor-management practices were transported to public education with relatively few modifications.

We are now witnessing departures from three of industrial unionism's most cherished assumptions and central organizing concepts, which are gradually being replaced by an emerging set of beliefs about what unions should do and be (Figure 1.1). First, unions are discarding beliefs about the inherent separateness of labor and management, teaching and administration. Emphasis is moving toward a collective mode of operation exemplified by site decision making, team teaching, and district-level councils and committees. Second, unions and managements are questioning the necessity of adversarial relationships. They have come to realize that educational improvement depends on care, dedication, and commitment rather than the observance of rules and the execution of preplanned routines. Third, ideas about teacher protection are being rethought. Unions are beginning to recognize that the quality and integrity of teaching, as well as the due process rights of individual teachers, need protection. Managements see that unions have a legitimate role to play in the protection of teaching, and that evaluation and assessment are not their exclusive prerogative.

Working Together

Where industrial unionism emphasizes exclusive domains and a relationship centered around negotiating and administering a limited economic agreement, professional unionism develops wide areas of joint operations. It defines education as a collective and shared enterprise.

The simple phrases "opening up the classroom doors" or "breaking

Old Industrial Style Teacher Unionism	The Emerging Union of Professionals
Emphasizes the separateness of labor and management: • Separation of managerial and teaching work • Separation between job design and its execution • Strong hierarchial divisions Motto: "Boards make policy, managers manage, teachers teach."	Emphasizes the collective aspect of work in schools: • Blurring the line between teaching and managerial work through joint committees and lead teacher positions • Designing and carrying out school programs in teams • Flattened hierarchies, decentralization Motto: "All of us are smarter than any of us."
Emphasizes adversarial relationships: • Organized around teacher discontent • Mutual deprecation—lazy teachers, incompetent managers • Win/Lose distributive bargaining • Limited scope contract Motto: "It's us versus them."	Emphasizes the interdependency of workers and managers: • Organized around the need for educational improvement • Mutual legitimation of the skill and capacity of management and union • Interest-based bargaining • Broad scope contracts and other agreements Motto: "If you don't look good, we don't look good."
Emphasizes protection of teachers: • Self-interest • External quality control Motto: "Any grievant is right"	Emphasizes protection of teaching: • Combination of self-interest and public interest • Internal quality control Motto: "The purpose of the union is not to defend its least competent members."

Figure 1.1   Industrial vs. professional unionism

down the isolation of teaching," which are at the heart of much of the teaching reform literature, become radical prescriptions when carried into organizational life. Teaching as we know it is isolated work. Both work rules and school curriculum support a division of labor that atomizes the school. Teachers may bargain collectively, but they work separately.

Working collectively means deciding collectively what should be done and how to do it. The admonition to work together inherently challenges centralized control and hierarchical authority. Rules that previously provided order and distributed fairness become impediments to change. Instead of providing rationalization they are seen as promoting rigidity. Unions and managements have sought ways to keep orderly development and continue to promote equity and fairness while allowing teachers the flexibility to invent their own solutions.

These cases illustrate the responses to the instinct to work together. Some of the responses have been structural, such as setting up joint labor-management committees, flattening hierarchies, and decentralizing decisions. Some are process oriented, such as training and development. And some are personal and interpersonal, involving new leadership roles for teachers and site administrators. As our colleague Byron King put it, "what's mostly getting restructured are people's heads."

Joint Committees. Joint union-management committees are universal, although their configuration and mission vary markedly. In Miami-Dade, the central committee combines legislative and conventional committee functions. Some subcommittees carry out traditional and noncontroversial activities, such as a recognition day for exemplary teachers; others act as clearinghouses for issues that will find their way into the revised labor contract. Miami created a Bureau of Professionalism to carry out most of the reform initiatives and then collapsed the bureau as finances tightened. Pittsburgh has a steering committee for its Professionalism in Education Partnership with 23 subcommittees and more than 300 people involved. Under Glenview's unique labor-management constitution, much of the district's decision making on instruction, personnel, and finance takes place in three joint committees.

One of the most interesting structural inventions is the Cincinnati Teacher Allocation Committee. The committee was established in the 1985 contract to administer a pool of resources earmarked for alleviating overcrowded classes. This committee functions in the place of the traditional class-size provision of the contract, under which an enrollment increase would automatically trigger a new teacher being assigned to the school. The Allocation Committee was designed to provide a more flexible response. It can allocate additional teachers, overload pay, or instructional aides, all within a fixed negotiated budget. It has reduced friction and eliminated grievances over class size.

Decentralization to School Site.   The relationship between professional unionism and school site management is more than coincidental. To countenance school site management, by whatever name it is known, the school district devolves decisional authority to the schools. To some degree, scheduling, budgeting, and curriculum decisions become a matter for direct discussion between principals and teachers.

Keeping work rules the same from school to school is a paramount goal of industrial unionism. It establishes a common rule for all and prevents either favoritism or coercion by principals. In the process of providing official permission to make decisions at school sites, districts and unions generally allow waivers of both district rules and union contracts. Thus, the departure from centralized control challenges the union as much as management. In abandoning this norm, union leaders are saying that they trust the rank and file to defend rather than debase unionism. School superintendents are saying that they can rely on principals to craft solutions as well as to be loyal.

Site management moves unionism to the workplace. The idea of uniformity across a large bargaining unit is discarded. Just as the NEA and AFT have developed a healthy dose of union democracy (much more so than most industrial unions), the professionalization of teaching calls for moving educational decisions, including the allocation of resources, into the hands of the people who carry out the work. Site management joins the design and execution of the work. It starts to link responsibility and resources.

To watch school cadres work in Miami is to see this happen. Within limits, they decide what new positions they want, whether resources are to be spent for personnel or material, and what programs to start.

Union stewards or building representatives begin to take on new roles: monitoring the process for shared decision making rather than enforcing work rules. They engage in problem solving and assistance more than confrontation and conflict.

Decentralization obviously creates tensions. These are present in virtually every city we visited, and they are particularly evident in one school in Louisville that opted out of participative management after three years to rethink its committee structure and decision process.

Teachers and administrators in Bellevue, Washington (see Appendix) and elsewhere had difficulty with the ambiguity of authority. The more radical the decentralization, the greater the need for training and process skills. Pittsburgh followed superintendent Richard Wallace's admonition to "train, train, and train some more," but it was still not enough. Louisville and Glenview have invested heavily in process skill training. In Chicago, where the restructuring has been most radical, the union is just awakening to its role as a primary source of teacher development.

Central Office Changes. Decentralization also changes school and union central offices. In some cases, such as Louisville, school central offices change dramatically. Louisville's 155 principals report directly to the superintendent through an ingeniously crafted system of lead principals and staff designated as "lightning rods" to solve service problems. Layers of central office bureaucracy have been pointed toward service rather than monitoring and compliance. Cincinnati has cut its central office staff in half; in other cities, economic recession is hastening decentralization.

Where there has been little realignment of the central office, such as in Rochester and Pittsburgh, central office opposition to site-based changes creates tension between teacher work groups and those trying to uphold existing programs and curricula. In Rochester, former superintendent Peter McWalters reports, "I'm having trouble getting the central office to stop acting like a central office."

Training and Development. Giving schools permission to change is insufficient. People who have not managed their own affairs — and teachers are amazed to find that principals generally have not been the masters of their own fates — do not possess the skills or instincts for problem solving. As the Greece and Glenview cases illustrate, unions and school districts that enter site management have to devote substantial time and attention to the basics: how to hold meetings, how to make decisions, how to think about new ideas. The first school decisions are inevitably small ones. The progression from concern about the Xerox machine and rules for meetings to clear-eyed analysis of educational programs generally takes about three years.

Training increases the capacity of teachers and site administrators to solve problems. Two of the more notable developments occurred in the Schenley High School Teacher Center in Pittsburgh and the Gheens Academy in Louisville. Both institutions predate the watershed collective bargaining agreements in their cities, but the strong commitment to training and development is one of the reasons that site management changes have proceeded as well as they have.

Staff education contributes two needed functions to reform. First, it helps each district and union develop a language of reform and change. In Louisville, Phil Schlechty's phrase, "every leader a teacher, every teacher a leader, every student a success," has garnered a place in the district's iconography. Second, staff education expands horizons. Training academies, such as Gheens, become places where teachers and principals directly confront the literature on teaching and school reform, and where teachers ask themselves what changes need to occur in their own schools.

The national teacher unions' roles in training and development are not reflected in the cases, but should be noted here. Both the AFT and the NEA have increased their efforts at education for school restructuring and change. The AFT holds a biannual Quality Education Standards in Teaching (QuEST) conference, and the NEA holds similar national meetings on educational issues. Both unions maintain networks of teachers interested in educational reform, and the NEA has plans for a large-scale information service to connect teachers nationwide. Both organizations are attempting to break down internal organizational barriers between professional development and collective bargaining. Over the past 20 years, these have been distant and sometimes warring camps.

Teacher and Principal Leadership. Through contractual and other agreements, unions and managements have created structures in which teachers can exercise both organizational and intellectual leadership. Unions have always created leadership positions *within the unions* (the NEA's enormous council and committee structure stands as a monument to the concept that everyone who wants to lead should have something to lead), but the change we have witnessed involves unions and administrations creating leadership positions *within schools and districts.*

The new agreements also legitimate intellectual leadership. Teachers and principals are being acknowledged as experts. Teachers are writing about reform and how to do it. In Miami-Dade, Elaine Lifton, who directs the teacher development center, coauthored a school site management manual used in the district and published nationally. Terry Wyatt (Waters & Wyatt, 1985) and other teachers from Toledo have become missionaries for the peer review process. In Chicago, the craft knowledge about managerial questions such as budgeting is moving from the central office to the sites as teachers on Local School Councils come to understand the new block budgeting system.

Unions aid this process by claiming teacher intellectuals as their own and providing places for them within the union. For years, an important characteristic of union leadership was the spunk to stand up against management in public. That spunk is what differentiated union leaders from other teachers. They were assertive, often noisy, and frequently troublesome. Sometimes these leaders were the most intellectually engaged teachers, but intellectualism or teaching ability was not what gained prominence. Now, at both the national and local levels, unions have begun to recognize the leadership of teachers who distinguish themselves through pedagogy, creativity, and scholarship.

Perhaps the most difficult challenge to creating collective workplaces relates to school principals. Generally, the agenda for teacher professionalism and empowerment has created substantial tension between the teachers' union and the principals' union or association in the cities we visited. In Rochester, principals sued and lost over the proposition that the new teachers' contract was an infringement of the principals' contractual rights. In Cincinnati and in other cities, the principals' association sees the decisional empowerment of teachers as cutting into the principal-as-hero status often inferred from the literature. As Marilyn Hohmann, principal of Fairdale High in Jefferson County, put it, "You can't be too hung up about authority."

Ironically, the cases show that working together requires stronger, not weaker, leaders. It would be difficult to look at the cases of Fairdale High in Jefferson County or Bunche Park in Miami and contend that they existed in the face of weak leadership.

Bargaining for the Same Goals

Industrial unionism assumes permanent adversaries. It organizes around vigorous representation of the differences between teachers and managers. In conventional labor relations, one of the damning charges made against superintendents or union leaders is that they "sold out" or "got soft on management." Unionists and managers engage in a rhetoric of mutual deprecation. It is difficult, for example, to pick up an issue of the United Teachers of Los Angeles newspaper and come away with the impression that the L.A. school district is being competently run. Most school board or administrator association journals tend to portray teachers as shallowly self-interested and incapable of considering the true needs of students and schools.

Permanent conflict was the strategy; cooperation was only a temporal tactic. However, the assumption of constant conflict, which is part of the structure of industrial unionism, underestimates the fragility of the institution of public education. It was never believed that school districts themselves — as opposed to the regime of a particular superintendent — might be vulnerable. It was never anticipated that large numbers of people would abandon the public schools or that private alternatives would be endorsed politically. Events of the last decade prove otherwise. In this environment, it is little wonder that some of the most innovative changes in labor relations have developed in the most troubled, frequently urban school districts, where poverty and race intersect to create the truly disadvantaged and the truly angry. In both Miami and Pittsburgh, restoring confidence in public schools and attracting new students and teachers were among the initial motivators for labor relations reform.

Unfortunately, organizations cannot be improved when the perception is that the people surrounding them are ill-intentioned or inept. Moving from a unionism built around diffidence and antagonism to one built around cooperation requires mutual respect; the vehicle for antagonism must be converted into a vehicle for getting things done. Toward this end, collective bargaining changes its function and meaning in two ways. First, bargaining techniques and practices change to allow for problem solving and mutual gains. In Cincinnati and Greece, bargainers schooled themselves in new techniques; in other cities, bargaining evolved a new tone. Second, the scope of interactions drastically increases either directly in the contract or through the use of agreements outside the contract. In Miami, the contract-making process has been changed to allow easy revision. In Glenview, the contract has become a statement of mission and principles. In Poway, Rochester, and Toledo, the contract serves as an anchor for reform, but nearly all the details are covered in other documents.

Bargaining Techniques and Practices.   Bargaining becomes more of a continuous problem-solving process and less of a periodic tournament. Cincinnati and Greece have trained in a bargaining technique called "principled negotiations." In Cincinnati, bargaining was facilitated by the direct intervention of a consultant who, in effect, stage-managed the process. In Albuquerque a process facilitator helped district and union through the first critical year. A number of similar techniques have been used in other districts under different names: win-win bargaining, interest-based bargaining, collaborative bargaining. Each is an effort to use bargaining to create mutual gain rather than divide a fixed pie of resources.

Under these new bargaining techniques, contracts become viewed less as treasure troves of victories and prerogatives and more as working documents. Miami is perhaps the best example; the thick Miami contract is changed as the district and union experience reforms. Much contract writing takes place within subgroups of administrators and teachers before the opening of the collective bargaining season. The continuity of discussions, along with provisions for contract waivers, add flexibility to the contractual process and to the contract's interpretation.

In several districts, basic contracts have been settled for long periods with the expectation that the parties could make incremental adjustments without reopening formal negotiations. In Hammond, Indiana (see Appendix), the current contract runs for a decade, and in Greece, the contracts for the administrator and classified unions have no expiration date.

Broader Scope and Different Agreements. Keeping the scope of bargaining narrow is a major management objective under industrial-style bargaining. As bargaining begins to symbolize problem solving instead of a tournament in which "we bargain and they collect," management's stand reverses. Issues are brought into the labor-management arena, and labor and management simultaneously establish new arenas. Labor's long-standing belief that it isn't real unless it's in the contract is supplanted with the idea that different agreements work for different purposes.

In all the districts illustrated in this book, educational policy is a legitimate and expected subject of collective bargaining. However, the agreements reached are commonly agreements to work on the problem rather than answers that convey a property right or cement an organizational practice. Most often the contract settlement establishes the beginning of a series of problem-focused meetings between teachers and school managers rather than signaling the end of negotiations.

Agreements Outside the Contract. Practices vary on how much school reform is written into the "traditional" collective bargaining agreement. In Miami, the contract keeps the record of reform. Virtually every reform change, including waivers of the contract, is recorded in the contract itself. Other districts take a different approach. The peer review process in Toledo, for example, is triggered by a single sentence in the contract. In Toledo, as in Poway, California, negotiators created the essence of peer review away from the negotiating table.

For five years we have been guiding and watching ten school districts experimenting with educational policy trust agreements in California (Koppich & Kerchner, 1990). The idea behind the trust agreement is to deliberately create a new forum in which labor and management can meet to place resources "in trust" to be used to work on pressing educational problems. This nomenclature has been used in other districts, notably Cincinnati, as a way to develop a reform agenda.

The extracontractual agreements appear to have several effects. First, they involve a different assumption about who is supposed to benefit from labor-management interactions. Teachers do not negotiate these agreements in their private interests, and self-interest seems to be conspicuously absent in negotiations we have witnessed.

Second, the extracontractual agreements involve a new arena. Conventional bargaining proceeds according to internal rules that are inherently positional and tactical. Team leaders, bargaining chairs, and chief negotiators speak; others watch. Leaders take positions and modify them in exchanges with the other side. Information is strategic. Extracontractual negotiations have a different logic. Participants do not sit in teams; they represent a principle or a problem. They brainstorm, try out new ideas, and talk whenever they want, sometimes at great length. In short, they do not behave like disciplined bargainers.

Third, negotiations tend to be additive rather than subtractive. Most bargaining assumes a win-lose distribution of fixed resources. Even high-trust negotiations, where there is no quarrel about the resources available, are largely about reaching a just division of available resources. Extracontractual bargaining tends to be about an expanding pool of resources, a win-win relationship in which both parties can wind up better off.

This change is extremely important because most school district resources are already allocated, mostly in personnel, and the solutions to problems inevitably involve adjustment of existing allocations rather than importation of new resources. One example: At the Lassiter Middle School in Louisville, teachers voted to depart from their long practice and contractual right of a duty-free lunch period. They did so to gain additional preparation time in which they could meet in teams to plan their activities. The teachers valued their team arrangement more than they valued a free lunch period. Moreover, they found that by meeting in teams they retained one of the best features of the duty-free lunch: a time to leave the world of children for a few minutes and enter a world of adult conversation. The change did not symbolize a defeat or a take-back or giving something up, because the teachers made the decision themselves.

Why develop new structures, which are time-consuming and sometimes cumbersome? Why not simply expand the scope of agreements under the existing contract, let the union have its say, and allow management to carry out its traditional role of contract implementation? The reason lies in an important recognition about the nature of school problems: They have no known answers. If the answers were simple and straightforward, the questions could be easily reduced to writing and inserted in a contract. The process we have witnessed is substantially different. People are working on the edge, contemplating problems that have no ready solutions. Essentially, they are doing research in their own organizations. They try out solutions, contemplate them in verbal debate and in position papers, and initiate pilot tests. In almost every case they are re-creating the notion of what a school district should be and how it should work.

Contract Waivers. Contract waivers are common. Almost every school district we visited had provisions for individual schools to seek waiver of portions of the district-wide contract to craft local school plans. In Miami-Dade, schools that are a part of the School-Based Management/Shared Decision Making project can submit school plans that request variation in the union contract, school board rules, or even state law. In essence the school site plans represent a set of subsidiary work rule arrangements.

Balancing Public Good and Teacher Interest

Industrial unionism arose to protect teachers from the whims of managerial and political behavior and to advance teachers' interests. Professional unionism is called upon to balance teachers' legitimate self-interests with the larger interests of *teaching* as an occupation and *education* as an institution.

Just as political scientists and economists have increasingly recognized the necessity of institutions that act beyond self-interest (Mansbridge, 1990), unionists and managers have come to recognize that they hold public as well as private-interest responsibilities. As Pittsburgh Federation of Teachers president Albert Fondy notes, "If there are problems in the school system, and the union is strong, then the union is responsible either for the fact that the problems exist in the first place, or at least responsible for the fact that they are not being addressed."

Making the leap to public interest profoundly complicates the job of teacher unionists. Teacher unionists must attend to the advance of the profession without appearing to disregard their memberships. Teachers in Greece, New York, turned out their union president because he appeared too distant from the rank and file and spent too little time "minding the store." Interestingly, Richard Bennett's electoral defeat did not portend an end to the union's involvement in educational reform.

Part of the conflict between representing teachers and representing teaching is resolved by declaration — an announcement that the union will defend the quality of teaching in the district. As Fondy puts it, "A union is not conceived with the primary mission of protecting the least competent of its members."

Nowhere is the movement toward representing both teachers and teaching seen more clearly than in the union's embrace of peer review and other forms of teacher participation in the evaluation of other teachers.

Peer Review.   Not every district in our study has embraced peer review. Some union leaders remain opposed to the practice on the grounds that it breaks down teacher solidarity and cooperativeness, but in every district we visited, some form of coaching and intervention is taking place. Teachers' unions have become *organizationally* responsive to the quality of other teachers' work.

Peer review is interesting because we can pinpoint where and when it started: Toledo, 1981, with a one-sentence reference in the contract that cemented an agreement under which teachers agreed to police the ranks of their veterans in return for the right to review new teachers. Since then, peer review has spread widely among progressive districts within the AFT, and the Toledo idea has been examined seriously in scores of other locations. The NEA still officially opposes peer review, but teachers in a number of districts have begun to engage in less judgmental forms of peer coaching and assistance. Louisville, Glenview, and Greece have such programs.

Peer review changes both the substance and the symbolism of teacher evaluation and assessment. The concept of teachers making substantive judgments about the quality of teaching places them in a new social and intellectual position. For such an idea to emerge from labor relations suggests a vastly different viewpoint about the function of unions. Traditionally, unions are built on internal cohesion: solidarity. Placing a union member in a position of judgment over another violates the existing norms of solidarity, and many unionists believe

that it will wreck the organization. But peer review has not wrecked
the unions that practice it, because teachers have a deep understanding
of the dualism of their professional and personal interests.

Still the symbolism is clouded. In Pittsburgh the evaluative work
of teachers was seen as administrative work rather than an expansion
of teaching work. The existing social system was so rigidly divided
into teacher and administrator castes that when teachers took on roles
formerly played by administrators, they were perceived as "little administrators" rather than as teachers doing professional work.

One union leader asked, "What's the big deal about peer review;
it's just teachers carrying out the same lousy evaluation system that
administrators used." This comment misses the important symbolism of
teachers taking on peer roles, but more importantly, it is wrong on
its face. The evaluation system *is* changed by teacher involvement.
Sometimes these changes are explicit, as in Miami, where teachers and
administrators negotiated, outside the contract, a new evaluation format and training for administrators and teachers in how to use it. But
the more interesting change has taken place gradually within the process of evaluation itself. No administrative system that we are aware of,
even in the days before collective bargaining, has been able to sustain a
substantive program of formative assistance for new teachers or a system of intervention for senior teachers whose performance has deteriorated to the extent that they were in danger of losing their jobs. These
systems exist today because the union and supporters within the administration were able to sequester funds to support the activities and protect the activity from other claimants. In Toledo, the teacher union
threatened a strike to preserve funds that supported the peer review
system.

In establishing and protecting funds for peer review and evaluation, these districts have developed new norms of caring for novice
teachers. Not only are new teachers evaluated, they receive scores of
hours of formative help. And teachers are willing to vote to fire other
teachers because they have been given the means to help them succeed.

Symbolism meets substance when teachers are dismissed for bad
teaching. Tenure statutes predated teacher unions, and unionism has
not changed the rules of dismissal very much. But unions do provide
teacher advocates, field representatives and lawyers, who understand
the burden of proof the school district has to meet for dismissal.

The question is not whether unions have protected incompetent
teachers. Certainly they have on occasion. Unions point to obvious flaws
in districts' dismissal cases, such as years of satisfactory performance ratings during a period in which a teacher was supposedly going to seed.

Union representatives, like lawyers, even get pleasure out of winning these contests. At one level it *is* a game. Drubbing management is fun.

Some union representatives have always stepped outside their advocacy roles. More than a few teachers have been counseled in union offices to get out of the classroom, and more than a few union leaders have moderated the extent to which they defended teachers whose performance was notorious. However, it is a different situation when a union's role in evaluation is made explicit.

In Miami and Rochester (as in Toledo, Poway, and elsewhere), peer review is connected to intervention: Teachers are responsible for assisting new teachers or veterans who are having difficulty. The record of those interventions becomes admissible evidence in disciplinary or dismissal hearings, showing that attempts at remediation and progressive discipline have been made. In Pittsburgh and some other cities, the labor contract specifies that peer observations can be used in dismissal hearings.

Teachers gain authority within the evaluation process. In Toledo, Poway, and other districts that have adopted peer review, teachers have enormous influence over who becomes a second-year teacher. Theirs is the dominant voice. But in no case do they have unfettered authority to fire a teacher. In every case we have seen, the peer review process is a formal recommendation to the school superintendent and the board. But as is the case with tenure reviews in colleges and universities, top administrators and boards nearly always accept these recommendations, overturning them at their own peril. The system expects teacher recommendations to be given great weight.

Rules about Conflict.   Managing conflict and decision making within the new coalition requires a departure from old modes of behavior that have been particularly beneficial to unions. Verbally thrashing the management and trashing the school district—a historic troop-rallying tool of unions—has become a dangerous undertaking. Continued coalition support requires a belief that the schools are making progress.

None of the districts we visited has had a strike during the reform period. Although we do not believe that union participation in reform makes overt labor conflict impossible, it appears to change the rules for carrying it out. Straightforward economic disagreements are possible and allowable, and a straightforward economic strike may be permissible, but activities that block progress on educational issues are highly suspect.

Consensual decision making has emerged as a decision style designed to support reform. Consensus, which is the rule in many school site management plans, is designed to prevent sabotage of decision implementation. When applied to community-level decisions, it means that decisions cannot be the product of a minimum winning coalition; efforts toward finding common ground are required. The political system appears to punish those who play by other rules. In two cities, dissident school board members, who are perceived as representing single interests, are being targeted for electoral opposition. Opposition candidates are supported by both business and teacher unions.

CONCLUSION

Together, these cases trace the outlines of a worker organization designed to fit the unique characteristics of teachers' work lives and the demands of public school settings. They tell us what a union of professionals believes, what one does, and, most importantly, that such an organization is possible. The school districts and unions you will read about all face the gritty urban reality that characterizes our times. Some are in central cities where the politics of race, class, poverty, and despair are most acute.

People who work in these schools, and those who lead movements attempting to reform them, need to believe that their efforts can produce change. This need is deeply psychological for those personally engaged in reform and highly informational for school reformers in general. In the beginning, those who would undertake such a venture need convincing proof that reform is possible — tangible proof that change can take place. As time passes, they need to understand that effective change is grindingly difficult work that requires a long haul. As a student wrote recently, "coming up with the ideas isn't so hard, but getting the job done is a bitch."

These schools have not "broken the mold." They are changing the mold's contours from the inside. They are building schools that are less centralized and more democratic. They are becoming more conscious of the need for continual assessment of learning and teaching practices. They have invested themselves in the infrastructure of educational change in functioning schools. They are, in their own words, rebuilding the airplane as it's rolling down the runway.

REFERENCES

Bolman, L. G., & Deal, T. E. (1991). *Reframing organizations: Artistry, choice, and leadership*. San Francisco: Jossey-Bass.
Koppich, J., & Kerchner, C. (1990). *Educational policy trust agreements:*

Connecting labor relations and school reform, annual report. Berkeley: Policy Analysis for California Education.

Levinson, H. (1972). *Organizational diagnosis.* Cambridge, MA: Harvard University Press.

Mansbridge, J. J. (Ed.). (1990). *Beyond self-interest.* Chicago: University of Chicago Press.

National Commission on Excellence in Education (1983). *A nation at risk: The imperative for educational reform, a report to the secretary of education* (226006 ed.). Washington, DC: U.S. Department of Education.

Waters, C. M., & Wyatt, T. L. (1985). Toledo's internship: The teachers' role in excellence. *Phi Delta Kappan, 66*(5), 365–68.

Yin, R. K. (1984). *Case study research.* Beverly Hills: Sage.

2

Louisville

PROFESSIONAL DEVELOPMENT DRIVES
A DECADE OF SCHOOL REFORM

Charles Taylor Kerchner

Our journey into educational change and restructuring begins just down the road from Churchill Downs. Louisville (Jefferson County), Kentucky, is a logical starting place, because it typifies established ideas about progress and alliances between communities and schools. Louisville is a city with a relatively tight and unified elite. As one observer put it, "If you want to get something done [in this city], there are six or seven people you have to involve." By gaining the backing of the community elite, the district and union have been able to implement reforms relatively free from external pressures. The dampening of public conflict has made internal changes relatively risk free for the teachers and administrators who try them. Under these circumstances, "little tries" can accumulate into something big.

Louisville has shaped staff development into a spearhead of reform. What is often considered a school district's least influential activity has become its most powerful. The visible symbol of this reform is the Jefferson County Public Schools (JCPS)/Gheens Professional Development Academy, which provides a safe haven for teachers and administrators to read, think, and challenge their prior assumptions about schools and their operations. Gheens Academy, along with a powerful superintendent and a progressive teacher union, have become the keystones for business partnerships, central office restructuring, and a site-based management plan.

25

THE LOUISVILLE CONTEXT

The Jefferson County Public Schools were formed in a shotgun marriage of the city and county school systems following a 1975 desegregation order. It became the nation's seventeenth largest school system, enrolling approximately 91,000 students in 160 schools. For the last decade, approximately 30 percent of the student population has been African-American. Tension, hostility, and "white flight" followed the court order, accompanied by a growing sense that the school district was in shambles. The Jefferson County Teachers Association (JCTA), a National Education Association (NEA) affiliate, mirrored teachers' discontent and frustration during the middle and late 1970s. Tremendous disruption followed the desegregation order, which also required staffs to be racially balanced. Teachers felt lost, as if their voices were not being heard.

Today, with about 11,000 employees and 5,400 teachers, the school system is the second largest employer in Jefferson County. In recent years, the district has hired approximately 200 to 400 teachers annually. About 22 percent of the teachers are African-American — enough to make the school district the largest employer of college-educated African-Americans in the state.

School politics in Louisville is largely elite, quiet, and middle-of-the-road. The district, which does not seem to have vocal, credible critics, has become part of a civic renaissance.

Board membership has changed almost totally during the last decade, but there has been remarkable political stability around the consensus that the school district is moving ahead. Superintendent Donald Ingwerson is known for making repeated adjustments in an idea until a workable consensus emerges.

This seemingly placid political picture masks enormous activity. Ingwerson described his management style thus: "Just because the duck looks calm doesn't mean he isn't paddling like hell under water."

TURNING POINTS

The story of change and development in Louisville is marked by five crucial events: (1) the district's formation, in 1975, as a step toward racial integration; (2) the 1981 arrival of Donald Ingwerson as superintendent; (3) the 1983 initiation of the Gheens Academy for staff development; (4) the negotiation in 1988 of a teachers' collective bargaining contract calling for participative management; and (5) the state supreme court's 1989 declaration that the state's school finance and operations laws were unconstitutional.

1975: School Integration and Consolidation

A 1975 U.S. District Court integration decision required that by September of that year, all schools in the county reflect a 70 percent white, 30 percent black student balance. Staffs were also to be balanced. Students were bused, teachers were transferred, and many parents abandoned public schools for private ones. Relations at some of the newly integrated schools were tense.

However disruptive it may have been at the time, the merger of the city and county school systems and the busing plan for racial balance gave suburban white families substantial incentives for concern about the quality of education in inner-city neighborhoods. Their children were now in the same financial and educational boat as black students, and they would certainly share classrooms for at least part of their school years.

1981: Ingwerson's Arrival

When Ingwerson arrived on the job in 1981, he faced a business community that was ready to publicly renounce the school district. His first tense meeting with 400 business representatives resulted in an agreement to find out how Louisville stood in relation to cities of comparable size. When the data were in, Louisville was not at the top of the heap, but not at the bottom either. More important, by responding to their challenge, the new superintendent had forged the beginnings of a working relationship with the civic elite.

In 1982, the Jefferson County Public Education Foundation was formed. Spurred by a consultant's advice about the link between information technology and the region's economic development, the public schools and the foundation invested heavily in computer labs at each school. School and business partnerships, now numbering 600, were begun with organizations as diverse as the Junior League and the Louisville Gas and Electric Company. By 1989–90, contributions totaled $9.6 million. The civic partnerships represented a way of demonstrating to the public that the district was making progress, and business involvement became an indication of progress in its own right.

1983: The Founding of Gheens Academy

The JCPS/Gheens Professional Development Academy venture was another sign that the school district was moving ahead, and it provided an organizational home for school development. Gheens fostered what Ingwerson called "a transparent umbrella," a common language, and a repeated belief system telegraphed by the motto, "Every leader a teacher, every teacher a leader, every student a success."

Much attention has been paid to communicating this belief system, and in this Gheens found a master in its first executive director, Phillip Schlechty. A self-described fast-talking Southerner, Schlechty possesses an unusual ability for synthesizing and communicating ideas to teachers and administrators. His earlier work (Schlechty & Whitford, 1983) had convinced him that staff development could be legitimized by school goals and that staff development activities could be an incentive for reform. Schlechty's philosophy has subsequently been given added status among the principals by Terry Brooks, Gheens' current director.

One clear characteristic of Louisville is that reform is not contained in a single program. Both at Gheens and at the schools, there is a whirlwind of reform in what at first appears to be confusing and chaotic innovation. However, a reform effort that encourages the initiation of many programs sends two signals to schools and teachers.

The first signal is captured in Schlechty's phrase "little tries"—the idea that significant change comes about through many small changes. Individually, the changes need not be particularly heroic or radical, but the combined effect is significant. And making many changes insulates schools from the accusation that any single change has failed. Allowing schools, teacher teams, and individuals to initiate new programs creates broad responsibility and widespread psychological commitment.

The second signal sent by the multiple-change approach is that of great freedom at the school sites. No central body reviews or approves a reform plan; schools opt into reform by faculty vote, and they can opt out the same way.

Although Gheens Academy has had many activities, its largest single innovation was the idea of Professional Development Schools. The venture started in 1986 as a way to create "teaching hospitals" for education, places where best practices would be exemplified and new teachers socialized (Olson, 1989). To be exemplars of best practice, Professional Development Schools would have to depart substantially from classic bureaucratic management and structure. Schools would have to reinvent themselves rather than point with pride to their past.

1988: The Participative Management Contract

In 1988 the Jefferson County Teachers Association negotiated a contract that spread the site management ideas begun in the Professional Development Schools and legitimated the concept in the eyes of many teachers. In all respects but one, the contract appeared to be a normal collective bargaining agreement. That one difference was Section K of the employee rights article of JCTA Agreement 1988–90, where innocuous-sounding words placed the union squarely in the school reform business. Section K began, "Both Parties to this Agreement endorse participatory management at the school level."

The contract specified some of the structures of site management: Two-thirds of the employees at the school had to vote by secret ballot to participate, deviations from the contract were allowed if approved by vote, and representatives to site-based management committees (if the site chose to have a committee) were to be elected by the employees at the school. The contract called for a district union-management oversight committee to resolve problems, but that committee was not particularly burdened, and it did not function as a board of control or central planning agency.

June Lee, past president of the JCTA, said that one surprise in the 1988 contract negotiations was the district's receptivity to the union's site management proposal. According to Lee, the district wanted to put it into effect at all the schools right away, but the two parties eventually negotiated a graduated plan for 24 schools the first year, 48 the second, and 96 the third.

The significance of the union's role in instituting school-based management depends on viewpoint. To one administrator, the contract change "mostly legitimated that which went on before." However, for some, Section K changed the meaning of labor relations altogether. One teacher remarked, "June Lee is a hero in this district. We fought hard for the things in that contract, and teachers are cautious about doing things that would undermine it. If June says that making changes in the contract in order to develop programs at the school is okay, then it's fine with me." The role of union leadership had moved from one of creating and enforcing work rules to one of being an agent for organizational renewal.

1989: Statewide School Finance and Structure Reform

The Louisville reforms helped set the statewide pattern of change in the monumental Kentucky Educational Reform Act of 1990. In November 1985, 66 poor, mostly rural school districts went to court alleging that the schools as constituted failed to provide the constitutionally required "efficient system of common education throughout the state." Annual tax support differences as large as $1,200 per student were cited. In June 1989, the Kentucky Supreme Court ruled the entire state public school system unconstitutional, declaring, "This decision applies to the entire sweep of the system — all its parts and parcels." Some 700 statutes fell.

Besides tax equalization, the 1990 reform act ushered in a new structure for the state's school system and new ideas about what education should be. Curriculum scope and sequence requirements were swept away, ungraded primary schools were ushered in, and school-based management became the law. The new Kentucky law also expanded statewide the idea of investment in education. To pay for the changes, the General Assembly increased the state sales tax from five to six cents on the dollar, raised the corporate income tax by one percent, eliminated the federal income tax deduction on state tax returns, and made Kentucky's tax code conform with the federal code.

TEACHER-DISTRICT LABOR RELATIONS

Louisville is a union town in a state that is generally hostile to unionism. Kentucky has no educational collective bargaining law. A lower court decision held that teachers cannot bargain, but Jefferson County bargains anyway — a reflection of the union's political strength. Agency shop is illegal for public employees in Kentucky, but 4,700 of the district's 5,400 teachers pay dues, and the union has an annual budget of about $500,000.

The union is politically active in school board elections. Five of the seven serving board members were endorsed by the JCTA. None of the current board members is considered an implacable foe of the union.

There have been two strikes. The first, in 1976, clearly symbolized the union's new-found aggressiveness. Teachers refused to ratify a contract, and the school board refused to return to the bargaining table. June Lee, president-elect of the union, responded by leading 4,000 teachers in a protest at the education center. Bargaining resumed and then broke down, and there was an 11-day strike — in effect, a recognition strike.

Since 1976, there has been only one other job action, a one-day strike over wages in 1979. June Lee served her term as JCTA president and went on to become president of the Kentucky Education Association. In 1987 she again became president of the Jefferson County association, an office she vacated in June 1991. During her term, she made a determined effort to change labor relations.

June Lee's retirement as president in 1991 might well have brought on a backlash, antireform presidency. But the new president, Bettie Weyler, who had served as Lee's vice president for four years, is strongly identified with reforms and is moving to strengthen and expand them. The union's reform agenda faces no active opposition among union staff or the elected executive board.

According to Steve Neal, JCTA's executive director, the participative management changes and the organizational elements that have been crucial to the success of the union's reform movement are:

1. The district puts $300,000 into school-based management, giving each school between $2,500 and $3,000 for released time and other process costs of the program.
2. JCTA and Gheens Academy representatives jointly train teachers and managers.
3. Participative management is anchored in a document, the contract, which gives teachers grievance recourse against any principal who tries to undermine the participative management approach.
4. Each program sunsets at the end of the year and has to be revoted by the faculty.
5. Voluntary participation is stressed, and support is broad-based.
6. There are virtually no rules about the subjects of joint decision making or school programs.
7. Through the Gheens Academy, linkages are formed across schools.
8. The union, through the *Action* newsletter, and the superintendent, through an interdistrict communication called *Monday Memo*, keep lines of internal communication open.

THE REFORM PROGRAMS

The changes in Louisville's labor relations are played out largely within three major reform programs: Gheens Academy, participative management, and a flattened hierarchy that is unique to Louisville.

Operations and Programs of Gheens Academy

Two years after coming to Jefferson County, Superintendent Ingwerson was approached by the Gheens Foundation, a legacy of a local family, which was interested in assisting the school system. The first

$5 million in Gheens Foundation grants came in 1983, just after the psychological downwash caused by the *Nation at Risk* report (National Commission on Excellence in Education, 1983). The school district renovated a closed elementary school, and Phillip Schlechty was hired as Gheens Academy's first executive director.

Although Schlechty brought entrepreneurship and national visibility, it is Terry Brooks, the current director and deputy superintendent, who gave the new venture status and legitimacy among principals. Brooks had spent most of his career within the district as a respected teacher and middle school principal. He brought to his job at Gheens Academy years of association with teachers and principals, many of whom he had mentored.

Setting as Strategy.   Gheens Academy works partly because it looks like a place for adults. Although it is not plush, it is sparkling clean and attractive. The facility has an auditorium with comfortable seats, seminar rooms with chairs that fit adult backs and bottoms, and a seemingly endless supply of coffee, soft drinks, and cookies. The facility announces itself as a place where teachers and administrators are welcome. The building also announces the district's commitment to development. The district's professional library, which rivals the education collection at a small college, is housed at Gheens, as are the curriculum resources center, the Exceptional Child Education Center for special education, and the district's computer education facility. Facilities are open in the late afternoons and evenings so that teachers can easily use them after school.

Creating an adult setting instead of a laboratory or demonstration school was part of the Gheens strategy. The idea was to create both physical and psychological space in which teachers and principals could take on strategic planning roles and momentarily set aside the rush of daily activities.

Evoking Systemic Change.   Gheens Academy is not a teacher or principal center or a district in-service education center. Gheens encourages the *entire* adult decision-making body of the school to spend time together on an equal footing in pursuit of ways to increase school effectiveness.

Gheens Academy *allows* symbolic changes to take place. No school was ever ordered to innovate, no curriculum mandate was ever developed, no common teaching format was created. Most of the training involves organizational process work or expanding educational horizons for teachers and administrators. The academy seeks to be a way to *invent* excellent schools rather than simply to identify and teach promising practices (Schlechty, Ingwerson & Brooks, 1988).

Gheens has several major programs and a bulletin board of activities each week. Although the academy has long-term objectives, it achieves them through short-term programs. For example, 11 high schools are members of the Coalition of Essential Schools, a program to deepen the curriculum and strengthen relations between teachers and students. Eighteen middle schools participate in the Middle Grades Assessment Program. The academy has also grown to include a joint project with the University of Louisville that allows principals and teachers to attend national and regional conferences and supports innovation at schools.

Twenty-five schools take part in Learning Choices, a U.S. Department of Education-supported program in which cross-school teams of teachers enrich the curriculum in various areas, including math and science. Wheatley Elementary has developed full-fledged science labs, an environmental courtyard, and a small zoo. Englehard, Shelby, and Breckenridge Elementaries are developing math and science magnet programs to feed into the Meyzeek Middle School math, science, and technology specialization. The 24 Professional Development Schools are actively searching for a "new paradigm, a new way of thinking about schools" (Gheens Foundation, 1988).

As free-form and responsive as its programs are, Gheens has consciously stayed away from organizational and curriculum maintenance activities—such as redoing a curriculum just because it happens to be the year for textbook adoption. In a system whose hallmark is decentralized site management, Gheens has actually recentralized some staff development resources, combining little $100 caches of staff development money sitting around at individual school sites into meaningful amounts of money at the academy.

In sum, Gheens Academy has taken what has historically been the weakest operation in urban school districts—staff development—and turned it into the centerpiece of an effort to change schools. It has done so by bringing together what would otherwise be scattered resources; creating a physical and professional environment where teachers, administrators, and classified staff feel welcome and appreciated; and offering programs that are interesting and intellectually substantive.

Participative Management, Louisville Style

Jefferson County school-based management is held together by board-adopted district goals, the programs initiated at Gheens Academy, and the will of the superintendent. The goals are very general ones—academic growth, shared decision making, innovative leadership, positive student environment, accountability, and efficiency—but they serve as a touchstone and a way for the school board to preserve a basic identity for the district.

Entry into any particular program is voluntary and nonjudgmental. However, an administrator who fails to understand the direction in which the school district is moving places his or her tenure at risk. Although Louisville is a "many chances" school district and the word *failure* has been virtually banned from conversation, principals say that Ingwerson can be quite firm about performance. Several principals took early retirement in the face of the reforms, and several central office administrators and principals have been reassigned.

Louisville's style of site management is shown in the stories of three schools: Byck Elementary, Lassiter Middle, and Fairdale High. These schools are not academically elite, magnet, or specialty schools. They are not in affluent neighborhoods, and their students' test scores are not at the top of the charts. They are among the district's restructuring stars: in Louisville parlance, "good schools getting better." They represent the direction in which Louisville is heading.

As distinctive as each school is, however, a number of common characteristics of school-based management emerge:

1. *In each school, the initial reform emerged from the immediate concerns of teachers.* People describing these schools' histories smile with amusement at how small the first steps were, but they are adamant about the logic and wisdom of small first tries. The lesson appears to be that you can't force people to undertake reforms that are larger than they can conceive of or that they think they are incapable of achieving. Be patient—vision and scope increase over time.

2. *No school explicitly forbids any topics.* This is not to say that there are not implicit limits. Teachers in Louisville approach the job of dividing scarce resources very gingerly. But few rules prevail.

3. *The nature of leadership by the school principals is different.* Principals are expected to develop, not to announce, the vision and mission of their schools. Principals say that they hold back so that ideas can emerge from the faculty and a consensus can form around decisions. Some report that they have implemented decisions they would not have chosen. Faithful implementation of school committee decisions is a distinguishing characteristic of school-based management.

4. *Consensus decision making is becoming the norm.* Not everyone assembled agrees with every decision, but everyone *consents* to it.

5. *Teachers and administrators give free gifts of their time to make*

the system work. Without question, reaching consensus is slower than giving orders, and committee work is more time-consuming than solo decisions.

6. *There is what one respondent termed a "flag and apple pie" vision about undertaking reform in the name of student success.* Reforms are not being undertaken to make educators' jobs more pleasant. "The union has never talked about participative management as just making life nicer for teachers," said Brooks.

These principles inform developments at all three of the following schools and characterize the whole of Louisville reforms.

Byck Elementary. The Dann C. Byck Elementary School enrolls 650 students in an old, poor Louisville neighborhood on the west side. Students from a somewhat more affluent neighborhood are bused in as part of the district's racial balance integration plan, but 83 percent of the students still qualify for free or reduced-cost lunches. Matt Benningfield, Byck's principal for 28 years, has well-established reformist credentials.

Byck's story is unusual because its faculty was one of the first to vote itself into participative management (PM). In spring 1991, however, it narrowly voted itself out after three years in the program. Benningfield saw the decision to leave participative management more as a chance to reflect and regroup than as a rejection of the idea. Still, the teacher vote sent waves of surprise through the district and the union.

Stephany Hoover, a second-grade teacher and former chair of the school's steering committee, described the experience:

> Participative management is like having a little child. During the first year, it's cute, everyone likes it, and you like to show it off to strangers. But then you hit the terrible twos. That was where we were. The kid starts to act up and throw tantrums. At the end of the school year we had what everyone calls "the faculty meeting from hell." Everyone was angry, and we still can't quite figure out why. We quickly decided that we hadn't mastered the participative management business yet, and we sent a group of people to Gheens to work on consensus decision making.

During its three years in PM, Byck — like other schools — started by making easy decisions. In the first year, the biggest decision was where to put the copy machine, and during the second year the committee worked on what it called staff perks. In the third year, teachers took on more substantive programs, such as personnel and resource allocation.

The whirlwind of reform that characterizes activities at Gheens Academy is also present at Byck. The school presents parents with choices of many different instructional programs. In addition, with corporate cooperation, Byck has established an in-school, student-run Kmart.

The participative management program has given rise to a score of teacher initiatives in the classrooms. Byck teachers created a four-teacher, cross-age team to encourage students from kindergarten to grade 5 to work and learn together. Two other groups of teachers created interdisciplinary teams at the third- and fourth-grade levels. Two first-grade teachers and their assistants knocked down the wall between their classrooms, creating an open-space learning environment for small homogeneous groups.

None of these programs is unique. But each is a local invention — a "little try" — that gives teachers ownership of an academic enterprise. Not all the programs follow the same pedagogical assumptions. Some involve increasing the homogeneity of teaching groups; others do the opposite. Some involve intensifying instruction in basal text-driven instruction; others discard texts. The common thread among the programs is that they seem to elicit high levels of commitment from the teachers who originated and operate them.

Principal Benningfield looks at the respite from PM as a time for regrouping: "We'll have a time to reconsider this, and [I] wouldn't be surprised if we rejoined."

Lassiter Middle.   Lassiter Middle School is located in southwestern Jefferson County in what is primarily a white working-class neighborhood. The school enrolls 730 students in grades 6–8; about 75 percent are white and 25 percent black. Approximately 50 percent of the students qualify for free or reduced-cost lunch.

Lassiter was one of the original Professional Development Schools and is also one of the 24 schools taking part in the NEA's national Mastery in Learning project. Like Byck, Lassiter has undertaken numerous program innovations: multiage teams, a new student lounge, teacher-based guidance, a dropout prevention program, conflict resolution training, an attendance incentive program, cooperative learning, and peer tutoring.

Lassiter adopted participative management the first year and grafted PM onto an already complex organizational structure and a history of teacher participation. The school had previously added a seventh period to its daily teaching schedule, in violation of contractual language calling for no more than 25 teaching periods per week. "We've not had a grievance at this school since I've been here," said Fred Harbison, in his fourth year as principal. And if any teacher had indicated that a grievance would be filed over the seven-period day, then "that program would have gone." In addition, teachers had voted to give up their duty-free lunch period so that teams could plan together.

We asked teachers why they were willing to teach more classes and give up their free lunch periods. Their universal answer was that in the larger scheme of things, their sacrifices didn't matter very much. The larger scheme of things was the development of a new-style middle school built around teacher teams that planned and coordinated learning for a group of approximately 120 students. These teams are the fundamental organization of instruction at Lassiter. They vary in their academic emphasis and teaching style, but they have in common the fact that they were teacher invented.

Participative management at Lassiter is coordinated by a steering committee, which includes a representative from each academic team, two administrators, representatives from Gheens Academy, two students, three parents, and a representative from the office, custodial, or cafeteria staff. However, all meetings are open, and *any staff member attending has voting privileges*. The steering committee chair is elected from the members, and decisions are made by consensus.

One effect of participative management has been to create a situation in which teachers perceive how the entire school works. "It makes me question more than it used to," said one teacher. "We began to realize how connected things are . . . how setting up multiage teams affects the flow of students into other grade-level teams. It forces you to get involved in the workings of the school."

Still, teachers are not totally comfortable with putting power in the hands of other teachers. Part of the uneasiness is summed up in one teacher's comment: "It's new." There is also some trepidation about trusting the judgments of other teachers. Another teacher contemplated the growing role that PM will have in budgeting, saying, "It's a sobering thought to know that other teachers will tell me what my budget for next year will be."

So far, the most substantive thing the committee has done is to work on the school's goals. These goals were an explicit PM decision, and some teachers see these macro-level decisions as the most important contribution. "We don't want to run the school on a daily basis, but we want to be in on the big decisions about direction." Building trust was a continuing theme among teachers and administrators as they described the PM process.

Fairdale High.   Fairdale High School is also in southwestern Jefferson County. The surrounding town is a tightly knit working-class community; it is a separate municipality, semirural, and mostly white. During the early days of school integration, National Guard troops were called on to keep the peace. Now, enrollments are racially balanced: approximately 70 percent white and 30 percent black among the school's 1,200 students. Most of the black students are bused from other parts of the county.

The local economy has also changed radically. The loss of factory jobs has caused real economic suffering, which is one of the motivators of change at the school. Historically, the community valued Fairdale High more for its athletic teams than for its academics. The Fairdale Bulldogs still win, but part of the Fairdale story is a conscious turn toward building support for academic quality tied to a changed workplace.

Fairdale can accurately be called a turnaround school. Principal Marilyn Hohmann recalls, "When I was brought in, the superintendent told me that things needed to change." The change process began in 1986 with membership in the Gheens Academy Professional Development Schools group. One of the first things the school realized was that it did not know much about itself. "No one had ever given [evaluation] information to teachers; their perception was that we were doing OK," Hohmann said.

As part of a self-study, ten teachers followed ten children through a school day. When it was over, teachers said things like, "It was boring," or, "You know, this isn't a very humane place to be." Another teacher reported that no adult had spoken to the child she was following the entire day.

Another activity that brought teachers together was reading about education and teaching. The teachers who went to Gheens Academy read and began to trade articles from *The Kappan, Educational Leadership,* and *Education Week.*

Even before participative management was initiated at Fairdale, the teachers started changing things. In 1987 a steering committee consisting of elected teachers, students, administrators, support staff, and parents adopted operating procedures and set up task forces to study, design, and implement program changes generated from staff brainstorming sessions (Fairdale High School, 1990). The next year, Fairdale joined the Coalition of Essential Schools. Changes in pedagogy, use of time, and student testing have flowed from incorporating coalition principles into school practice.

The Professional Development School and the Coalition of Essential Schools experiences encouraged Fairdale to deal with its beliefs and belief statements. "Make no mistake about it," Hohmann said, "we are into culture building here. We are building a community culture outside and a professional culture inside."

The PM committee setup is much like that at Lassiter and clearly reflects the influence of Gheens and the union. The steering committee functions as more of a sounding board than a deliberative body. Importantly, teachers reported the most satisfaction with participative management the closer it comes to dealing with student achievement questions.

The Union's Role in PM.   In addition to its historic role in founding participative management, the union plays a daily operational role, largely through the work of its five field representatives. Traditionally, union field representatives are grievance chasers. This role has not disappeared with the onset of PM; rather, it has been adapted to the reform process itself. Union field representatives do a lot of counseling. As one said, "Sometimes [teachers] will not feel comfortable making decisions. And the administration has been under a certain mind-set, and it is not going to change simply because there is PM. We often come in to buoy the faculty . . . give them some assertiveness training, or a good talk so they don't have PM in name only."

Is the union staff entirely at ease with the new order? No, no more so than the administrators. Staff members, like central office staff, are concerned with the lack of uniformity across schools. Union strength has been built on the strength of common rules applied to all, but when it comes to substantive educational issues, there are no cut and dried rules. The union can't decide for the teachers what they want; they have to decide for themselves.

Flattened District Hierarchy

The superintendent has created a highly unusual relationship with the 155 principals: They all report directly to him. This arrangement, which violates all conventional span-of-control rules, was sought by the principals early in the reform era and seems to be working well.

The principals themselves worked out a cluster arrangement through which they communicate on district policy matters, and superintendent Ingwerson meets with the leaders of the clusters periodically. The clusters — called School Based Administrative Teams — are based on principal affinity, and are balanced by race and sex rather than being geographic groupings.

The most innovative aspect of the direct reporting relationship is how they go about solving daily service-delivery problems. "I [asked] the principals how they would get everyday problems solved," said Ingwerson. They said, 'Well, who do you call when you have problems, and can we have those phone numbers?'" The result was that the superintendent passed his contacts — people who handle air-conditioning, roofing, school safety, equipment, and public-relations problems — over to the principals.

They created a standing rule. When a principal has a problem, the first call is directed to the person in the central office who is assigned to handle that type of problem. If the problem remains unsolved, the second call goes to the superintendent directly.

It is evident from conversations with principals that they cherish their direct contact with the superintendent. "We like to hear what he says directly; it's different than getting his thinking second or third hand." At the same time, Ingwerson, like most executives, has a reputation for not liking bad news. So principals are developing networks of knowledge about how to solve particular problems, and they share these solutions among themselves.

Along with the structural change came a major shift in central office command and control. The district has moved from management of processes toward a concern for results. The central office went from telling people what to do to counseling and providing services.

For principals, these changes increase ambiguity. The system has not entirely moved to results-oriented management, and principals still worry about doing the right thing.

CONCLUSION: NEW ROLES FOR THE UNION

Successful school reforms, like successful children, have many elders. And so it is in Louisville. Those close to the Gheens Foundation claim some of the credit. The superintendent's supporters say that the school-business coalition made reforms possible. But it is the role of the Jefferson County Teachers Association that is of particular interest to us here. Its role in supporting and legitimating reforms has been unmistakable. In the process of change, the union has taken on some new roles and used some traditional labor mechanisms, such as grievances, for new purposes.

In Louisville, the lack of public conflict has been most notable, and it fits perfectly with the community ethos of quiet problem solving. JCTA has abandoned public belligerence. No one suggests that it does not have the capacity for concerted action — even for a strike — but the union has not found it necessary to carry out even ritual saber rattling. There is no pretense of personal closeness with the superintendent; these are not comrades in arms. Rather, this is a recognized organizational relationship in which the union plays three key roles: legitimator of reform, communicator, and infrastructure supporter.

Legitimacy flows, in part, from the credibility of union leadership. June Lee's "hero" status made it possible for teachers to depart from traditional concerns about wages and hours and to take on responsibility for forming teacher work groups, starting new projects, and helping schools operate. Legitimacy is also anchored in the contract. June Lee is retired from office now, but the 1988–90 contract, especially Section K on reform, is a reminder that the union *as an organization* is committed to participative management.

In labor relations systems that work, unions have always served as a mechanism for communication with top management. Jefferson County's reforms focus these communications on educational issues instead of solely on teachers' working conditions. Simultaneously, the union has taken on the task of changing teachers' perceptions of themselves and increasing their willingness to undertake reforms.

The union has not suffered a major backlash from its cooperative stance with school management. As JCTA executive director Neal put it, "I am asked questions about why we were not visible in fighting the district, and I have to respond, 'What is our goal?' If our goal is to have program influence and get a 10 percent raise, then we are doing all right. If our goal is to kick ass, then we aren't."

The pattern of change in Louisville is instructive. Reforms have been under way for a decade. One of the elements that made long-term change possible was *not* focusing on test results in the early years. "We were culture building for the first four years," Regina Kyle, the Gheens consultant, said. Confidence in the district has increased, and innovative programs have spread to many schools. Just in the last year, reform has moved from structural change — site management and flattening the hierarchy — to a substantial focus on work-force education. "[But] we need exponential change, and we're not there yet," said Kyle.

NOTE ON FIELD INVESTIGATION

Charles Kerchner visited Louisville in spring 1990 and fall 1991, each time for four days. The superintendent, board members, union leaders and staff, and several principals were interviewed, as were a panel of central office staffers and staff from Gheens Academy. Three schools were visited.

REFERENCES

Fairdale High School. (1990). *Fairdale High School: An essential school where success is no longer a secret*. Louisville: Fairdale High School.

Gheens Foundation. (1988). *Innovation in education: A report on the JCPS/ Gheens Professional Development Academy*. Louisville: Gheens Foundation.

National Commission on Excellence in Education. (1983). *A nation at risk: The imperative for educational reform, a report to the secretary of education* (226006 ed.). Washington, DC: U.S. Department of Education.

Olson, L. (1989). A "teaching hospital" model. *Education Week*, November 19, p. 1.

Schlechty, P. C.,Ingwerson, D. W., & Brooks, T. I. (1988). Inventing professional development schools. *Educational Leadership* (November), 28–31.

Schlechty, P. C., & Whitford, B. L. (1983). The organizational context of school systems and the functions of staff development. In G. A. Griffin (Ed.), *82nd yearbook of the National Society for the Study of Education* (pp. 62–91). Chicago: NSEE.

3

Pittsburgh

REFORM IN A WELL-MANAGED PUBLIC BUREAUCRACY

Charles Taylor Kerchner

In many ways, Pittsburgh is a test case of whether reforms in urban school systems can work. Pittsburgh is clearly an old central city, but it draws on an unusual confluence of resources. Thus, Pittsburgh's labor relations and educational reforms show what can be accomplished under the most favorable conditions. The Pittsburgh case also illustrates the abilities and, in some ways, the limits of the existing mode of complex public bureaucracies.

THE PITTSBURGH RENAISSANCE

For a dozen years, school reform in Pittsburgh, Pennsylvania, has focused on instruction and achievement. The district has created a nationally recognized teacher center, a student performance-monitoring system, and a program for school site management — innovations that are beginning to change the character of administrative and teacher leadership in Pittsburgh. Agreements with the Pittsburgh Federation of Teachers (PFT) have served as vehicles for creating and expressing this reform.

Pittsburgh is nearly the archetype of industrial America. But Pittsburgh has enjoyed a renaissance during a generation in which most U.S. cities have decayed. "Big steel" — which fed three generations, fouled the air, and poisoned the rivers — has virtually vanished, replaced by high-tech industries, a sparkling downtown, and recognition as "America's most livable city."

The Pittsburgh Public Schools is a large public bureaucracy. Yet, at about 40,000 students, it is neither unmanageable nor chaotic. Its

43

superintendent has served for more than a decade, and its schools have enjoyed fiscal support that allowed both program expansion and real wage gains. Likewise, the Pittsburgh Federation of Teachers has enjoyed stable leadership, and both the district and the union are considered progressive and capable. Like other city districts, Pittsburgh suffers from urban stress. Yet the middle class has not abandoned the city's residential neighborhoods, and students in the schools are about equally divided racially between black and white.

FOUR PILLARS SUPPORTING REFORM

Pittsburgh's reforms are being made within the framework of a public bureaucracy whose goals are to make public schools productive, caring, and responsive. All the traditional trappings of public schooling remain in place — a large central administration, whose role prescriptions have changed relatively little during the decade; a well-articulated scope and sequence curriculum; a district testing program; and a centralized budgeting system. The reforms of the last decade took place within this framework. Four institutional pillars — superintendent, board, enrollment and finance, and union — have stabilized school reforms.

The Superintendent

Superintendent Richard C. Wallace, Jr., has been a highly visible symbol of change since his arrival in Pittsburgh in 1981. Data-driven change and careful, rational planning have become articles of faith for Wallace and guide the operating procedure for new programs within the district.

The Board

Until the mid-1980s, the board retained its traditional civic elite characteristics. But then district boundaries were redrawn so that three incumbents were forced to run against one another, and there was a wholesale replacement of board members. Four of the current board members have a background in community organizing and are considered representatives of particular communities and constituencies. This rise of special-interest politics has clouded the board's relationship with the superintendent, culminating in a series of public confrontations and a slander suit brought by Wallace against a board member.

Enrollment and Finance

Pittsburgh's enrollment has stabilized after a long decline. Enrollment in 1991–92 was 40,137, down from approximately 76,000 in 1966 (Public School Student Information Management Division, 1989). The change in enrollment is reflected almost entirely in a decline in the number of white students; black enrollment has remained relatively stable. Schools have achieved reasonable racial balance through a voluntary integration plan, although some elementary and senior high schools remain racially isolated.

Pittsburgh provides a relatively high level of financial support for its schools. The 1990 operating budget was $313.6 million, or approximately $7,979 per student, reflecting per-pupil support that is substantially greater than the national average.

Importantly, the Pittsburgh school board has independent taxing authority that lets it respond to financial needs. At the same time, elected board members are politically sensitive to tax increases. The tax rate is now at its legal limit, and the board is reluctant to raise it, even though an increase is considered to be inevitable in the near future. Budgets since 1990 have reflected fiscal tightening; some reform ventures have been scuttled, and all are being scrutinized.

The Union

The Pittsburgh Federation of Teachers (PFT) is a strong union in a strong union city. Teachers have a history of militant action. The PFT struck to gain union recognition in 1968 and hit the streets twice more, the last time for 33 days in 1975. But the union in Pittsburgh has always had an educational agenda, and since the mid-1980s, labor and management have worked hard to forge a productive relationship.

Like the school district, the PFT has enjoyed stable and energetic leadership. Albert Fondy has been its president for nearly a generation.

THE STAGES OF PITTSBURGH REFORM

The Pittsburgh story unfolds in three roughly chronological stages: a mandate for change within a supportive political and economic environment, a focus on educational leadership, and an explicit connection between labor relations and reform.

Creating a Mandate

Creating a mandate placed the reform agenda on a plane above business as usual. First, the reform mandate rested on data — consciously gathered and applied information about the district, its priorities, and its performance.

Second, the reform involved focusing activities on the instructional process. The Pittsburgh Federation of Teachers had a long history of interest in educational issues, but only since the mid-1980s had that interest clearly become part of the union identity in the school district. The union began to describe itself as a professional organization, and its leaders announced a philosophy of professional obligations.

Third, as education came to the forefront under the instructional leadership banner, district reorganization proceeded through labor relations. The district was not changed by circumventing the union, but by acting *with* the union. Partnerships with the union were put into place at the district level through steering committees. At the school site level, teachers took on contracted leadership positions through instructional cabinets.

Pittsburgh's mandate for reform has been characterized by movement of the superintendent's attention away from what Wallace (1985) calls the four B's of administration — buses, budgets, buildings, and bonds — and toward instructional leadership. The use of organizational information to drive reform has been a hallmark of the decade. In 1980, Wallace commissioned a district-wide needs assessment. The results led the school board to adopt six main goals: improving student achievement, improving staff and personnel evaluation, managing student population decline, improving the ability of the district to attract and hold students, improving the quality of school discipline, and improving the performance of low-achieving schools (Wallace, 1983). Attaching programs to goals became a way to focus attention and gain approval.

Focusing on Instructional Leadership

Wallace did not coin the phrase "instructional leadership," but he has made it his own. His idea of instructional leadership is visionary and data driven: "The superintendent of education must constantly seek and process data and inquire as to its meaning. Planning must be data based" (Wallace, 1985). Teachers, administrators, and perhaps parents should take part in planning: "It is imperative that those who are to use an innovation or a new program alternative must acquire some sense of ownership" (Wallace, 1985).

Educational leaders must have a vision of "good education." In addition to acting on their visions, leaders must follow through: "If a program is begun, it is important to pay attention to that initiative, to modify it, and see it through its cycle of completion" (Wallace, 1985).

Pittsburgh's reforms did not begin with a labor-management treaty. Early on, superintendent Wallace and PFT president Fondy each found the other someone he could do business with, but the opening labor-management act in Pittsburgh was to create the Schenley High School Teacher Center as a way of upgrading secondary schools. The teacher center, which opened in the fall of 1983, provided eight-week sabbaticals for teachers, during which they were involved in seminars, classes, and a clinical training program based on the Madeline Hunter model of instruction and classroom observation.

Schenley also symbolized a commitment to professional development. Its programs operated "on company time." Teachers were released from their regular duties for a period of intensive education. They could study and think during substantial blocks of time in comfortable settings rather than receiving the usual in-service training in late afternoon or evening classes. At the same time, the teacher center represented a mutual obligation. The district provided the teacher center and supported it financially, but participation was mandatory for every high school teacher in the district.

The second leg of reform was a testing program designed to provide timely data feedback to teachers. Monitoring Achievement in Pittsburgh (MAP) is arguably the most comprehensive internal assessment program in any U.S. school district (LeMahieu, 1984). Wallace believes that what gets tested gets taught. So students are tested up to five times a year in all academic subjects, and teachers receive detailed feedback about student performance on test items that are closely aligned with the district curriculum.

The district has also been a leader in developing innovative teaching and assessment practices in the arts and humanities. Project Arts/ PROPEL, run cooperatively with Harvard University and the Educational Testing Service, adapts some of Howard Gardner's performance teaching and testing ideas to urban classrooms.

Linking Labor Relations and School Reform

The relationship between the Pittsburgh public schools and the Pittsburgh Federation of Teachers rests on a common concern for the institutional fate of public education. As PFT head Fondy (1987) put it, "A union shares the responsibility for assuring the effectiveness, sta-

bility, and long-term viability and success of the institution or enterprise in which its members are employed."

The Major Players.   To a large extent, the relationship between
the administration and the union is an extension of the relationship
between the two men who lead them. Wallace and Fondy share a
working relationship rather than camaraderie. They disagree in public,
sometimes heatedly, and they have very different working styles.

Wallace is precise and tightly controlled. His unemotional speech
pattern masks what Wallace and others call a terrible temper. Wallace
has also earned respect by sticking with the job. Says PFT vice president
Paul Francis: "He has the interest of the kids at heart, and it didn't
seem to us he was going to come here just to get his ticket punched as a
big city school superintendent."

Fondy, in contrast, is a bear of a man, expressive in speech and
gesture. Where Wallace projects a calm deliberateness, Fondy is a
whirlwind of activity. Aside from his family, the union he has headed
since 1968 constitutes the major interest of his life.

The two share an instinct for politics and the political fray. Fondy
runs an explicitly political organization. He has repeatedly been elected
president of both the Pittsburgh and the Pennsylvania Federations of
Teachers. The union supports political candidates and is an important
force in Pittsburgh Democratic Party politics. (Eight of the nine incumbent school board members received the union's endorsement during
their campaigns.) But Wallace is no less a politician. A school watcher
in Pittsburgh commented, "Most people say that if you scratched Wallace you'd find an intellectual underneath; *I* think you'd find a street
fighter."

Strength and Responsibility.   Both Fondy and Wallace link labor
relations and instructional leadership by connecting union strength
with a willingness to take responsibility. Wallace asserts that he has
never read the union contract, and says that he never intends to: "I do
what I think is right, and if I'm off base somebody's going to tell me
about it!" His goal is to form a working relationship.

Fondy (1987) expresses the union's viewpoint: "A union must always conscientiously and scrupulously fulfill its fundamental responsibility to represent and service its members. . . . At the same time, a
union is not conceived with the primary mission of protecting the least
competent of its members." Fondy believes that "if there are problems
in the school system, and the union is strong, then the union is responsible either for the fact that the problems exist in the first place, or at

least responsible for the fact that they are not being addressed." Union strength, in Fondy's mind, is the key to teacher engagement in restructuring.

Wallace also recognizes the union's responsibilities: "The bedrock of a professional union is in the willingness to police their own troops . . . and take the responsibility for it. They have to be willing to be held accountable publicly."

Both Wallace and Fondy understand the necessity of personal risk involved in reform. Says Wallace (1985), "One must attempt the impossible." For Fondy (1987), it is a question of "taking internal political risks, if necessary, to strengthen the enterprise in which members work, to improve the quality of the services which members provide to their clientele, and to stabilize and build the union."

Professionalism and Education. Both Wallace and Fondy view professionalism as a means to an end, and both believe in visible progress. Wallace is very specific on this point: "There's a growing awareness in this district . . . that teachers are being very well paid. [But] there is beginning to develop a medium-level grumble that if [people] don't start to see teachers being more hospitable, putting in longer days, being more accommodating to parents and kids, then there is going to be a rebellion." Fondy agrees that salary increases cannot go on without the teachers "making some kind of an argument that the productivity of what [they] are doing is increasing."

THE GROWTH OF UNION STRENGTH

Labor relations in Pittsburgh schools have followed a common developmental pattern, growing from an informal and associational past, progressing to militancy to achieve a contract, and culminating in the demonstration of picket line and political power. The federation was chartered in 1935, but for the first 30 years of its existence it was not the leading teachers' organization. The majority of teachers belonged to the National Education Association–affiliated Pittsburgh Teachers Association until the mid-1960s.

Union organization in Pittsburgh was spurred by successes in New York and Philadelphia. American Federation of Teachers (AFT) staff came to town with an organizing effort in 1967, and a strike for union recognition was called in 1968. It was the first of three walkouts.

The PFT called the first strike even though it had a membership of only 700 of the district's 3,500 teachers. About a third of the teachers stayed out of school. After several days the teachers went back to work, and a date was set for a representation election, which the PFT won. Superintendent Sidney Marland (who later became U.S. Commissioner of Education) called the election illegal and left the district. In 1971, there was a one-week strike over economic issues.

The school district's angriest labor dispute took place in 1975. Teachers stayed out of school from 1 December to 26 January. Court injunctions to end the strike were ignored. The union was fined, the union office was padlocked, and its officers had already made plans to go to jail when a settlement was finally reached (Pittsburgh Federation of Teachers, 1985).

The vivid signal that labor relations were changing came a decade later, in 1985, when the PFT and the district reached a contract settlement that contained an internal mechanism for dealing with educational issues. The more public and dramatic aspect of the contract settlement was that it was achieved early, a full year before the old contract expired. The early contract symbolized "labor peace," which was, in the words of the *Pittsburgh Post-Gazette* (5 September 1985, p. 6), destined to give the schools "even more national visibility."

As a part of the 1985 contract, the PFT and the district executed a memorandum of agreement that launched the Teacher Professionalism Project. In 1988, the name was changed to the Professionalism and Education Partnership (PEP). The initial agreement pledged joint effort toward several objectives: greater teacher professionalism and a strong, accepted, professional role for practicing classroom teachers; a fundamental teacher role in staff development; career-type, expanded professional responsibilities for continuing classroom teachers; and teacher involvement in and responsibility for the induction of new teachers into the profession.

A second early contract agreement in 1988 included large salary increases. Top salaries increased by 25 percent over four years, and starting salaries jumped 40 percent over the same period (Pittsburgh Federation of Teachers, n.d.b). Teacher professionalism became part of the contract.

A third early contract, signed in December 1991, extends through 1994. This latest contract is notable because it freezes salaries for the last four months of 1992, allowing the board to postpone a tax increase during an election year (Zlatos, 1991). Still, the wage freeze is temporary. Top teacher salaries (for a master's degree and ten years' experience) will rise from $51,000 to $58,500 over the course of the contract. Teachers ratified the contract 1,023 to 440 (Gigler, 1991). Union president Fondy called the settlement an "unprecedented example of effective labor relations."

By the contract's expiration it will have been more than a decade since a teacher contract was negotiated using traditional team-based, positional bargaining. The style of negotiations — private, involving only the superintendent and union leader instead of large teams — has been criticized, but it has not hurt Fondy's popularity with the teachers. In 1991 he was reelected for his thirteenth two-year term.

FOUR NEW REFORM STRUCTURES

Four major structural changes followed the 1985 agreement: (1) a *district-level steering committee* moved the PEP project forward; (2) *instructional cabinets* were established in each school; (3) the job of *instructional teacher leader* (ITL) was created; and (4) time for teacher interaction was created by *an agreement to extend the school day* to allow for weekly meetings.

The Steering Committee

The enlarged structure of labor-management interaction uses a central steering committee. Twelve members are appointed by the superintendent and 11 by the PFT. Unlike the situation in many other districts, the Pittsburgh Administrators' Association is a member of the partnership and is represented on the steering committee. (The weighting of membership is of no particular significance. Decisions are consensual, and differences of opinion frequently do not follow labor-management lines.)

The committee is charged with handling the overall management of PEP activities and with making final recommendations, including those involving changes in the language of future labor contracts. It develops an annual statement of priorities and supervises the design and implementation of PEP project activities. The committee, which meets about once a month, is cochaired by assistant superintendent Stanley Herman (until November 1990, James Angevine) and PFT vice president Paul Francis, but its schedule is affected by a standing agreement that the committee will not convene unless Wallace and Fondy personally attend.

Both teacher and administrator representatives report that the steering committee operates differently from collective bargaining. The parties do not enter the room with preestablished positions, and the traditional restrictions on team members voicing individual opinions do not exist. Francis saw the steering committee invention as a necessity: "We found that in talking about educational issues at the bargaining table [under the old rules], even when the other side agreed, they couldn't agree because of the discipline involved in the process."

Members sit where they want to sit, talk when they want to talk, and take whatever position they want to take. At times Wallace and Fondy have even found themselves in agreement with each other but not with the rest of the team.

Subcommittees. The steering committee handles some issues itself. However, most of the broad-scale involvement takes place through a large number of subcommittees, whose total membership of teachers and administrators exceeds 300. Probably the most significant subcommittee was the one that explored school site management. This subcommittee worked for two years before recommending the instructional cabinet design now being implemented city-wide. In a joint letter, Wallace and Fondy emphasized their resolve "to restructure the teaching profession in Pittsburgh in order to give teachers more authority and responsibility for the education of students. An integral part of this restructuring of authority and responsibility is power sharing through collaborative decision making. The vehicle . . . is the school building instructional cabinet."

By 1990, the steering committee had spawned 16 subcommittees, each with a specific charge and a set of reporting dates. Subcommittees are composed of volunteers solicited by a joint letter from the superintendent and the union president. Although each subcommittee has met and produced written reports, universal opinion is that they are slow and hesitant to reach conclusions. Fondy attributes the slowness to the sporadic timing of committee meetings: "The committees have to meet on their own time. That's not the best way, but it's the only way. We started out having released time for the steering committee, but we cut that out. Once you start giving people time off for meetings the process becomes too expensive."

The trend now appears to be toward a leaner structure. For example, the steering committee now uses the cumbersome subcommittee system less and concentrates on fewer issues. A substantive discussion of school restructuring occupied the committee during much of the 1990–91 school year. Using external grant funds, the steering committee issued requests for proposals from two development teams to plan the reopening of two elementary schools. Team members, mostly teachers, were released from other duties to plan full time during the 1992 spring semester. Discussions about the autonomy of school sites, particularly the extent of their budgetary freedom, have significance beyond these two sites.

The Instructional Cabinet

The instructional cabinets were a goal of the 1985 agreement, and some schools moved quickly to institute them. The one at Schenley High School, home of the high school teacher center, was among the earliest and most comprehensive. Definitive direction came from the October 1987 subcommittee report and a position paper written by Wallace the following spring. By spring 1991, instructional cabinets were operating in all schools, with varying effectiveness.

Membership consists of all instructional teacher leaders (ITLs), additional teacher representatives of programs, the principal and other administrators, representatives of support services, and the PFT building representative. The cabinet, whose size is set by the principal as a function of school population, reviews existing instructional policies, programs, plans, and procedures and develops new ones in areas such as curriculum and instructional materials, staff development, and school activities. Leadership rotates, and meeting results are shared. Cabinets may meet on school time or beyond the regular workday if members choose.

Wallace (1988) made clear his expectations of shared decision making and its systematic use. From the outset, the superintendent called attention to the *quality* of decisions that would be made, not simply the act of teacher participation.

However, the key structural element, and the one most quickly internalized by the schools, was the degree of shared decision making accorded the instructional cabinet. Control over the level of teacher and staff involvement was placed firmly in the hands of the principal, who was to make a determination in accordance with "time availability, degree of expertise, and appropriateness of faculty involvement," among other factors (Wallace, 1988). Seven degrees of involvement were described, ranging from no involvement to total consensus.

The levels-of-involvement scale allowed the district to sidestep the ambiguity of principal control that has troubled other districts involved in school-based decision making. Technically, the school principal has veto power in the school's instructional cabinet and can claim control by declaring an item off the agenda or by allowing only perfunctory consultation. In practice, most cabinets operate around jointly made decisions.

Cabinet Training. Cabinets also take time and training. Wallace's motto, "Train, train, and train some more," is played out in the extensive preparation given to ITLs and facilitators and in the training and evaluation of whole cabinets.

Some participants have criticized the cabinet training as too narrow in scope. Indeed, training has had more to do with process facilitation than with strategic planning at schools or rethinking school missions from the ground up.

Assessment of Cabinet Operations. The district has carried out two studies of instructional cabinets: One followed cabinet activity, topics, and leadership over a two-year period, and the other assessed the quality of cabinet decisions.

The 1988–90 study of cabinets showed that their activities were concentrated on making decisions rather than making announcements (Pittsburgh Public Schools, 1991). Over the two years, agendas became less crowded and more focused. Cabinet agendas reflected the normal operations of a school: curriculum, organization, schedule, special events, professional development, and school climate. Interestingly, teachers in their new roles placed far more items on the agenda than did the principals. In both years, cabinet meetings were usually chaired by teachers.

In the second study, principals and teachers, most of whom had not served on the cabinets, were asked to evaluate the quality of the cabinets' decisions, based on their awareness of the outcome and rationale, their belief that individual needs and opinions were accommodated, their satisfaction with the rationale and outcome, their willingness to facilitate decision implementation, and their perception of the decision's success. Overall, participants ranked decisions made by consensus significantly higher than those made by principals.

At a more global level, we heard repeated self-criticism that cabinets have been slow to grasp fundamental issues. The cabinets seemed to operate in a predictable way, spending time initially on items of teacher discomfort and then on concerns about students' emotional well-being before taking aim at student achievement. However, when teachers turned their attention to student achievement, they typically took a sophisticated approach that placed learning within the context of the students' world as opposed to adopting simple techniques for curriculum intensification.

Cabinets cannot by themselves transform schools. In Pittsburgh, cabinets are very much an instrument of the existing school organization, operating within the goal framework of the board and the central administration. But the school district has begun a school restructuring effort that, at least potentially, offers schools a much broader mandate for change.

ITLs and Their Monitoring Roles

Instructional teacher leaders fill two roles — "both first-line, non-commissioned officer and liaison in shared governance" (Mooney, 1990). However, given the symbolic emphasis on teacher willingness to assume evaluative roles, it is not surprising that most of the training and attention has centered around the ITLs' instructional monitoring roles. The other two roles established by the labor-management steering committee — leader in school renewal and leader in curricular matters — have received less attention. The result has somewhat clouded the identity of ITLs.

The teachers seemed somewhat ambivalent and unresponsive toward the ITLs — even some teachers who were ITLs themselves. They seemed rather passive, as if waiting for someone to define their role for them rather than defining it for themselves. Attempts have been made to define what an ITL is and does. More than in any other district we visited, Pittsburgh has made explicit attempts at role definition — through union and management public statements and through training. Still, the district has not brought ITLs together regularly enough to form a group identity.

ITL Training. An ITL first receives training in the Pittsburgh effective teaching model, in models of pupil growth and development, and, importantly, in the process of giving feedback to peers. The first summer's intensive sessions included an introduction to the ITL role expectation, leadership skill training, peer observation models, and the use of instructional data. These skills are reinforced during the school year. In the second summer, skill training is updated and conflict management is added.

However, several aspects of the practice cloud the status of ITLs. For example, in some high schools, filling the ITL positions simply meant designating the existing department chairs and thus carrying forward the old status and identification, which sometimes included a learned sense of incapacity.

Negotiations Over Time and Leadership

For the cabinet-shared governance system to work, two important operational changes had to occur. Teachers had to take on official leadership roles, and teachers had to have enough time to meet as groups. Moving from agreement in principle to agreement about practice gave the professionalism partnership its most tense negotiation moments.

The issue was not money or the creation of teacher leaders. Instructional teacher leader positions had been created in the 1985 contract, and the salary for such positions had been set. But the union and administration were far apart about how the school day would accommodate the program and how teacher leaders would be chosen.

The union's initial position, voiced by Fondy, opposed lengthening the school day. Yet all sides questioned whether substantive teacher interactions could take place during the existing 40-minute preparation period. (The high schools had preparation periods; the elementary schools did not.) The compromise position was to lengthen the teacher workday to eight hours on Wednesdays and to recapture some of the time by shaving a minute off each class period.

The discussion then moved to the selection of instructional teacher leaders. The union proposed selection by teacher vote; management wanted selection by school principals. The compromise selection process, described in a joint union-management statement, provides for departments or other groups of teachers to identify *two* potential candidates for the building principal's review and selection (Pittsburgh Federation of Teachers, 1988). If a team leader or department head already exists, the group can indicate whether it wishes that person to continue. If teacher consensus cannot be reached, a third-party team of PFT and administrative representatives makes the decision. Such a team has been used in only three cases.

Agreements over time allocation and the teacher leader selection process signaled that union and management were invested in the project. Both sides had compromised, but more importantly, the PFT began to play a mediating role in the process, "creatively moving its representatives toward a participatory role in teacher evaluation" (Engle, 1987).

PFT members overwhelmingly ratified contract changes relating to the schedule changes and the new ITL roles (Pittsburgh Federation of Teachers and Pittsburgh Public Schools, 1988). Part of the union's job was, in effect, selling new teacher roles to a sometimes skeptical and reluctant audience. Both the union and the administration had to convince teachers that the higher salaries — $50,000 to over $60,000 — would create public pressure for taking on new roles (Pittsburgh Federation of Teachers, n.d.a).

Also, the union was concerned that failure to agree on additional time to meet would create a difficult obstacle in the upcoming collective bargaining negotiations. The school board had grown critical of the city schools' relatively short school day compared with that required in suburban locations (Pittsburgh Federation of Teachers, 1987). Beyond immediate practicalities, however, listeners to union statements and readers of its newsletter were brought back to the central question of professionalization: "Clearly, if teachers are to be accountable for the quality of instruction, then we must dialog with one another — about what we do best; about the most effective means to do it; about what to do if what we did didn't work; about what is best for children" (Gensure, 1987).

SYMBOLS AND REALITIES OF TEACHER PROFESSIONALISM

How is the professional partnership faring? The usual answer says that one-third of the schools are getting along well, another third have constructed skeletal cabinets, and the rest are still struggling with the idea. Not all the principals were crazy about the idea, and a rash of retirements followed its implementation. The larger message about the need for concerted cooperation to restore confidence in the schools is not universally heard at the school sites.

At the Ground Level

In some locations, the cabinets have instituted virtually no change. Here the former department heads became instructional teacher leaders and, rightly or wrongly, are seen by their colleagues as symbols of the school's continuing inaction. In other settings, change is quite visible.

Although none of the cabinets actually ran the schools in which they were located, most of them changed the ways in which their schools were run. They rearranged authority, increased teacher involvement in decisions, changed the way decisions are made, reallocated time, and learned from their own processes.

Clearly, teacher voice and decisional presence increased. Teachers were heard on more subjects than before, and principals came to understand that *careful listening* was part of the faculty's expectation of them. A principal's unilateral decision about the school's direction or a major change in operations would not be accepted at any of the schools we visited. In several cases, principals reported that they even brought issues to the cabinet that they had the legitimate authority to decide without consultation.

The decision-making process has changed. Group decision making by consensus is both preached and practiced. In terms of labor relations, the word *consensus* appeared for the first time in the 1988 Memorandum of Agreement (Mooney, 1990).

Some measure of the value ascribed to cabinets may be found in the willingness of faculty to extend their workdays to participate in them. At all but one of the schools visited, the staff scheduled meetings in the early morning hours to avoid interfering with other school activities.

Cabinets also redefine the measure of a good principal. Whereas cabinets may be seen as vehicles for teacher empowerment, it is the principal who is held accountable for how they work. Cabinet activities are monitored by the district's staff development department, and staff observations become part of principal evaluations.

In Union Operations

The professionalism agenda adds to the union's roles. The PFT still does the things that unions used to do, and with increased intensity, which taxes its six-person professional staff. Grievances are filed, and the union represents teachers who receive unsatisfactory performance ratings. The number of grievances going to arbitration has actually increased because the union is somewhat more willing to take "judgment call" grievances to arbitration to show that it is still fulfilling its duty to provide procedural due process for members.

But it is the committee work that most stresses the union staff. Committee membership is not the difficult part; finding time to do the necessary staff work between committee meetings has been an exhausting challenge.

CONCLUSION: SHAKY PILLARS

Three of the pillars of stability that underlie Pittsburgh's reforms are shaking. Superintendent Wallace retired in 1992.

The fiscal support that nurtured the district during the past decade is threatened by recession and tax nervousness. It is likely that the school board will increase taxes in 1993, but the extent of revenue needed — and the threat to established reform programs — is partly a function of state appropriations in a commonwealth where the recession has hit hard. Perhaps most threatening to districts that invest heavily in education, such as Pittsburgh, are the proposals for statewide funding equalization.

The school board is fostering a more populist approach to reforms, with heavier levels of parent involvement. We cannot know whether this push will tear at the seams of the professionalism partnership or help re-create the mandate. One significant unknown is the fallout from Wallace's slander suit filed in April 1991 against board member Valerie McDonald. On its face, the suit seeks damages for McDonald having called Wallace a racist at a board meeting and subsequent press conference (Donovan, 1991). This is the political context in which the roles of the superintendent and the board in school reform will be decided, as well as the extent to which the board will be divided by racial and special-interest politics and the extent to which the schools will be able to reach a compatible working definition of equity.

The PFT, the fourth pillar, remains largely unchanged in leadership and operations, which may suggest its stabilizing value in long-term organizational change.

NOTE ON FIELD INVESTIGATION

Charles Kerchner made four trips to Pittsburgh from December 1989 through May 1991. These visits were supplemented with telephone interviews and personal conversations at professional meetings and other settings. Interviews were held with the superintendent, board members, union president and staff, central office personnel, several principals, and approximately 40 teachers. Five school sites were visited.

REFERENCES

Donovan, D. (1991). Members of city school board sued by superintendent. *Pittsburgh Press*, 9 April, p. B1.

Engle, D. (1987). *Documentor's Notes*. Pittsburgh Professionalism Project.

Fondy, A. (1987). *The future of public education and the teaching profession in Pennsylvania*. Pittsburgh: Pennsylvania Federation of Teachers.

Gensure, K. (1987). The TPP and teacher interaction. *The PFT Point* (September).

Gigler, R. (1991). Teachers to get $58,000 by '94. *Pittsburgh Press*, 9 December, p. A1.

LeMahieu, P. G. (1984). The effects on achievement and instructional content of a program of student monitoring through frequent testing. *Educational Evaluation and Policy Analysis* (Summer), 175–87.

Mooney, J. E. (1990). *Ideology in school governance*. Ph.D. dissertation, University of Pittsburgh.

Pittsburgh Federation of Teachers. (1985). *50 Years of service to Pittsburgh's children: Pittsburgh Federation of Teachers 50th anniversary, 1935–1985*. Pittsburgh: PFT.

Pittsburgh Federation of Teachers (1987). *Facts and considerations on the proposed changes in high school time schedule*. Pittsburgh: PFT.

Pittsburgh Federation of Teachers. (1988). *New article, high school time schedule, teacher interaction period, and related matters*. Pittsburgh: PFT.

Pittsburgh Federation of Teachers. (n.d.a). *Important notes for instructional teacher leader presentations*. Pittsburgh: PFT.

Pittsburgh Federation of Teachers. (n.d.b). *A unique and national significant education/negotiations achievement in Pittsburgh*. Pittsburgh: PFT.

Pittsburgh Federation of Teachers and Pittsburgh Public Schools. (1988). *Joint statement of position*. Pittsburgh: PFT and PPS.

Pittsburgh Public Schools (1991). *Descriptive analysis of instructional cabinet activity and group interaction: Comparison of 1988/89 and 1989/90 data* (unpublished study).

Public School Student Information Management Division. (1989). *Membership report as of October 2, 1989*. Pittsburgh: Pittsburgh Public Schools.

Wallace, R. C., Jr. (1983). *School district initiatives in response to board priorities*. ERIC No. ED 233 471.

Wallace, R. C., Jr. (1985). *The superintendent of education: Data-based instructional leadership*. ERIC No. ED 256 060. Pittsburgh: University of Pittsburgh, Learning Research and Development Center.

Wallace, R. C., Jr. (1988). *The instructional cabinet and shared decision making: A position paper*.

Zlatos, B. (1991). City school taxes won't rise in '92. *Pittsburgh Press*, 20 December, p. B1.

4

Cincinnati

BETTING ON AN UNFINISHED SEASON

Byron King

Four aspects of the Cincinnati story are particularly distinctive. First, the relationship between the union president and the superintendent has been unusual. Most breakthroughs in labor relations are the products of a "deal made at the top," in which the union president and the superintendent agree on the broad outlines of a new relationship and a direction for the district. But not in Cincinnati. Cincinnati Federation of Teachers (CFT) president Tom Mooney and now former superintendent Lee Etta Powell often held different opinions about reform, their personal relationship was cool, and the union, not the district, is credited with driving reform and forging a business and civic coalition.

Second, the political and financial environment is hostile. Voters rejected a tax levy in November 1990, forcing the district into bankruptcy. Faced with the prospect of massive program cuts, voters finally approved a new tax levy in November 1991.

Third, despite these handicaps, negotiated reforms are making progress. Peer review is in place. The joint teacher-district Teacher Allocation Committee has created a flexible response to class-size limitations that has been written into recent contracts. The Career in Teaching program is in place, and a high school that would train students for the teaching profession is on the drawing board.

Fourth, the district has been reorganized, drastically decreasing the size of its central office and transferring authority to school sites.

Change came to Cincinnati after a decade of acrimonious labor relations. Breakthrough contracts were signed in 1985 and 1988. An era of good feeling and educational reform seemed sure to follow. The settlements were hailed as agents of change that "could reshape the work of teachers and the education of children" (Johnson, 1989). A "community of professionals" was being created (Rodman, 1988).

Change is still under way in Cincinnati—a new contract was signed in June 1991—but no one talks any more about an easy finish. The district is broke, the business and political community is restive, and the superintendent has been replaced. Nonetheless, much in Cincinnati serves as a model.

THE CINCINNATI ENVIRONMENT

Cincinnati is an extremely livable city. With a population of 374,080, it retains the flavor of a prideful regional municipality. Elegant restaurants, restored hotels, first-line department stores and specialty shops, and the designed-to-impress corporate headquarters of Procter & Gamble dot the city. Riverfront Stadium, home of the Reds and Bengals, is within walking distance of downtown office buildings.

Economic diversity prevents major "smokestack" recessions. The Greater Cincinnati Chamber of Commerce reports steady job growth from 1986 to 1989, and the unemployment rate dropped from 6.2 to 4.9 percent. The five largest employers are General Electric, Procter & Gamble, the University of Cincinnati, the federal government, and the Kroger Company. Procter & Gamble, founded and still headquartered in Cincinnati, employs 13,000 people. These employers are historically nonunion. Procter & Gamble in particular has actively sought human resource management alternatives to unionism.

Although population in the greater Cincinnati metropolitan area has increased, the central city's population has declined by more than 50,000 since 1970. Hills and housing patterns have created 44 distinct, economically disparate neighborhoods within the city's 78 square miles. Many neighborhoods are racially integrated. Middle-class African-American families live in neighborhoods throughout the city. The inhabitants of some of the poorest areas are Appalachian whites. Class, rather than race, identifies the people in greatest need of improved educational and social services.

The small-city character of Cincinnati gives it an insular quality. Newcomers are viewed suspiciously and are generally kept at the fringes of power and influence. This insularity would challenge any incoming school superintendent, but particularly Lee Etta Powell, who was both an outsider and one of only a handful of African-American women in the nation to hold that position.

SCHOOL DISTRICT OVERVIEW

Cincinnati is the third largest school district in Ohio, following Cleveland and Columbus. Student enrollment in 1989–90 was 51,606, down slightly after six years of stability. Enrollment is projected to increase somewhat through the rest of the 1990s. Approximately 61 percent of students are African-American and 38 percent are white, a ratio that is almost the inverse of the city's population: 65 percent white and 34 percent African-American. Less than half of the students rank at or above national norms, as measured by the California Achievement Test. There are 3,080 certificated, nonadministrative staff, mostly teachers, in five primary, 55 elementary, nine middle/junior high, ten senior high, and several special schools.

Superintendent Powell divided the district into three administrative regions, each with its own assistant superintendent. In theory, each area was conceived as a minidistrict. The rationale for the move was to decentralize the district, but former school board president Virginia Griffin charges that it has had the opposite effect: "It's another layer [of bureaucracy]. Somebody cut the school system in half, separated it, and shoved another layer in."

The Issue of Race

The issue of race has dramatically affected the district over the last generation. The district settled a ten-year-old school desegregation case with the National Association for the Advancement of Colored People (NAACP) in February 1984. The so-called Bronson Settlement requires the school district to "make significant progress in reducing racial isolation" (Cincinnati Public Schools, 1989).

The primary means of improving racial balance have been magnet schools — called alternative schools in Cincinnati. Each alternative school has a special program: Mortimer Adler's Paideia program, Montessori, performing arts, health professions, and German language. During 1989–90, an estimated 20,000 students — about 40 percent of the total enrollment — were involved in such programs. These alternative schools enjoy an excellent reputation nationally and are a source of substantial community pride.

Although the alternative schools promote racial integration and quality instruction programs in some neighborhoods, many predominantly African-American schools remain unaffected by the reforms. In 1984, the CFT surveyed 18 schools having seventh and eighth grades and found that most of the schools not offering algebra and foreign languages had predominantly black student enrollments. Providing quality instructional programs for predominantly black neighborhood schools remains a major equity issue for the district.

Race has also influenced unionism. Observers say that Mooney's leadership of the CFT is based on an alliance between African-American and white teachers who hold strong antidiscrimination positions. Four of the seven elected union officers are black. Mooney's continued leadership is considered remarkable because the faculties at many schools are said to be racially divided. In fact, his reelection as CFT president in 1981 was opposed in part because of his support of desegregation and affirmative action.

District Finances

This district, like many, is once again facing tight fiscal times. Between 1968 and 1980, seven proposed tax levy increases were defeated. In December 1979, the district declared itself bankrupt and closed down for 15 days. Former school board member G. David Schiering points out that during this time, "persistent myths [in the public's mind] about 'hidden funds' and 'administrative fat' could not be dispelled." To restore public credibility in the district, Local School Advisory Committees were established in 1980. Each committee, composed of staff, students, parents, local businesses, and community members, is involved in setting school planning goals and some modified forms of site-based budgeting (Morgan, 1982).

During the 1980s, voters once again began to approve tax levies to increase the operating budget of the district. However, toward the end of the decade, the margin of support was very slim. The total annual operating budget of the district was $252 million for 1989–90, with a per-pupil expenditure of $5,146. Revenue to the district comes from local property taxes (48 percent), the state (39.9 percent), the federal government (8.3 percent), and other local sources (3.8 percent). A $12.5 million capital improvement levy passed in 1989 yields $2.5 million annually.

In November 1990, the voters again rejected a tax levy increase, forcing the district to apply for a state loan of nearly $30 million to operate during 1991 (Weisman, 1990). The state agreed to support a $27.1 million loan for the district from the Fifth Third Bank of Cincinnati, provided the district agreed to make budget cuts equaling the amount of the loan over two years.

The *Cincinnati Enquirer* (8 November 1990) called the tax defeat a "vote of no confidence" in the school system: "Cincinnatians told the board of education and the school administration that the school system is not doing the job Cincinnatians want done. They simply decided this week that non-performance should not be rewarded."

Although superintendent Powell's leadership was not criticized outright, the *Enquirer* (7 November 1990) placed her photograph in the middle of the editorial. In contrast, CFT's Tom Mooney was portrayed positively and quoted as saying that "there need to be some basic changes in policy and structure of the school system to restore public confidence before another [tax levy] effort is made."

The Board of Education

The seven school board members are chosen in a city-wide, officially nonpartisan election for staggered four-year terms. The average current board tenure is 7.1 years, although Virginia Griffin, the former board president, has been on the board for more than 22 years. Members are paid an $80 stipend for each twice-monthly meeting.

Board member Virginia Rhodes calls the board an "old boys' club" that is "corporate blessed." Indeed, Cincinnati has a long history of business and professional leadership control in selecting school board members.

Politics have limited the board's role in leading reform. Votes tend to split 4–3, and, as board member Griffin says, "It's difficult to build consensus." CFT's Mooney believes that the board is out of touch with the day-to-day issues that are important to teachers and parents.

The Business Community

The Cincinnati Youth Collaborative is a cooperative effort among the district, the city, and the business community to address the dropout problem. Efforts have been focused at Taft High School, which has a high dropout rate, poor attendance, and low academic performance. Executives from Procter & Gamble, interested in the concept of shared decision making, play a leadership role in the group.

A second business intervention, the Cincinnati Business Committee, composed of the CEOs of the city's 22 largest businesses, studied the district's organization and practices. Chaired by Clement Buenger, chairman of the Fifth Third Bancorp, the committee included participants from Procter & Gamble, Kroger, Cincinnati Bell, General Electric, and Cincinnati Gas and Electric Company. Although billed as "free consulting," the committee's intent "to cut costs and improve efficiency" was more suggestive of an organizational audit (*Cincinnati Post*, 31 March 1990, p. 6A). Its report, released in fall 1991, was critical of school district functioning and suggested major structural reforms (Buenger, 1991).

HISTORY OF CINCINNATI LABOR RELATIONS

When Lee Etta Powell came to Cincinnati, she said she found "a mind-set that administrators were in one group and teachers were in another group and that they were natural enemies as opposed to being allies." Indeed, before the mid-1980s, relations between the teachers and district could only be described as adversarial.

Bargaining with teachers began in the late 1960s, well before a 1983 state law required that school districts recognize unions. From the late 1960s through the mid-1970s, teachers were represented by the Cincinnati Teachers Association, an affiliate of the National Education Association (NEA). The district currently negotiates with the CFT; American Federation of State, County, and Municipal Employees (AFSCME); Local 20 Operating Engineers; and the Building Trades Council.

The 1985 Contract

The 1985 teachers' contract moved beyond economic issues and established the union's right to bring issues of educational policy to the bargaining table (Johnson, 1989). While the union was creating the public agenda for educational reform, the district was unable to articulate a clear vision of the future. By the time contract negotiations began, the *Cincinnati Enquirer* was running editorials outlining the union's contract position. Comments were favorable: "It speaks well of Cincinnati's teachers and their professional commitment that they see the improvement of educational standards as *the* most important issue on the bargaining agenda" (*Cincinnati Enquirer*, 16 December 1984).

Among the reform issues ultimately included in the 1985 contract were (1) establishment of class-size limits and a joint CFT-board Teacher Allocation Committee to redistribute resources among schools, (2) a procedure to allow teachers to decide on student promotions, (3) an agreement to pilot test a peer review plan, and (4) the right of the CFT to appoint all teachers participating in joint teacher-administrator committees.

Organizationally, the 1985 agreement fell between administrations. The previous superintendent had died, and most of the negotiations proceeded under the guidance of deputy superintendent Lynn Goodwin. Lee Etta Powell became superintendent on 1 October 1986.

Powell came to the district with the agenda of improving student achievement. The inequities between magnet and neighborhood schools had already surfaced as an issue. In addition, the district lacked a unified K–12 curriculum. Using committees of administrators and CFT-appointed teachers, the district devised curriculum frameworks and selected textbooks for reading, language arts, mathematics, and science.

But Powell arrived to find a history of teacher and administrator antagonism and enmity. She hoped to change that. In a 1989 interview, Powell spoke of her philosophy of "inclusion" regarding decisions: "Teachers should participate in the issues affecting the running of schools. . . . Administrators and teachers need to believe 'sharing is the normal thing,' instead of 'tug of war'" (Trotter, 1989). Teacher inclusion, however, was to be in the context of a chain of command. The style was to be traditional. District direction was to be established by the superintendent.

The 1988 Contract

Contract bargaining in 1985 had been an unpleasant experience for the district. The CFT had convinced the community that the union was more concerned about student welfare than was the district. But by fall 1987, the district had become open to new bargaining approaches. District and union representatives participated in training sessions conducted by Conflict Management Incorporated. The sessions, based on the concept of "principled negotiation," emphasized negotiation to produce a just agreement that enhances and preserves a positive relationship between the parties (Fisher & Ury, 1981).

Lynn Goodwin played a major role in guiding the district's bargaining in 1987–88. Board member Virginia Rhodes believes that Goodwin was "one of the few people in the administration who understood what was wrong in 1985. It was really his leadership that enabled us to get into a different process."

Goodwin sought to open up bargaining. He observed that "if the teachers don't get to talk about it [reform] at the bargaining table, then they're never going to get to talk about it." Part of the 1988 negotiations involved a conscious search for ways to solve problems away from the bargaining table so that issues didn't build up over three years.

Lee Etta Powell became superintendent after the 1985 bargaining, and she did not participate directly in the 1988 negotiations. According to Rhodes, her absence meant that the superintendent was not on the "same wavelength as everybody else was as to how important it was to make the stuff we were doing in 1988 work."

Not all teachers were satisfied with the direction taken by the contract settlement. In fact, an unusually large number voted against ratification. Tom Mooney remarked that some teachers still believed that they would not receive all they could from bargaining unless they publicly bashed the district and the school board. Mooney's 1989 reelection bid itself was contested, with the principled bargaining strategy the main issue. Mooney's opponent received one-third of the vote.

THE REFORM FEATURES

The 1988 contract, which expired 31 December 1990, both improved traditional teacher work rule protections and expanded moves toward teacher professionalization begun in the 1985 contract. The contract established the Career in Teaching Program and formalized the Peer Assistance and Appraisal Program. In addition, the 1988 contract (1) required that nonteaching supervisory duties be assigned to nonteaching personnel, (2) expanded teacher involvement in recommending teaching assignments for the next school year, (3) mandated significant increases in teacher preparation time, and (4) limited the total number of students secondary teachers could see in a single day to 150 (down from 180).

As an addendum to the contract, a trust agreement considered educational reform issues that had been raised in the bargaining process: teacher recruitment and training (including exploring the concept of a professional practice school), early childhood programs, educational program initiatives (middle schools and participation in the Coalition of Essential Schools, a national effort by Brown University's Ted Sizer to reform secondary education), and professional services (a variety of activities including improved parent-teacher contacts and clerical assistance to teachers).

The name "trust agreement" was borrowed from a California experiment in which ten districts and unions negotiated educational policy issues, such as peer review, staff development, and school site management. Operating plans and resource allocations for these ventures were written into labor-management pacts called "educational policy trust agreements" (Koppich & Kerchner, 1990).

The contract also continued the Teacher Building Committee

(TBC), which met monthly to review the contract implementation and "educational policies and programs in the building" (Collective Bargaining Agreement 1988, pp. 10–11). Regular contact between the central office and the union was also established, including a monthly meeting of the union president and superintendent.

Implementation of the major reform issues in the contract was slow. Board member Griffin says that the trust agreement elements were delayed because of "foot-dragging by our administration for two and a half years at least." Roger Effron, the personnel director, disagrees: "We just bit off more than we could chew. The delays occurred because the committees had lots of issues to resolve." Nonetheless, further negotiations on trust agreement items, including the career ladder, were delayed until February 1990, the last year of the contract.

Several theories have been proposed to explain the delay in implementing reform sections of the contract. Although Goodwin was the district spokesperson during bargaining, he moved to the sidelines when it was time to administer the contract. At the same time, Powell restructured the district office, resulting in some confusion about who was responsible for implementing which contract articles.

The district and the union held monthly problem-solving sessions, but superintendent Powell did not attend regularly. Some teacher activists theorize that the district delay was because "Lee Etta bought into things [empowerment of teachers] she did not understand. When she realized the implications of the contract [i.e., that teachers would have more authority], she slowed down the process."

Moreover, Powell did not believe that it was necessary to apply the principled negotiation model to problems involving the daily operation of the district. As a result, middle-level managers, principals, and teachers never received training in the process. This gap made it difficult for them to understand the spirit of the collaborative 1988 bargaining experience.

Peer Assistance and Appraisal Program

The 1988 contract continued the Peer Assistance and Appraisal Program (PAAP), expanding it to "all teaching fields and to educational service personnel" (Collective Bargaining Agreement 1988, 20–27). In describing the rationale behind peer review, the CFT points out that "the principal's lack of time and expertise are considered among the important reasons for the failure of evaluation programs. Principals are not experts in all subjects on which they must evaluate their staff nor is evaluation their prime responsibility" (Morgan & Froelich, 1990).

Peer review of teachers is conducted by 14 consulting teachers who are released full time from the classroom. They serve for a maximum of two years and may not take an administrative position during the following year. Consulting teachers, who have a maximum caseload of 14 teachers, earn $5,500 stipends in addition to their regular salaries.

The peer review program has two components. An intern component uses consulting teachers to provide "guidance and orientation into the teaching profession" for first-year teachers, much like an apprenticeship program (Morgan & Froelich, 1990). The intervention component assists teachers who exhibit serious teaching deficiencies. In both situations, consulting teachers provide a number of services, including "helping to formulate job targets, plan lessons and locate needed materials, and arranging visiting days for appraisees so that they may observe successful teachers in classroom situations similar to theirs" (Morgan & Froelich, 1990). At the end of the year, the consulting teacher writes a summary evaluation that includes a recommendation for renewal or nonrenewal of the teaching contract.

A principal generally refers a low-performing tenured teacher to the peer assistance panel, which determines whether intervention is needed. A teacher also can recommend another teacher for intervention through the CFT building representative, but so far none has done so.

The Peer Review Panel, composed of five teachers appointed by the CFT and five administrators appointed by the superintendent, governs the program. Responsibilities include the selection and evaluation of consulting teachers and approval of consulting teachers' recommendations for nonrenewal of teachers' contracts. Peer reviewers average five recommendations a year for nonrenewal of employment for probationary teachers. Of the permanent teachers recommended for intervention, one-third have not been accepted by the review panel because the evidence did not appear compelling, one-third have undergone supervision and been released from the program based on improved performance, and one-third have resigned or been discharged. The superintendent can overturn the panel's recommendation but has done so only once, terminating a probationary teacher the panel had recommended for continued employment.

Personnel director Roger Effron has been involved in multiple levels of peer review: as a school principal serving on the 1986 bargaining team, as a member of the first peer review panel, and, since 1987, as a personnel director. He points out that many teachers and principals were worried about the process at first. Principals would call him, saying, "You gave this [teacher evaluation] away. The union is going to run this." Also, it was difficult in the beginning to establish guidelines for peer review because teachers and administrators were not accustomed to working with one another.

Many, but not all, Cincinnati principals are now comfortable with the peer review process. Some say that it means one less headache for them, though they also claim that they could do a better job of evaluation if they too had only 14 teachers to evaluate. However, Henri Frazier, president of the Cincinnati Association of Elementary School Principals, believes that although consulting teachers provide a valuable service for reviewing teacher performance, principals should have more control over the final evaluation.

Administrators have raised two criticisms about the role of consulting teachers. First, administrators must be trained in an evaluation process, such as clinical supervision, before they are allowed to evaluate teachers. But consulting teachers are not required to be certified before they begin evaluation duties. Second, consulting teachers are not directly supervised by anyone except the Peer Review Panel, which meets monthly and does not monitor consulting teachers' daily activities.

CFT representative Irene Thorman explains that consulting teachers are "exposed to, but not trained in" several observational methodologies during the summer before they assume their duties. But the real training comes through informal acculturation — interaction with veteran consulting teachers — rather than formal instruction. One of the pluses of the program is that even though consulting teachers have the power to recommend termination, classroom teachers seem to open up to consulting teachers more often than they would to a principal.

Career in Teaching Program

The CFT's drive to establish a career ladder is attributed to the Carnegie report on the teaching profession (Carnegie Forum on Education and the Economy, 1986). The goal of the CFT is to develop teachers who are leaders, suggesting that the concept of "principal as educational leader" is unrealistic: "A principal of a modern school faces too many administrative tasks. Further, schools are too large and teaching fields too specialized for a principal to provide the instructional leadership that is needed. Instructional leadership must exist within every department, team and unit" (Mooney, 1990).

The 1988 contract established a joint union-administrator committee to develop a teacher career ladder. Four levels were identified: intern, resident, career, and lead. A Career in Teaching Panel was formed to oversee the assessment process, credential lead teachers, and recommend additional roles and responsibilities for lead teachers. The goal was to have the first lead teachers in place by September 1990. But the initiation of the Career in Teaching Program was delayed. Board member Griffin said, "We were supposed to start studying it immediately after the negotiations were completed, and [we did] nothing about it for at least a year and a half. Then they finally got a committee set up and the superintendent wouldn't let them meet." The school board and CFT finally approved the Career in Teaching Program in February 1990.

The certification process has two phases. The first is a "paper screening" of applicants by the panel. Candidates for lead teacher certification must have at least ten years of teaching experience, including five years in Cincinnati. In the second phase, applicants are assigned to a trained teacher observer (TTO), who prepares a report on the applicant's potential to be a lead teacher (Cincinnati Public Schools, 1990). The report is based on four classroom observations, a review of the personnel file, and interviews with the applicant's coteachers and principal. The TTO then makes a recommendation, which is reviewed by the Career in Teaching Panel.

The lead teacher selection process in spring 1990 caused some frustration. Principals complained that clearly qualified teachers had not been certified as lead teachers. Teachers on the selection panel countered that some teachers did not take the completion of the application form seriously and did not complete important sections or failed to meet application deadlines.

Each school site was allocated a set number of lead teacher positions. Once the list of certified teachers was published, the placement process began. A panel of three teachers interviewed each candidate and recommended three to the principal for final selection.

By January 1991, 39 school-level lead teachers and four trained teacher observers had been selected. The school-level positions are primary- or intermediate-level leader at elementary schools, middle school interdisciplinary team leader, and senior high school subject area leader.

Effron views the development of new relationships among the lead teacher, principal, and other staff as one of the upcoming challenges for the Career in Teaching Program. He wonders whether the job descriptions will become a "boundary or a foundation" in the relationship between principal and lead teacher. Without a good working relationship focusing on what is good for children, "we're not going to have a very successful program." And, he adds, the lead teacher risks being identified as the "principal's puppet" by the other teachers.

Teacher Allocation Committee

Some of the best examples of district-union collaboration for educational reform are found in the many district-wide joint committees. At least 37 different committees, with teachers appointed by the CFT, have been formed to address a variety of issues, including curriculum reform, textbook selection, staff development, Chapter I (federal funds earmarked for students of low-income families) planning, and the school calendar.

Most notable among the joint bodies has been the Teacher Allocation Committee. A predetermined set of resources is placed in the committee's hands to solve class-size problems that occur between enrollment projections and staffing assignments in the spring and actual student attendance in the fall. The district agreed to leave decisions solely in the hands of this joint labor-management committee. The union agreed not to grieve the committee's decisions.

The resources available to the allocation committee to reduce class sizes at individual school sites include (1) a reserve pool of 35 teaching positions, (2) up to 50 instructor assistants who can be placed in classrooms with above-formula enrollments when extra teachers are not available, and (3) direct overload payments made to teachers who do not get relief from extra teachers or assistants.

The committee, which meets six times a year, has eight members: the two cochairs (one teacher, one administrator), and three members representing teachers, and three representing the district. As is the case for all joint committee responsibilities, teacher members receive no added compensation.

Soon after being established, the allocation committee designed procedures for schools to report enrollments and request class-size relief. Early in the fall, each school reports student enrollment and class loads. Given that information, the committee determines where teachers must be moved or whether a school qualifies to receive extra resources.

The committee's procedures require collaboration among principals and CFT representatives. Both sides are required to sign the school staffing enrollment report and validate its accuracy. The procedure encourages an open exchange of information between principals and teachers.

The biggest challenge the committee faces is making sure that teachers and principals understand the process. CFT members on the committee have been equally critical of administrators and teachers who do not follow the time lines.

The committee is a real success story, according to teacher cochair

Bebe Freeman. "When we first negotiated joint committees everyone was a little edgy about 'Can this really work, will we be able to jointly make decisions with our administration?'" Participants believe that the committee has been successful because it is grounded in clear contract language and collaboratively developed operating procedures. According to the cochairs, both teachers and administrators realize that the process is helping schools and students.

Professional Development School

Plans for a Professional Development School are now moving forward, largely because the University of Cincinnati allocated $2 million to support the project. The Professional Development School, staffed by lead teachers who would also have adjunct teaching positions at the University of Cincinnati, would encompass the final phase of training for intern teachers. The district wants to connect this concept to a preprofessional high school for the teaching profession. And, in an effort to create a larger pool of African-American teachers, the district would guarantee employment to any of the program's graduates who become teachers.

Shared Decision Making

When shared decision making occurs, it appears to be more the result of teacher and principal interest than of any consistent expectation from the central district office. But shared decision making has yet to be implemented in a meaningful way at school sites. One abortive attempt was made in 1987 to use shared decision making at two elementary schools. Mooney attributes the failure to a lack of consistent district support. Griffin says that "no effort was made by the administration to get principals in those schools who had the faintest notions about what shared decision making was or an interest in doing it."

Powell's philosophy of inclusion did not accommodate the expanded decision-making roles described in the contract. Under Powell's leadership, the administration made concessions but still wanted to keep control. Shared decision making foundered.

ROLE SHIFTS CAUSED BY CONTRACTUAL CHANGES

Many staff positions within the district are being redefined. Two groups in Cincinnati experiencing the strain of role shifts are school principals and union activists.

Principals: Left Behind or Opting Out?

School principals give mixed reviews to Cincinnati reforms. They are concerned about what teachers have gained as well as what they perceive themselves to have lost.

District director of communication and labor relations Gerald Varland points out that the big contract issues may have had support from the top leadership of the district, but that support did not necessarily filter down to principals and supervisors. Principals were not made aware of the impact of the principled negotiation experience; they were not sold on the new collaborative attitude toward teachers implied by that bargaining process.

Goodwin, the architect of the district's negotiations for the last three contracts, notes that traditional collective bargaining offered little involvement for principals. The current reforms are intended to create settings in which both principals and teachers can discuss educational policies. But, he says, "The principals have not used these very effectively; they tend to be whiny and reactive."

The CFT has successfully negotiated contracts that both improve teacher work rules (preparation time, supervision, teaching load) and expand reform issues, such as peer review and the career ladder. These changes make it difficult for principals to manage schools in the traditional manner. One principal said that field-level administrators believe that teachers have "walked away with the kitchen sink."

Ray Finke, principal of Western Hills High School and president of the Cincinnati Association of Administrators and Supervisors, is skeptical about the value of the last two contracts: "We've done absolutely nothing with these new contracts to guarantee that we're going to improve any of the results by which we measure student progress." Finke views the contract as limiting the "amount of work teachers do outside the classroom."

Bebe Freeman, however, points out that no teachers serving on joint committees receive additional pay, even though many such committees involve long hours and difficult decisions. Her theory is that the amount of effort teachers expend on their work is related to the leadership of the principal. Freeman believes that principals who want to dominate and make all the decisions "attract the teachers who only want to do the minimum because they aren't the ones making decisions anyway."

Henri Frazier of the Cincinnati Association of Elementary School Principals expressed frustration with district emphasis on the lead teacher program. She is not opposed to the concept, but sees it as a distraction from the more important issue of providing equitable funding for elementary school programs. She does not think elementary schools will gain anything from having lead teachers and believes that the money would be better spent hiring counselors.

Union Activists: From Outsiders to Insiders

The reforms in Cincinnati are redefining the term "union activist." Mooney notes that "the change in the union's focus . . . brings out a different set of people to be active." Teachers are spending a great deal of volunteer time on committees generated by the contract, as well as on district curriculum and program development committees. "The more the union has tried to push professionalization and reform efforts," says Mooney, "the clearer it becomes that the traditional political leadership of the profession cannot handle [all] the leadership roles that need to be played if the teaching profession is really going to take on a central role in driving school improvement and ultimately in running schools better than they're run now."

CONCLUSION

The 1990–91 school year ended with a series of mixed signals. In April 1991, superintendent Powell resigned. She had lost support on the school board and was increasingly criticized by business and community leaders. However, the circumstances of her leaving ignited another controversy. The board, in the midst of cutting the budget by more than $15 million, agreed to a $200,000 severance settlement. (The settlement was challenged in court, and an anonymous private donor provided a settlement believed to be substantially lower than the original.) Unionists and parent activists, who had seen cherished programs cut back, were furious.

In June 1991, the teachers and district approved a new three-year contract that made a 4 percent wage increase contingent on the tax levy's passage in November 1991. The negotiations themselves presented a series of mixed images. The use of the principled negotiation technique expanded. The superintendent (prior to her resignation) and board participated in negotiations training, and Ray Finke of the administrators' association became an observer at negotiations. Yet negotiations were tense and publicly acrimonious. Mooney accused Powell and the school board of backpedaling on promised administrative cutbacks. Former board president Virginia Griffin accused Mooney of harming the tax levy's chances by questioning the board's integrity.

Beneath the fuss, the contract that emerged continues the trend toward negotiated educational policy and joint operations begun in 1985. It includes a greatly strengthened discipline policy, including a union-district panel to review all discipline procedures.

The contract created an Education Initiatives Panel to support changes already under way and to begin new restructuring efforts to improve educational outcomes. Shared decision making will be instituted at one high school and two middle schools based on a plan jointly developed by the union and administration. The plan anticipates waivers of existing board and union rules. Meanwhile, a task force continues to work on recommendations for a city-wide site management plan.

Nonetheless, some individuals view the new agreement, expanding reforms, and increased teacher authority with uneasiness. School board president Robert Braddock remarks, "These are teachers. They are not elected officials. They are not answerable to the public the way we are." Still he recognizes, "This is a new era. They say 'if you give employees more say so, you're supposed to get a better operation.' We're trying it" (Clark, 1991).

Shortly after contract agreement was reached, the board appointed Michael Brandt, a respected high school principal, as superintendent. The CFT looked on the appointment with great favor.

In May 1992, superintendent Brandt attended to the business committee's Buenger report (Buenger, 1991) in a drastic reorganization that slashed the number of central office jobs in half, from 127 to 62 positions (Gursky, 1992). Several layers of administration have been eliminated, including the area superintendents.

NOTE ON FIELD INVESTIGATION

Byron King and Charles Kerchner visited Cincinnati in June 1990, and several subsequent personal and telephone interviews were conducted. Interviews were conducted with the superintendent; central office staff; union leadership, including bargaining team members and joint committee members; leaders of principals' organizations; and several civic leaders. Site visits were made to three schools.

REFERENCES

Baden, P. L. (1991). Deal angers parents: Some say Powell retainer dooms next levy. *Cincinnati Enquirer*, 20 April, p. 1.

Buenger, C. L. (1991). *The Cincinnati business committee task force on public schools, report and recommendations.*

Carnegie Forum on Education and the Economy. (1986). *A nation prepared: Teachers for the 21st century*. New York: Carnegie Corporation.

Cincinnati Public Schools (1989). *Summary budget presentation: 1989–90 operating budget*. Cincinnati Public Schools.

Cincinnati Public Schools. (1990). *The career teaching program*.

Clark, M. D. (1991). Teachers get raise if levy wins. *Cincinnati Post*, 29 June, p. 1A.

Fisher, R., & Ury, W. (1981). *Getting to yes: Negotiating agreement without giving in*. Boston: Houghton Mifflin.

Gursky, D. (1992). Cincinnati cuts more than half of central office. *Education Week*, 20 May, p. 1.

Johnson, S. M. (1989). Bargaining for better schools: Reshaping education in the Cincinnati public schools. In J. M. Rosow & R. Zager (Eds.), *Allies in education reform: How teachers, unions and administrators can join forces to better schools*. San Francisco: Jossey-Bass.

Koppich, J., & Kerchner, C. (1990). *Educational policy trust agreements: Connecting labor relations and school reform, annual report*. Berkeley: Policy Analysis for California Education.

Mooney. T. (1990). *CFT Bulletin: Career Ladder Update*. Internal publication, Cincinnati Federation of Teachers.

Morgan, J. (1982). Local school goal setting: A new approach to development of school district goals. ERIC No. ED 218 759.

Morgan, J., & Froelich, A. (1990). A look at the real issues: Why peer review? *Federation Teacher*, 12 April.

Rodman, B. (1988). Hopes for a "team of fellow professionals." *Education Week*, 9 April, p. 1.

Trotter, A. (1989). Lee Etta Powell. *Executive Educator* (November), p. 14.

Weisman, J. (1990). Cincinnati seeks state loan in wake of tax-levy defeat. *Education* Week, 14 November, p. 5.

5

Greece Central School District

STEPPING BACK FROM THE BRINK

Anthony M. Cresswell

A visitor to the Greece Central School District looking for traditional styles and forms of labor-management relations would be in for a big surprise. In a fairly low-profile but effective manner, the staff and board have crafted major reforms in bargaining and overall management and governance. Over a period of about seven years (1984–91), the staff and board have redesigned the bargaining process, forged creative new agreements (with several unexpected provisions), and expanded the reform process to affect most of the internal governance of the school district. In doing so, they have had to reexamine and often abandon traditional ways of doing business. It has been an eclectic, opportunistic process. They have borrowed freely from outside the district and, when necessary, created new methods of their own. Although not uniformly smooth or trouble free, the process has been remarkably collaborative and successful. As such, a description of it offers valuable insights into the potential for major school and bargaining reforms within the existing framework of labor-management relations.

DYNAMICS OF REFORM

"We went up to the brink and looked over, and we didn't like what we saw," said Richard Bennett, former Greece Teachers Association (GTA) president. Looking over that brink and backing away from it began a period of major change in the teacher-board bargaining relationship and in the governance of the district. Two questions about the district and the players in this process of change emerge: What brought them to the brink? And how did they manage to draw back and find another path? The answers to these questions involve the positive, constructive convergence of events, opportunities, and personalities. Some of the convergence was fortuitous; much has been the result of conscious decisions and planning by some of the major participants.

DISTRICT CONTEXT

The town of Greece, which is served by the Greece Central School District, is a fairly affluent, stable, middle-class, predominantly white, suburban area of upstate New York; the 1990 population was 91,000. Located in Monroe County, Greece borders Rochester to the east and Lake Ontario to the north.

The district is generally free of large concentrations of poverty, conflictual relations among racial or ethnic groups, and other social problems that often plague school districts. It provides a hospitable environment for reforms to emerge and succeed. More recently, though, substantial growth in enrollment and state budget problems have increased stress.

The 1990–91 enrollment of approximately 12,500 students is distributed among 19 buildings. The district projects an increase of about 2,900 students by 1995. Operations in 1990–91 involved an annual budget of approximately $84 million and 1,500 employees, about 800 of whom are teachers.

THE HISTORY OF REFORMS

Reform in Greece has three main phases, covering about seven years: a period of conflict and confrontation (roughly 1984–86); one of trust building and experimentation (roughly 1987–89); and one of testing, refining, and attempting to institutionalize reforms (1989 to the present). In the first phase, external financial and political pressures interacted with the personal styles and attitudes of key players to produce high levels of conflict and hostility. The two main constituencies involved, the board and the teachers' union, were dissatisfied with the conflict. Their dissatisfaction led to changing some key actors and emphasizing different goals, values, and ways of playing the game. The result was a shift in the organizational culture away from adversarial and toward much more collaborative norms and patterns of behavior. With the new actors and expectations in place, opportunities for trust building and collaboration were more readily recognized and exploited in work toward restructuring.

The processes of restructuring both the bargaining relationship and the district administration went hand in hand. The result has been a fairly rapid movement toward site-based management and enhanced decision-making roles for teachers and other staff within school buildings. Widened participation has also opened decision making at the district level. A dramatic example of this decentralization was the relinquishing of all planning and staffing for a new building to a committee of teachers and parents. In addition, the increased participation included changes in program monitoring and evaluation and the development of an incentive system for teachers to participate in decision making.

Restructuring has clearly gone far beyond the bargaining agreement. A much broader collaboration among the district and the teachers' and administrators' unions has emerged.

Phase 1: Conflict and Confrontation

The early 1980s were years of deteriorating relationships among the main participants in the district's governance. The conflicts were not simply labor-management disputes, but also included basic issues of control and policy. The board was strongly influenced by a faction (four of the nine members at the time) that wanted to participate actively in the operational management of the district and keep expenditures low. The current superintendent referred to this style as "micro-management," and it extended to such details as what make of truck the district should buy to replace one taken out of service. This micro-management brought the faction into conflict with the superintendent and the rest of the board, who favored higher expenditures and less board involvement in managerial details. The factional conflict within the board soured board-superintendent relations and added considerable tension to bargaining.

In 1983, during this period of tension and conflict, the superintendent retired. A new superintendent, recruited from Michigan, was hired for the 1983–84 school year and given an initial three-year contract. Jerry Herman had a reputation for tough relations with unions. Some referred to him as a "union buster" and to the style of the board as "union bashing."

Conflict and confrontation characterized both the superintendent's and the board's approach to bargaining. They planned to force major concessions from the GTA in the negotiation of a successor to the agreement expiring in June 1985. They hired a professional negotiator, Jim Stanton, and the bargaining began in spring 1985. As might be expected, the negotiations proceeded to impasse with a high degree of acrimony and open hostility.

By this time, the board had grown disillusioned and angry with Herman's performance. The bargaining strategy had not produced the expected major board gains, only more impasse and stress. The hostility had spilled over into the day-to-day operations of the district. The situation had so deteriorated that the normally divided board factions agreed that the superintendent had to go. Even though Herman was only partway through his initial contract, the board offered to buy out his last year if he would resign. The board asked John Yagielski, the long-time assistant superintendent for business, to take over.

But Yagielski was not willing to take over and continue with business as usual. He had his own ideas about how to improve the situation, and he insisted on some commitments from the board. He asked for and received a firm promise that the board would move away from adversarial roles in bargaining and internal relationships. The board agreed to seek new ways of bargaining and to increase decision participation within the district. With this agreement in place, he began as superintendent in the fall of 1985 in the midst of the impasse with the GTA. However, Yagielski was not able to get directly involved in the bargaining because the board instructed him to leave the negotiations to the hired gun. Yagielski was thus not able to begin the search for improved methods during that round of bargaining.

And improved methods were clearly needed. Negotiations for a successor to the 1983–85 agreement were long and difficult, extending from 1985 into January 1987 for the ratification of a two-year agreement for 1985–87. By then, Yagielski had been in office for over a year and was pushing for changes in bargaining and decision making. But some extra time was needed to restructure things, and that time would not be available if the district and the GTA plunged right into new negotiations in the spring of 1987. To buy some time for restructuring, Yagielski and then-GTA president Bea Ruford decided to try a different approach. After the contract ratification, the two met privately to work out an extension of the 1985–87 agreement. They hoped that the extension would create a grace period during which a better basis for future negotiations could be established.

Although that goal was certainly worthwhile, the political and organizational support for that tactic was not in place. GTA president Ruford had misjudged her membership; she had not consulted adequately with the GTA or prepared the members to accept this kind of clandestine process. When they heard about the ploy, many GTA members felt betrayed and refused to ratify the extension. The membership was angered by what it viewed as a high-handed attempt by the president and the superintendent to circumvent members' participation in the bargaining. Tension was high and trust was even lower than before as the district and union faced a new round of negotiations. Most signals pointed to even higher levels of conflict and hostility to come. They were standing at the brink.

What saved the district from a plunge into destructive confrontation was a complex mix of good strategy, good intentions, and good luck. As the district faced the brink, some basic processes of change had begun that would let the players move in new directions. Significant changes were taking place in the board itself. In 1986, the cost-cutting adversarial faction lost control. Through a series of retirements, only two of the incumbent board members remained by 1988. The working style of the board also began to respond to pressures and initiatives for change. John Yagielski started training activities to expose the board members to a more policy oriented concept of their role. In addition, the negative GTA reaction to the contract-extension ploy had precipitated a new slate of challengers running for GTA office.

At almost the same time, George Vito, president of the Greece Association of School Administrators (GASA), introduced the district to alternative approaches to bargaining. At a professional conference, Vito had encountered the "principled negotiations" and "win-win" approach promoted through the Harvard Negotiation Project and Conflict Management Inc. (CMI) of Boston (Fisher & Ury, 1981). He was impressed with their work and invited CMI to submit a proposal for working with the district. Vito passed the proposal on to Yagielski, who promoted it with the board. These efforts resulted in a joint board-GASA-GTA training session with CMI. The training led to the fundamental restructuring of the bargaining process, which later produced the successful 1989–94 agreement.

Phase 2: Experimentation and Trust Building

By late 1987, the labor relations in the district had begun to move back from the brink. Business as usual was no longer satisfactory. The desire for a different approach was reflected in the change in superintendent two years earlier, changes in the board's style of work and membership, and pressure for new leadership within the GTA. These changes eventually combined to produce major restructuring and reformed relations. But first a transitional period was needed. The desires and pressures for reform were present, but the parties had yet to translate their desires into the foundations of trust and organizational tools required for major reforms.

The negotiation and ratification of the 1987–89 agreement resulted in two major steps toward change, largely due to Yagielski's use of the negotiations to encourage the GTA to accept an expanded concept of the teachers' role. One result was the creation of the Council for Change, a joint GTA-board committee responsible for promoting change throughout the district. But creating the Council for Change was not enough.

The GTA was not yet ready to fully embrace the expanded responsibility concept, although it was not opposed to it in principle. The union had encountered a clear mandate for change in that direction from the spring 1987 elections. New officers and an almost entirely new executive council were elected, including Dick Bennett and Peter Schramm as president and vice president. They were elected on a platform that promised to seek a new approach in bargaining, but with no clear details of what that meant. They had also identified a new dual role for the GTA: continuing to serve the traditional trade union interests of the membership as well as pursuing their professional interests. But this dual role was not sufficiently defined or accepted for Bennett and Schramm to push for major restructuring in negotiations.

The superintendent tried to make economic gains for the GTA contingent on acceptance of this new role and expanded responsibility. But this pushing was largely ineffective. The new GTA officers were reluctant to commit the GTA to instant, full-fledged cooperation. As president Dick Bennett described it, that first summer's bargaining between the new participants was a "dance where we were trying to figure out what we were doing, where we both were coming from." Without a solid basis of understanding and trust, neither party was willing to take major risks or make major concessions. As a result, the bargaining lead to impasse again. The mediator's proposal served as the basis for an agreement on another two-year contract, settled in November 1987.

However, the new agreement for 1987–89 did not go far enough for many of the teachers. Although it contained several new ideas, it did not deliver major new benefits or fulfill expectations. As a result, the agreement almost failed ratification by the GTA, passing by 5–4 in the executive council and by only 21 votes in the general membership. This split in the GTA posed serious problems for the new officers. They recognized that they had been elected to initiate changes, but few had resulted from the first negotiation. The Council for Change therefore decided to produce a new statement of goals for the GTA. The council met with the board, the Parent-Teacher Association (PTA), and administrators to discuss these goals before formulating the document, which was made public in January 1988.

That document was the *Renewal Plan*, the second building block for reform. It called for greatly increased shared decision making by teachers at the building and district levels, which the executive council believed should be the foundation for the new GTA. The superintendent was pleased with the plan, which he saw as the green light for reform he had been looking for. The *Renewal Plan* indicated that the superintendent and the GTA were working on the same basic reform agenda and could be partners rather than adversaries. That partnership has been the basis for much of the reform success.

In the implementation of the *Renewal Plan*, the GTA identified the Council for Change as a major mechanism. The GASA was somewhat unhappy about this implementation strategy because it had no power to appoint members to the council. Unlike the teachers' union, which appointed five members to the council, the five administrators were appointed by the superintendent, not chosen by their peers. However, GASA did not block the plan or its implementation. The organization was willing to take a risk to let the development go forward.

Phase 3: Building Reforms into the Structure

The GTA and the district entered the process of negotiating a successor to the 1987–89 agreement with significant changes in personnel and attitude but few changes in structure. Aside from the Council for Change, the arrangements for bargaining and the conduct of district affairs had felt little impact. A spirit of and commitment to reform had emerged but had yet to find its way into the structure of the system.

The initial focus of attention was the bargaining process. The changes in the bargaining process were possible because the parties had developed trust and a desire to collaborate. These structural reforms can be seen as steps to institutionalize the new bargaining relationship and avoid unnecessary recurrence of destructive confrontations.

The actual revisions in the bargaining process followed the concepts introduced in the district by CMI. In essence, this approach is based on four points elaborated on by Fisher and Ury (1981): (1) separate the people from the problem; (2) focus on interests, not positions; (3) generate a variety of possibilities before deciding what to do; and (4) insist that results be based on objective standards.

To operationalize these points, the district changed the structure and procedures of the bargaining process in line with the recommendations of the CMI consultant. The structural changes included the creation of joint union-board teams to gather background data, prepare the informational base of the negotiations, and develop alternative approaches to resolution. The procedural innovations included prenegotiation sessions in which the parties developed the bargaining agenda and carefully defined the time frame for the actual negotiations to ensure that unnecessary ploys and maneuvers were avoided.

The training and preparations for this new approach took place during the 1987–89 agreement. Participating in the training process with CMI seemed to be an essential part of the trust-building process. Although the techniques and procedures taught in the training are useful in their own right, the common experience and shared language developed by participants went a long way toward building a working relationship. Simply by participating in the process together they were pursuing a more collaborative pattern of behavior and cementing a commitment to change.

The new bargaining approach has been used only once by the GTA. It appears to have been successful; the long-term agreement (1989–94) suggests considerable strength of commitment. The process moved to conclusion without impasse and resulted in many significant changes in the agreement, which was ratified 9–0 by the board and 555–171 by the teachers. But one successful use does not ensure institutionalization, especially with the long interval between negotiations. It remains to be seen whether the main elements of this restructuring endure.

Results from the negotiations with two other unions, the GASA and the Association of Greece Central Educational Personnel (AGCEP), indicate that the basic approach will continue to be successful. The two agreements, effective in January and December 1988, respectively, are unusual in that they have no expiration date. Annual salary increases are determined by a cost-of-living adjustment. Although the exact schedule was not specified, the parties agreed to meet regularly to discuss matters of mutual interest. Other language allows individual clauses to be altered by mutual agreement and allows either party to dissolve the agreement, effective one calendar year from the date of written notice.

The reforms addressed in the 1989–94 GTA agreement fall into three general groups: (1) new approaches to increased decision participation by teachers, (2) increases in the flexibility of the agreement to accommodate change and within-district variation, and (3) changes in teacher roles and compensation. Each of these sections includes fairly general provisions that establish goals and principles and suggest future or continuing reform directions. Although it supplies some details on implementation, the agreement itself does not fully specify the nature of the reforms. The full definition and implementation of these reforms have taken place outside of bargaining and involve more direct union-management collaboration on changes in district policy and organization.

A separate section of the agreement, called "Commitments for the Future," contains eight items identified as future projects that address the need for continual improvement. The items involve, with one exception, additional joint committee assignments on topics the parties wish to pursue during the term of the agreement. No specific deadlines for action are involved. The one exception is support for a grant application to the state education department to finance a teacher mentor-intern program.

Commitment to Participation in Decision Making. The agreement sets the framework for major reforms in the role of teachers in district management. That framework consists of statements of goals, beliefs, and basic principles for the development of "shared decision making at the school and district level" (Art. XXV, Sec. A). The agreement articulates a general commitment by both parties to work collaboratively toward these ends, but it does not specify the full range of actions, procedures, or timetables to be used. The Council for Change is continued from the previous agreement. As for the remaining details, the parties were apparently content to trust the council and their otherwise generally cooperative orientation.

The agreement commits the GTA and the district to develop and implement school-level decision participation for teachers. It is, in fact, a dual commitment to site- or school-based management in principle and to the substantial participation of teachers in that process. The agreement does not, however, spell out in detail how to achieve these goals. Rather it provides general statements of beliefs and goals and leaves the details to individual schools to work out. That process is still under way.

The agreement is somewhat less extensive and forceful with regard to district-level participation. It establishes the Council for Change as a district-wide body with a narrow focus on contract matters that is instructed to "consider and make recommendations with respect to proposed changes within the District affecting terms and conditions of employment prior to their implementation" (Art. III, Sec. A.1). A later section, "Professional Participation in Decision Making" (Art. XXV), refers potentially to all district-level decisions but spells out no specific means of implementation.

Contract Flexibility and Waivers. Significantly, the agreement opens the door to flexible, creative approaches to working out the details by providing for departures from the usual contractual constraints.

The language allows individual schools to take approaches not necessarily consistent with the agreement. One section states, "During this period of working to establish shared decision-making . . . neither party will hold the other to any past practice, precedent or changes due to attempts within each school to work together" (Art. XXV, Sec. A.2). This statement clearly attempts to reduce the likelihood of grievances emerging from and impeding reforms.

The importance of keeping the contract from impeding reforms is even more dramatically illustrated in the provision for contract waivers. The agreement includes a formal procedure (Art. XXV, Sec. 3) for individual schools to obtain waivers that allowed them to change or ignore contract provisions that interfere with a school-level reform. The waivers are not available for so-called collective areas of the agreement such as salary, benefits, the grievance procedure, and so on. A waiver is good for a year and may be extended one year at a time by the same procedure.

The waiver process is not just window dressing. It has been used repeatedly and successfully — and for some unexpected purposes. To date, approximately 12 waivers have been requested, and all were granted. Of these, eight dealt with compensation variances, four of which changed or increased the stipend arrangements for summer and extra work. Another waiver relaxed contractual requirements for teacher planning time. Two others allowed hiring of a part-time teacher at over 60 percent of the full-time equivalent, which is otherwise prohibited.

Four other waivers are worthy of special note: They allowed the stipends provided to teachers who participate in building management to be extended to *nonteaching* staff. That is, the teachers waived portions of *their* agreement to obtain benefits for members of *other* bargaining units. The supporting documents argued that the effectiveness of decision making would be improved if *all* involved parties participated and they debated the fairness of compensating some and not others. These statements provide persuasive evidence of some teachers' commitment to the reforms in general and recognition of the important role of nonteaching staff in decision making at the building level.

Teacher Roles and Compensation.   Besides the changes implied in increased decision participation, the agreement takes an additional step in the direction of further teacher role changes. The section called "Additional Responsibilities and Compensation" establishes a joint committee to oversee three small pilot projects that change the definition of and compensation structure for some middle and high school positions. It also calls for a study with recommendations involving all teacher leadership positions and redefinitions of teaching roles. The new master and lead teacher positions, established unilaterally by the district, could thereby come under the review of joint committees. Because most of this work is still in progress, it is unclear what the outcome of these small steps will be.

Under the principles and goals of the agreement, teacher role definition and responsibilities are expected to change as a result of increased decision participation, whether at the school or district level. Moreover, time and effort spent on decision participation are typically viewed as additions to work load, which raises questions of compensation. The agreement makes general references to further study and development of compensation for these added professional responsibilities, but spells out no specifics. The details were worked out not during bargaining, but by collaborative efforts afterward.

THE DETAILS OF RESTRUCTURING

A high degree of integration and interaction has emerged between the initiatives and ideas found in the agreement and other restructuring and policy reform implemented through extracontractual decision making. As a result, the boundary between the formally negotiated change and the more generalized collaborative restructuring of the district is not clear or consistent.

In addition to the negotiated material described, the full range of recent reforms in the district includes restating and redefining district goals and beliefs, changing the board-superintendent relationship, opening a new school with a radically different approach, implementing a new instructional assessment system, and significantly expanding parent and community involvement in the schools.

District Committees

The new district committee structure provides impressive evidence of the magnitude of the reform efforts. The committees represent a systemic structural change in terms of participation in district-wide decision making. And as is true of some other changes, the committee system was not simply the result of bilateral negotiations. Rather it was the result of superintendent, board, and staff initiatives and collaborative decision making through the Council for Change. Again, the council, a negotiated element of structure, was employed for reform activities that went well beyond its contractual purpose.

The result is a highly complex committee system. In addition to the Council for Change, there are 26 standing committees and 19 ad hoc committees distributed over six areas of management. There are five committees on goals and planning, 15 committees address instructional management, five involve student management, 14 relate to personnel management, four involve resource management, and two deal with partnerships between the school district and other organizations. Although the number of committees seems extraordinary and possibly burdensome, there are no reports of difficulty. About half of the committees are short-term, ad hoc groups, and not all the standing committees meet frequently.

The Point Value System

Participation in this expanded decision-making process is more than just empowerment; it is an addition to work load. The board and the GTA developed what they call a *point value system* to recognize and reward this additional professional activity. After ratification of the 1989–94 agreement, the district and the GTA formed the Professional Point Value Committee to develop a system of points representing the relative value of district-sponsored professional development activities. The points could then be translated into extra compensation of various sorts. Although committee work was not part of the original charge, the committee decided to include participation in district-wide committees in the definition of professional development, along with other staff development activities. The resulting point value system thus became an incentive system for both formal professional development activities and decision participation.

Under the point value system, a certain number of points is assigned to each recognized decision participation or professional development activity. For example, service on a "Type B" district-wide committee (one that meets for more than six after-school or three full-day sessions) is worth 20 points, attendance at a five-session after-school workshop at the Teacher Center is worth 10 points, and so on. Each set of 25 points is worth $200. The holder of the points can redeem them for classroom supplies or equipment, professional development expenses, or simply as additional pay.

Site-Based Management

The establishment of a school-based management structure was also a creature of the agreed-upon principles, but it was not operationalized in the GTA or GASA agreements. The board, the superintendent, the teachers' union, and the administrators' union all shared a commitment in principle to move toward a site-based management system. Beginning in 1989–90, they created a process for building that system. Again, the Council for Change had a central role as the forum in which the plans were conceived, reviewed, and eventually approved. As with the district-wide decision process, this role is outside the specific contractual purpose of the council but fully consistent with its emergence as a tool for collaboration.

The process, in general, was to create what were called joint *ad hoc* teams of teachers and administrators for each building. After approval by the Council for Change, these teams were to create a *school management team plan*. They would have training and a facilitator to support this process. The resulting plan would go to the Council for Change for review and eventually be adopted as the basis for site-based management.

The joint *ad hoc* teams had very broad discretion in designing their plans. The work was based on the assumption that each building would have different needs and preferences, and thus no single plan would work for all. Although all plans were to deal with the structure, membership, and responsibilities of school management, no particular details were required. A building could even opt out of site-based management altogether and leave the principal fully in charge.

As a result of this discretion, the process has taken considerable time to complete and has produced a wide variety of results. However, all the district's schools have completed management plans and have begun to put them into operation. The plans vary from structures in which a single committee make most decisions to complex systems of roles and subcommittees involving all types of school staff and parents. This reform is an ongoing process, and the full details of its structure and outcomes are yet to emerge. It is clear, however, that the goal of creating site-based management systems, mediated and reviewed by the Council for Change, is succeeding.

Administrator Organization Support

One reason for success is the considerable support from many principals and the lack of serious organized resistance from their organization. The GASA has been a supporter of the reforms in general and in basic detail. Once the board and superintendent decided that site-based management was a district goal, its implementation became a part of the principals' performance objectives. Because principals are paid entirely on a merit system and their compensation is tied directly to their performance evaluations, they have a direct interest in the overall success of the process.

The School of Choice

Enrollment increases in the district created another opportunity for a collaborative approach to management. The district projected that it would need to add several new elementary classrooms by the fall of 1990. It decided to reopen the West Ridge building, which had been taken out of service in 1983 due to falling enrollments. In addition, the district decided to make West Ridge a "school of choice." All staff and students for the school would be chosen from volunteers. This approach avoided the problems of reassigning staff or changing the attendance boundaries for the other elementary schools.

The methods used to plan and staff the new school illustrate the district's extraordinary level of commitment to collaborative, building-level management of the operation. In June 1989, a letter went out to all teachers inviting them to make a firm commitment to devote a year to planning an as-yet-unspecified school of the future. The teachers would then transfer into the new school when it opened. Thus, the planners would have to live with their design. About 40 teachers decided to take the risk and applied. From that group, the district chose a core team of ten, roughly representative of all the schools. The PTA added four parents who were prepared to commit their children to the new building. The core team of 14 then went to work developing and staffing the new school.

The district provided both wide discretion and substantial support to the core team. The superintendent took an active role, and a support team of other teachers, administrators, community members, and University of Rochester faculty was available. The core team attended a week-long retreat in August 1989 to begin, and each teacher received one release day per month for the work. The team had full discretion to decide on program structure, staffing, and student admission. They spent the remaining 12 months preparing for a September 1990 opening.

One of the key features of the core team's approach was taking pains to ensure that all staff shared a common vision of the school and its mission. First, the team forged its own consensus, which became the basis for developing specifications for hiring a principal and reviewing teacher applicants. Each teacher applicant had to submit a written statement of his or her vision for a school of the future. The team interviewed the applicants. As new staff were added, they joined the team and helped choose the next additions. Thus, the full staff had a strong shared vision of the school's design and mission. The core team was also responsible for recruiting the principal. They searched for and found one who shared their enthusiasm for the participative design.

The shared vision and collaboration have produced a thoroughly innovative and exciting school operation. The usual grade structure was abandoned in favor of a multigrade, team-taught "family plan" organization with a heavy emphasis on new instructional technology and extensive computer facilities. The school also places strong emphasis on parent involvement in both day-to-day instructional matters and overall operations. In addition, West Ridge School is a district showcase with a steady stream of outside visitors.

The new school is not a direct product of collective negotiations. Nothing in the agreement specifically addressed it. However, it is clearly a concrete manifestation of the principles of collaborative decision making worked out in the bargaining process.

District Facilitator

The wide range of reform activities occurring in the district added significant work load at the central office. In response to the increasing communication and coordination demands, the board created the job of district facilitator to deal with the variety of tasks. Peter Schramm, the GTA vice president, was hired in 1990 to fill this role. He remains in it part time, even though he is no longer a GTA officer.

Schramm's experience in the reform process and the teachers' organization gave him valuable insights and access. Even though he is no longer an officer, he is still in an excellent position to assist communications between the district and the GTA on the detailed issues and questions that arise in normal school operations. But his, or any other GTA member's, value in such a role derives in large part from the willingness of all parties to keep adversarial concerns out of consideration. The adversarial aspects of union-board relations will not go away completely. As a result, he risks losing credibility as a GTA member (which the election results detailed below suggest) and risks being viewed with suspicion by district administration.

TESTING INSTITUTIONALIZATION: SPRING 1991

The degree to which these reforms have become thoroughly institutionalized is indicated by how well they have survived dramatic events in the district and changes in key personnel. The robustness of the reforms in light of such changes was illustrated by the spring 1991 elections for new GTA officers. In that election, Karen Alexander and Jim Maiorana defeated Dick Bennett and Peter Schramm in their bid for a third term as president and vice president. The defeat did not, however, signal a shift of the GTA membership away from general commitment to the reforms. The opposition candidates were not opposed to the reforms themselves, nor did the reforms become issues in the campaign. In fact, the new officers have been major actors in the restructuring movement from its beginning. They claim to be as committed to the basic reforms as were their predecessors, although they expressed some concerns about specific impacts of the changes on teacher work load and roles.

However, the defeat of the incumbent GTA officers does seem indirectly linked to their role in the reforms. Over time, the dynamics of the reform process seem to have changed how the GTA membership viewed Bennett and Schramm. Many saw a conflict between their roles as advocates for and representatives of GTA and their roles as advocates for the district and reforms. Members reported that Bennett and Schramm were more concerned with maintaining good relations with the district administration than with promoting GTA interests. According to the new GTA president, Bennett and Schramm were too concerned with the "big picture" of district issues and reforms and neglected the day-to-day details of GTA business, such as grievances.

Another possible factor was described as Bennett's and Schramm's indifference to teachers' problems with the reforms. These problems were not necessarily cases of general resistance to restructuring, but the normal rough spots of any large-scale organizational change. Some teachers resented the extra work load and being called "nonprofessional" if they did not embrace the expanded decision participation. Bennett and Schramm were seen as unresponsive to these problems and ineffective in communicating teachers' concerns to the district administration.

The level of dissatisfaction that resulted from these problems was not enough, in itself, to generate active opposition to Bennett and Schramm's reelection. However, the coincidence of the state budget crisis and the ice storm of 4 March 1991 created new, intense pressures on the district. The way Bennett, Schramm, and the district administration reacted to those pressures produced an angry response from many GTA members and mobilized the late challenge in the officer election campaign.

The Ice Storm and Makeup Days

Considerable teacher dissatisfaction was created by the district's schedule of makeup days following a major ice storm. The storm, which struck northern New York on 4 March 1991, did enormous damage in

Greece and a large surrounding area. All the Greece schools were closed for at least five days. As a result, the school calendar had to change to add makeup days.

Adding the makeup days turned out to be both complex and contentious. Three vacation days, including the last two days of the spring vacation week, were designated as makeup days and combined with the extra days in the calendar. Following the requirements of the contract, the superintendent met with the affected union presidents and they agreed to the revised calendar. The staff was informed of the calendar revision in a memo dated 18 March 1991.

If the story had ended there, it would have been an unpopular but probably not an explosive issue among the staff. Shortening spring break meant that many would have to abandon long-standing vacation plans, and some would lose money on air fare changes, lost reservation deposits, and so on. However, the 18 March memo left the door open to modifications by saying, among other things, that the district was seeking special legislation to use an alternative approach.

On 26 March, the district reversed its earlier decision and announced the new calendar, leaving spring vacation week intact and holding school on Good Friday-Passover and 21 June instead. But again, timing was a problem. The decision was announced to a meeting of all employee association presidents and a memo went out to employees the same day. But the message did not reach most teachers immediately, and many did not find out until just before the rescheduled day. By then some teachers had canceled spring vacation plans due to the uncertainty. Many had family plans for Good Friday-Passover that had to be changed. Moreover, the news got to bus drivers, cafeteria workers, and students before most teachers and principals learned of the decision. The teachers were described as "incensed" and convinced that no one in the administration cared about the impact on them. It also appeared to many that their officers had failed them as well.

Budget Crisis

At the same time, the district and employees were wrestling with a serious budget crisis. In early spring, the Greece district has been informed of a substantial reduction in anticipated state aid revenues for the coming school year. A loss of approximately $1 million prompted the district to begin discussions with employee unions, including the GTA. Bennett and Schramm represented the GTA in these discussions.

The situation came to a head in late March, at the same time as the makeup day controversy. The GTA officers called a special meeting of the representative assembly to deal with the budget cut and salary freeze issues. Although willing to make some salary concessions, the representatives were largely unwilling to give up salary increases simply to avoid a tax increase. The result was an impasse within the GTA.

To resolve the impasse, two more special meetings were held. But the representatives were still unwilling to agree to a salary freeze or concession without a tax increase. Bennett apparently believed that some kind of GTA salary concession was appropriate and resisted communicating a hard line to the superintendent. The superintendent, meanwhile, was pressing Bennett for a small GTA concession as a sign of good faith. All this discussion took place without any official proposals coming forth.

Bennett's resistance to communicating the GTA hard-line position to the district was seen by some GTA members as excessive advocacy for the board's position and raised questions about his loyalty. His loyalty came into even sharper question a few days later when a local paper published an article in which he seemed to disclose confidential information about the GTA position on the salary freeze from the previous meetings. Rather than giving a clear statement of the GTA position, Bennett was quoted as saying, "Some teachers say we ought to do what we can to save jobs." This disclosure angered many GTA members and galvanized active opposition to Bennett and Schramm, resulting in the candidacies of Alexander and Maiorana.

There is no evidence that the former officers actually betrayed GTA interests. The problems were more a consequence of conflicting notions about what the proper role of officers should be.

The success of the challengers appeared to be a result of some general dissatisfactions with the performance of the Bennett-Schramm team and some specific events surrounding salary negotiations and makeup days. The election did not signal a movement away from the basic principles or goals of the reforms. It does seem clear that the new officers will be devoting more attention to nonreform issues, adjusting the pace and direction of change to better fit the desires of the teachers. This change could slow or even redirect the restructuring process in some important ways, but not by abandoning or diverting attention from the basic goals. The teachers supported the process and participated actively with considerable enthusiasm. Only in some specific matters did their interests and the officers' diverge — perhaps more than the former union officers realized. That, more than anything, seems to account for their defeat. It also suggests that the relationship between union affairs and reform agendas may be rocky at times but can still lead to significant results.

The reform agenda may have a more serious test as a result of recent events. In 1992, Yagielski resigned to take a superintendency in suburban Albany, New York. His resignation was a reaction to a long and bitterly contested campaign to pass a school bond issue referendum for a new elementary school. Although the ballot issue passed in December 1991, Yagielski said he was "burned out" by the process, which he described as a highly personalized battle between himself and a number of senior citizens opposed to the project. His fatigue and disillusionment led him to consider overtures from other districts.

It is too early, of course, to judge the effects of his departure on labor relations. The political climate of the district seems to be growing more contentious, but if the reforms themselves are not the objects of conflict they may survive and prosper. The board and teachers have continued to cooperate on the referendum campaign and budget matters, which indicates that the foundation for cooperation remains intact.

NOTE ON FIELD INVESTIGATION

Anthony Cresswell made three visits to the district in spring and summer 1991, and several follow-up interviews were conducted. Administrators, teachers, and union officials were interviewed. A large body of reports, publications, agreements, and other union and district documents was examined.

REFERENCE

Fisher, R., & Ury, W. (1981). *Getting to yes: Negotiating agreement without giving in*. Boston: Houghton Mifflin.

6

Glenview, Illinois

FROM CONTRACT TO CONSTITUTION

Mark A. Smylie

In September 1989, teachers in the Glenview Public Schools ratified a new agreement with the board of education that turned their traditional contract into what the district calls its "constitution." This collectively bargained agreement signals a change in labor relations from adversarial pursuit of economic self-interests to collaborative restructuring of teachers' work and decision making throughout the district. The agreement exchanged traditional work rules for philosophical principles and professional responsibilities for the education and care of children. As a metaphor for change in the district, the constitution shifts emphasis from work rules to work goals, roles, and responsibilities in defining the professional lives and relationships of teachers and administrators.

THE GLENVIEW PUBLIC SCHOOLS

Glenview, a northern suburb of Chicago, is a predominantly white, professional, middle- and upper-middle-income community. Although several large Chicago-area corporations, including Kraft, Zenith Electronics, and Scott Foresman Publishing, are headquartered there, many residents commute to work in downtown Chicago. A Naval Air Station and large mobile home park make the community more racially and economically diverse than its location might suggest. Between 1970 and 1990, Glenview's population grew almost 50 percent, rising steadily from 24,880 to 37,090 people.

Glenview is served by separate elementary and high school districts. The Glenview Public Schools constitute the community's elementary district. Three primary schools serve students in kindergarten through third grade; three intermediate schools serve students in fourth through sixth grade. One middle school enrolls all the district's seventh- and eighth-grade students. The district employs approximately 220 classroom teachers and 13 school and district-level administrators.

Glenview's central administration has been remarkably stable over the past 20 years. William J. Attea, superintendent since 1970, is only the third superintendent in the district's history. Other district offices have witnessed equally long tenures.

Until recently, school-level administration reflected the stability and longevity of the central office. However, four of the district's seven principals retired or resigned in 1990. As a result of replacements and reassignments, five principals and two assistant principals were new to their buildings when schools opened in fall 1991.

The Student Population

Glenview Public Schools enroll 3,200 students in kindergarten through eighth grade. Between the late 1960s and 1980, enrollment declined from 4,800 students to 2,600, due primarily to changes in birth rates and age distribution. Since 1980, enrollment has increased steadily.

Like the community's population, the district's student enrollment has become more ethnically diverse. The student population has changed from almost 100 percent white in the early 1970s to 82 percent white, 2 percent African-American, 4 percent Hispanic, and 12 percent Asian-American in 1990–91. Thirty different primary languages are represented among Glenview's students, creating increased demand for English as a second language programs. In 1990–91, 6 percent of the students were eligible for the federal government's free or reduced-priced lunch program, the highest number of eligible students since the district began participating in the program. Although Glenview students generally score well on standardized tests of achievement — their scores rank in the top 15 to 20 percent in statewide comparisons — the district does not fare as well in comparisons with its more affluent, ethnically and socioeconomically homogeneous neighbors.

District Finances

The Glenview school district is fiscally healthy. Its fiscal health and stability have been important factors in promoting school reform over the past ten years. In 1989–90, Glenview spent $5,574 per pupil, compared to the state average of $4,808 per pupil. However, Glenview has the lowest per-pupil expenditure among the North Shore school districts.

The Glenview Education Association

Teachers in the Glenview Public Schools are represented by the Glenview Education Association (GEA), a local affiliate of the Illinois Education Association (IEA) and the National Education Association (NEA). Approximately 80 percent of the district's teachers are GEA members. Between 1983 and 1991, Marilyn Miller, a speech-language pathologist, served as GEA president. She was reelected for eight consecutive year-long terms without substantial opposition. In fall 1991, Miller decided not to seek another term and was replaced by Mary Stump, a first-grade teacher.

The GEA, which is supported by the regional IEA staff, is governed and administered by a 27-member executive board. The GEA has no paid staff and follows the usual practice in smaller NEA-affiliated locals of using the services of an IEA staff member. The GEA has traditionally focused most of its attention on supporting teachers within the district and has not regularly played an advocacy role in school board elections or administrative appointments.

The GEA has become a partner with the administration and the board in school reform initiatives. As such, it has come to play an active role in developing district programs and policy.

LABOR RELATIONS IN GLENVIEW

Labor relations have been a particular focus of superintendent Attea's administration. When he assumed the superintendency in 1970, Illinois had no collective bargaining law, and he initially delayed the district's entrance into collective bargaining. At that time, recognition of teachers' unions was a local board option. The GEA sought recognition in 1970 and began to negotiate a contract with a school board committee. But on his appointment, Attea reviewed the draft contract and retained a labor attorney who advised that the contract "gave away the store." The board refused to approve it, and the GEA maintained a relationship with the district but did not bargain contracts until 1976. For several years, Glenview was one of the largest districts in the state without collective bargaining.

The union negotiated three-year contracts in 1976 and again in 1981. In spring 1984, the GEA and the board began negotiating a new agreement. Talks proceeded without substantial difficulty until the board proposed that the contract incorporate a performance-based career ladder plan. This proposal became a serious impediment to settlement. Although the proposal was eventually withdrawn, the board and the GEA agreed to discuss it after formal contract negotiations. Those discussions eventually led to the creation of a teacher career development program, Project PEER (Promoting Excellence in Education through Recognition), which established new leadership roles for teachers at both school and district levels and provided the foundation for new teacher-administrator working relationships that would reappear in the 1989 constitution.

The new three-year contract, ratified in fall 1984, contained general work rule provisions related to compensation, leaves of absence, position vacancies and transfers, retirement, and grievance procedures. It also contained a provision to roll the contract forward without additional negotiations, except on salaries. On its expiration in August 1987, the contract was rolled forward for two consecutive years.

Toward Collaborative Labor Relations

In what became a distinctive feature of labor relations in the district, superintendent Attea and GEA president Miller were able to focus bargaining—as well as labor relations generally—on the achievement of educational goals for the district. Beginning in the mid-1980s, Attea and Miller discussed shared priorities for the district's students and for the professionalization of teachers. These priorities helped them relinquish "ownership" of traditional labor-management positions; they moved beyond using bargaining to win concessions and used it to pursue commonly held aims for the district.

Relations with the IEA and NEA

The IEA played an integral role in developing collaborative labor relations in Glenview. It assigned several staff members who had experience in alternative bargaining strategies to work in the district prior to the constitution. They helped the district develop and implement a teacher career enhancement program that was part of the 1984 contract. They helped the district adopt a collaborative bargaining strategy for its 1988 contract negotiations and facilitated planning groups of the GEA representatives, administrators, and board members that crafted the constitution.

GEA and district relations with the IEA have generally been positive. During negotiations for the constitution, several individuals among IEA's leadership expressed concerns about specific provisions of the agreement. However, those concerns were addressed in revisions. Some tension resulted from an individual IEA staff member who strongly opposed the constitution. This staffer had been assigned by the IEA to work with Glenview but left that assignment in the early stages of negotiations. Some teachers and administrators in the district allege an ongoing relationship between this individual and a small but vocal opposition group of teachers who attempted to block negotiations. While the IEA has not specifically endorsed the constitution as a model, it has profiled the agreement in its literature and at statewide conferences.

Likewise, GEA relationships with the NEA have been positive. NEA leadership has supported and recognized from the beginning Glenview's collaborative labor relations, teacher career enhancement initiatives, and constitution. Indeed, NEA has invited Glenview to make presentations at national and regional meetings and at its Mastery in Learning conferences. NEA has also featured the district in internal "think papers" on collaborative labor relations and membership publications.

THE CONSTITUTION AND SCHOOL REFORM

In summer 1988, after the 1984 contract had been rolled forward for the second time, the GEA, district administration, and board decided to craft a completely new bargaining agreement that reflected collaborative labor relations and new conceptions of teacher professionalism. According to one teacher, "We really didn't want another contract. We wanted a constitution."

Development of the Glenview constitution may be traced to the district's experience with new teacher leadership roles in Project PEER, the teacher career enhancement program initiated during 1984 contract negotiations (Smylie, Brownlie-Conyers & Crowson, 1991, 1992). These roles were planned by a committee of teachers, administrators, and GEA representatives in 1984 and 1985 and were formally established in a 1986 side-letter agreement. They involved the competitive peer selection of classroom teachers for "specialist" roles with incentives of added responsibility, recognition, and compensation.

Three types of specialist roles were established: (1) subject area specialist, (2) technology specialist, and (3) instructional specialist. As time for new contract talks approached, GEA president Miller recalls:

> We were fearful and reluctant to go back to the traditional bargaining. We didn't want to get into an adversarial role again. So we just started to brainstorm and talk about what were some other ways that we could negotiate. It was decided there by a couple of teachers that we would start meeting informally to talk about what we wanted teaching to be like in five to ten years.

During a discussion in Miller's living room, a junior high social studies teacher suggested developing a constitution rather than negotiating a new contract.

Planning and Development

Informal discussions among GEA leaders and members continued throughout the 1987–88 school year. GEA continued to explore different bargaining options (for example, "win-win," traditional negotiating, and "strategic bargaining") and key themes of teacher professionalism around which new negotiations might develop. In December 1987, these discussions broadened to include district administration. The discussions progressed so well that the GEA determined to craft a new agreement rather than extend the existing one. At the end of the summer union and district leaders reviewed their discussions with the board of education and presented different options for future negotiations. The board agreed and began working with this group of teachers and administrators to establish a framework for developing a new 1989–90 agreement.

Board members, GEA representatives, and district and building administrators served on three substantive issue committees — professional responsibilities, professional relationships, and finance — and a coordinating committee to develop what was to become the constitution. Each committee, which was composed of four teachers, two administrators, and two board members, was cochaired by a teacher and either a board member or a district administrator. Committee chairs served on the coordinating council, whose responsibilities included resolving differences among the committees and developing the final bargaining agreement.

The board and GEA adopted the "strategic bargaining" approach to guide their work. The intent of strategic bargaining is to place squarely on the table a set of organizational problems that are central to strategic planning in organizations. It focuses attention on the future of the organization rather than on the self-interests or concerns of individual parties.

Committees began meeting weekly in October 1988. Each committee was to brainstorm issues and make preliminary recommendations for the new agreement. Committee members received additional staff development in group processes and problem-solving skills. Regular feedback meetings were held at each school to inform teachers and principals of committee deliberations and to receive their ideas.

Jean Conyers, the district's director of instructional services and a member of the professional responsibilities committee, recalled the initial discussions:

> We talked about sabbaticals for teachers. We talked about being involved in action research. We got into discussions about restructuring the schools, having extended days, going 7:00 to 7:00 or whatever. We also talked about different roles and responsibilities of teachers and their involvement in the profession. We talked about responsibility for furthering the growth of one another and themselves, issues around mentoring and peer coaching and even issues around peer evaluation. Our discussions were quite global in nature.

Committee deliberations proceeded vigorously from October 1988 through February 1989. The early start of the discussions that year allowed teachers, administrators, and board members to work creatively without the intervening tension of the short-term deadlines of conventional collective bargaining processes. Members of different committees reported how close they had grown and how much of a support group the committees had become. The assistant superintendent observed how struck he was that after some initial expressions of territoriality, it was not long before "some of the teachers started to sound like board members and conversely some of the board members started to sound like teachers."

Adoption and Ratification

Following months of committee discussions and meetings with building faculties and administrators, the coordinating committee began to synthesize the work of the three issue committees and draft the full constitution. As Miller, a member of the coordinating committee, recalled: "We had to try to understand where everybody was coming from. It took a long time to put the actual framework of the constitution together. This was such a radical difference from contracts."

The constitution went to the district's teachers for ratification in May 1989. As they neared a vote, a group of teachers asked the board to consider whether more than the simple majority required by state law should be sought in a contractual change of such magnitude. The GEA executive board concurred and proposed that a two-thirds vote of approval be required for ratification.

On the first vote in June 1989, the constitution fell five votes short of the two-thirds needed for ratification. In analyzing teachers' concerns, GEA, the administration, and the board became aware of three specific changes that needed to be made to garner sufficient votes for ratification. These changes related to the constitution's requirement that teachers — including current teachers — hold master's degrees for continued employment in the district. The changes were made, and teachers ratified the revised agreement in July by a 79% majority. In August 1989, the constitution was signed by GEA and board representatives.

Principles and Provisions

Glenview's constitution is a legally binding, three-year collective bargaining agreement. It differs from conventional contracts because it contains statements about mission and principles, precisely those topics that labor attorneys, particularly attorneys for management, warn against.

The GEA and the school district agreed to "broad-based involvement in decision making. . . . We are committed to structures and processes which rely on collaboration and consensus in making educational decisions" (Glenview Public Schools, 1989, p. 3). Consensus decision making is not simply a vague word. It establishes a new process:

> Consensus means general agreement and concord. For consensus to exist, it is not necessary for every participant to agree in full, but it is necessary for every participant to be heard and, in the end, for none to believe that the decision violates his or her conviction. It is not necessary that every person consider the decision the best one (Glenview Public Schools, 1989, p. 3).

The constitution also commits the union and the district to the "growth of teaching as a profession" and to "holding ourselves and each other accountable" for the educational process. The agreement recognizes "the importance of teachers being involved in the setting and implementing of standards of professional practice" (Glenview Public Schools, 1989, p. 3).

The constitution also makes substantial changes in teacher work roles. The usual days and hours provisions are missing in favor of a general list of responsibilities. The constitution contains a set of bylaws that address conventional collective bargaining issues — work calendar, teacher leave and transfer policies, grievance procedures, compensation and benefits schedules, and retirement policies.

Expanded Teacher Work Roles.   The principles lay a foundation for expanded teacher work roles. The constitution sketches these roles in ambitious but intentionally general and ambiguous terms, as "expectations . . . to serve as guidelines to all involved in the implementation of this agreement." According to the constitution, teachers are responsible for defining specific standards of practice that articulate how these roles are to be performed.

The constitution states that teachers' work must be viewed in a "holistic professional manner." Work extends beyond interaction with students in classrooms to include developing productive working relationships with other teachers, administrators, and parents; engaging in career-long professional learning and development; and participating in planning and decision making at the school and district levels.

New Decision-Making Bodies.   Although the constitution affirms the board's final responsibility for district governance, it states that in exercising its role, the board "shares with the professional staff through a collaborative, consensus decision-making model the responsibility for determining how the goals and mission of the district might be achieved." To this end, the constitution maintains the PEER specialist roles and creates new opportunities for teachers to participate in and make program and policy decisions at the school and district levels.

Each elementary attendance area, consisting of one K–3 primary school and its paired grade 4–6 intermediate school, is to establish a local school council comprising four parents, four teachers, and each school's principal. The district's middle school is to establish its own council, with the same representation of teachers, parents, and administrators. Local school councils are to form goals and expectations for their schools and evaluate initiatives designed at the school level to achieve them.

In addition to these decision-making bodies, each school is to establish its own building council to develop strategies to achieve local school council goals. They are also to develop policies and procedures related to the organization, budget, and educational program of the school. The constitution permits each school's faculty and principal to determine the structure and composition of its building council.

The constitution establishes three district-level standing committees, each chaired by a teacher and made up of three teachers elected by district teachers, the GEA president, a principal, a district-level administrator, the superintendent, and board member. Decisions are made by consensus. The Personnel Committee is charged with addressing general issues of teacher rights and welfare, developing teacher personnel policies, and developing and monitoring the implementation of a new teacher evaluation system. The Finance Committee is responsible for developing policies and procedures related to salaries and fringe benefits and making recommendations to the board about the district's budget. The PEER Committee (renamed the Education Committee in 1991) is charged with responsibility for the district's instructional programs and teacher professional learning and development. Like the former PEER Steering Committee, this group is responsible for supporting, coordinating, and supervising the work of the PEER specialists. Subcommittees (reading, math, and so on) carry out the work of this committee. Decisions of these district-level committees require board approval only if they require adjustments in the budget or appropriation of additional funds.

A district-level Coordinating Council monitors implementation of the constitution and hears and acts on appeals to the actions of local school councils, building councils, or district-level committees and subcommittees. Membership of this council consists of the three teachers who chair the district-level standing committees, the GEA president, a principal, the superintendent, and the president of the board of education. Decisions of this body are final and binding.

These new bodies shift the locus of decision making and governance away from administration and traditional union-management negotiations. The constitution establishes new processes by which teachers — not the GEA or administration — assume primary responsibility for most decision making. It protects the fidelity of those processes by placing teachers in key leadership positions on decision-making bodies and by making them majority members. Importantly, the constitution shifts the roles of the GEA and district administration from being decision makers to being guardians of a process by which others make decisions.

Implementation

By most accounts of teachers and administrators, the first year of implementation was remarkably smooth. Changes contained in the constitution were slowly phased in through the 1989–90 school year.

The GEA agreed not to grieve anything related to the constitution that first year.

Initially, a district-level orientation team of teachers and administrators was created to establish guidelines and timetables for constituting various school and district-level committees and councils. In addition, the district conducted staff development sessions to prepare teachers, principals, and parents for consensus decision making.

Right on schedule in late fall 1989, the district-level committees and subcommittees began their work. In most of the committees, a substantial amount of time was devoted during the first year to developing goals, agendas, and working relationships among members. As the year progressed, these committees began to focus more on the substantive issues for which they were given responsibility.

The Personnel Committee. During the first two years of the constitution, the Personnel Committee addressed a number of issues including employee benefit claims, a no-smoking policy, teacher access to school buildings after hours, notification of within-district position vacancies, an employee assistance council, and nomination guidelines for various state and national teaching awards. The committee also heard several cases brought by individual teachers concerning leaves of absence, salary advancement, and tutoring district students after hours for extra remuneration.

A substantial amount of the Personnel Committee's work during the first year focused on developing a new district-wide teacher evaluation system that promoted instructional improvement and professional development. Consistent with the principles of collaboration in the constitution, the new system incorporated an interactive model of clinical supervision linked to improvement of job performance. Teachers, with their evaluators, would have opportunities to discuss performance, set goals, and develop strategies for improvement. As mandated by state law, the new evaluation system made provisions for appointing consulting teachers to work with teachers whose performance and improvement were rated unsatisfactory. The committee developed the roles and responsibilities of these consulting teachers.

The Finance Committee. During the first two years of the constitution, the Finance Committee was relatively inactive because the constitution had set salary schedules and benefits packages for a three-year period. Activity increased in the spring and fall 1991 when the committee focused its attention in two areas: health and life insurance provisions and policies for district personnel, and the long-term financial status of the district in light of recent property reassessments and proposed state legislation capping local property taxes.

The Education Committee and Its Subcommittees.   During the first year of the constitution, the Education Committee began creating guidelines to enable schools to develop plans for restructuring the school day, thereby altering teachers' responsibilities and class schedules to create more time to participate in professional development activities and to work collaboratively on curriculum development and instructional improvement. During the second year of the constitution, this committee began to assess the implementation of restructuring plans developed by each of the building councils.

Also during the second year of the agreement, the Education Committee focused generally on improving evaluation of curricular and instructional programs across the district. Finally, the committee began to redefine the PEER specialist roles to make them more compatible with broader-based participatory decision making established by the constitution.

The curriculum subcommittees of the Education Committee addressed most district-level decision making in curriculum, instruction, and staff development. The reading and language arts, math, social studies, and science subcommittees reviewed curricular goals and objectives, developed new scopes and sequences of subject matter and skills, examined different instructional materials, considered approaches to grouping students for instruction, and discussed teacher staff development activities to support implementation of curricular and instructional programs.

For example, the Reading/Language Arts Subcommittee (one of the most active curriculum subcommittees) shifted the curriculum away from basal texts and toward a literature-based approach to instruction. The subcommittee began to define what teachers should be teaching in their classrooms and how they should be teaching it. Indeed, in spring 1991 this subcommittee established a system to monitor teachers' use of recommended instructional strategies and materials during the upcoming school year.

The Math Subcommittee sought to revise the curriculum to reflect the goals and standards of the National Council of Teachers of Mathematics, which meant moving from arithmetic, rote learning, algorithmic-based instruction to more concept-based, problem-solving instruction. It also meant increasing use of manipulatives in the classroom, incorporating other new instructional materials and texts, and developing a new student assessment plan. In conjunction with these developments, this subcommittee realigned instructional objectives, subject matter content, and curricular materials to better meet students' learning needs in kindergarten through sixth grade.

Local School Councils. The local school councils, formed during the 1989–90 school year, spent the first year identifying and selecting council members, establishing meeting schedules and agendas, and developing procedures for conducting business.

During 1990–91, local school councils devoted most of their time to developing goals for educational improvement. By far the most commonly adopted goals concerned improving parent-school relationships. Two councils adopted goals of improving communication with parents; three adopted goals of enhancing parents' roles in the education of their children. Two councils proposed developing parent education programs.

Other goals set by local school councils included promoting community values through education, developing a new homework policy, developing curricular and extracurricular programs to promote student success and sense of well-being, and promoting applications of technology in all areas of classroom instruction. Councils monitored activities they had set in motion and used information they collected to reexamine and refine their goals for the 1992–93 school year.

Building Councils. Under the constitution, each school could choose how it established and structured its building council. Teachers and principals in each school spent considerable time planning the organization of their building councils and developing strategies for identifying and selecting members. In almost all schools, principals and faculty decided to open council membership to all teachers in the building. Perhaps because of its size and its "house" structure, the district's middle school opted to develop a representational form of council structure.

One of the primary substantive tasks of each building council was to develop proposals for restructuring the school day and expanding the amount of time available to teachers for collaborative planning and program development. These plans were submitted for approval to the district-level Education Committee in spring 1990, to be implemented the following school year. Building councils also addressed student assignment, staff selection and assignment, and budgets.

Over the next two years, building councils focused their activities in three primary areas: implementing proposals for restructuring the school day, developing and implementing strategies for achieving local school council goals, and initiating individual school improvements.

Initial Outcomes

Few data have been collected by the district to assess initial outcomes of district-level committee work and decisions. The most comprehensive information concerns decisions of the two most active curriculum subcommittees—the Reading/Language Arts Subcommittee and the Math Subcommittee. These data, based primarily on surveys and interviews, indicate that classroom teachers generally agree with the content of the subcommittees' decisions, perceive the subcommittees to be responsive to their individual concerns, and accept the legitimacy of teacher-made decisions and the committee decision-making processes.

Initial data also reveal that almost two-thirds of classroom teachers have made some change in their classroom practices consistent with the decisions of the two curricular subcommittees. Almost 60 percent reported changes in their thinking about students and teaching that were related to subcommittee decisions. And nearly 50 percent of classroom teachers attributed positive changes in their students' attitudes about school and learning to subcommittee decisions; 40 percent attributed some positive academic achievement effect to those decisions.

Although the district has not systematically evaluated the achievement of specific building council goals and activities, it has begun to evaluate schools' efforts to restructure the school day. The findings of an early evaluation by the Education Committee indicate that increased collaborative planning time led to positive outcomes. Teachers reported that they learned new techniques from collaborating with colleagues and that they had devoted more time to their own professional learning and development. Teachers also said that they have expanded their knowledge of individual students through discussions with other teachers and professional staff members, including social workers and school psychologists.

Faculty collaboration also seemed to improve the school climate. Teachers reported feeling more supported by colleagues and school administration and that communication among teachers and administrators had improved markedly. Teachers were beginning to move beyond sharing stories and strategies to work as teams to create new programs and address common educational objectives.

CURRENT STATUS OF LABOR RELATIONS

During the first three years of the constitution, labor relations in the district remained positive and productive. The GEA, district administration, and board continued to work collaboratively. In spring

1991, Miller decided not to seek another term as GEA president. Pro-constitution candidate Mary Stump was easily elected, despite the presence of an opposition candidate. Stump was reelected to a second term in spring 1992 by a 78 percent vote. Stump's assumption of leadership in the GEA did not cause any serious problems in union-administration relations. After an initial period of adjustment, Attea and Stump have developed the same open, amicable, collaborative working relationship that Miller and Attea had attained.

In spring 1992, the GEA (with the support of nearly 80 percent of GEA membership) and the board agreed to roll forward the constitution for the 1992–93 school year. At the same time, the finance committee entered into renegotiation of salaries and benefits. These negotiations were completed in June without serious contention or controversy.

The constitution has devolved many decisions and disputes that would traditionally have been resolved through bargaining to district-level and building-level committees. Instead of focusing on decision making through bargaining, the GEA and administration have assumed new roles of educating district personnel and the community about the constitution and promoting new decision-making processes.

ISSUES AND CHALLENGES

By both district and GEA accounts, the first two years of the constitution were extremely successful. The relative ease of implementation was attributed to several key factors. First, the constitution was developed and implemented on a foundation of collaboration, trust, respect, and stability in labor-management relations, community support, and district finances. Second, Project PEER promoted visions and expectations for teacher professionalism that were shared by GEA and the administration and that both partners wished to institutionalize through bargaining agreements.

Third, the district had developed, over the years, a strong infrastructure of professional support. Throughout the implementation of Project PEER and development of the constitution, teachers and administrators participated in substantial professional development activity led by district personnel, university faculty, and outside consultants. This activity helped develop group process and decision-making skills and also helped increase teacher and administrator knowledge and understanding of substantive issues that new decision-making bodies would address. In addition, the district found support from a network of suburban Chicago school districts—the Consortium for Educational

Change—initiated by Jo Anderson and other IEA staff and the College of Education at the University of Illinois, Chicago. The network provides Glenview administrators and GEA leaders opportunities to learn from other districts and to gain new perspectives on their own initiatives, achievements, and concerns.

But toward the end of the 1990–91 school year, a number of important issues and challenges began to emerge, signaling the end of the honeymoon period. The success of the constitution rests at the building level with the capacity of each school to broaden its decision-making structures and adopt consensus processes that work. The constitution gives individual schools wide latitude to decide the composition and the decision-making scope of their building councils. Nearly every school has wrestled with how to interpret and implement the consensus decision-making process contained in the agreement. A number of teachers and principals have begun to discover the many ways in which consensus decision making can be delayed, rechanneled, and sabotaged. One teacher observed, "I think because the honeymoon is over you find that some teachers aren't quite as earnest about participating as they once were."

In addition, individual schools have struggled with transitions in roles and responsibilities. The constitution strongly influences the role of the building principal, although implications for principals' roles are only now being discovered. Building councils have begun to struggle with which decisions are theirs to make and which remain the prerogative of principals and district-level committees and administrators. As one district administrator explained: "There have been a lot of questions from all people. Parents say 'What are you involving us for?' Teachers are saying 'We don't want to be involved in all the decisions.' Principals are saying 'What is my role?'"

Some teacher opposition to the "new unionism" also has developed, grounded in perceptions that the GEA has become too "cozy" with the administration and that the constitution is too open-ended in its demands on the time and energy of classroom teachers. Opposition seems related more to fear of problems in the future than specific concerns about the present. Opponents, for example, question whether the GEA will still be able to protect them if problems arise. If the four-to-one margins of support for rolling forward the constitution to the 1992–93 school year and for the reelection of pro-constitution candidate Stump as GEA president are indications, the strength of this opposition is not great. Yet incorporating disgruntled teachers in the changes created by the constitution remains an important issue for the district and the union.

Several issues have also arisen with respect to evaluation and accountability. As described earlier, the constitution shifts the locus of responsibility for decisions from school and district-level administrators to new teacher-dominated decision-making bodies. In one sense, this relieves administrators from accountability for specific decisions that are now shared among many. As one district administrator put it, decisions have less "adversarial impact" when shared. There is less need for administrators to find ways to protect themselves. They can point to other people to explain bad decisions.

Yet the constitution also increases administrators' accountability for following and preserving the fidelity of the decision-making process itself. According to one principal, "If you don't follow the system, you get into trouble." For principals, "trouble" can come from both teachers and district-level administrators. For district administrators, it can come from teachers, the GEA, and the board.

Accountability extends beyond playing by the rules. Administrators remain accountable for the results of decisions made by others. Attea describes the issue this way: "The bottom line is kids, what's happening to kids. If this isn't improving things for kids, it's not worth it. . . . Sooner or later the pie is going to hit me in the face and [the board is] going to say, 'OK, this has cost us a bundle over the past few years. What more are we getting?' That's a legitimate question."

The district grapples not only with who is accountable to whom for what but also with how evidence can be gathered to evaluate the effectiveness of the change. Evaluating the constitution poses both conceptual and technical problems, especially in attempting to map and empirically test the relationships among organizational changes brought about by the agreement, improvement in classroom learning opportunities, and the learning and development of children in classrooms. (Recently, the district has entered into a contract with a private research firm to evaluate all aspects of the constitution.)

Finally, Glenview faces what Attea calls its "education problem": the challenge to develop understanding and acceptance of the principles and provisions of the constitution among all faculty and administrators in the district and within the community at large. The GEA and district-level administration are well aware of problems that may result if they get "too far out front." Related to this issue is an observation made by IEA's Jo Anderson that the ultimate success of initiatives such as Glenview's constitution may depend on a district's ability to develop "external anchors." Such anchors include state policy to legitimize and support these initiatives over time, community perceptions and attitudes that these initiatives are consistent with expectations about proper roles of teachers and administrators and about what and whom schools are for, and community beliefs that at the bottom line, children will benefit from such fundamental changes in school organization and labor relations.

REFERENCES

Attea, W. J. (1970). *Professional development: The roles of the professional, the school, and the university.* Unpublished manuscript.

Crowson, R. L., & Smylie, M. A. (1989). *The Glenview constitution: An event history.* Unpublished manuscript, University of Illinois at Chicago, College of Education.

Education Committee. (1992). *Evaluation of collaborative planning time models.* Report to the Board of Education, Glenview Public Schools.

Glenview Public Schools. (1984). *Agreement between board of education, community consolidated school district #34, Glenview, Illinois and Glenview Education Association, 1984–87.*

Glenview Public Schools. (1989). *Constitution, an agreement between the Glenview Education Association and the board of education of the Glenview Public Schools.*

Glenview Public Schools. (1990). *District management document: Program descriptions and objectives for 1990–91.*

Smylie, M. A., Brownlee-Conyers, J., & Crowson, R. L. (1991). *When teachers make district level decisions: A case study.* Paper presented at the annual meeting of the American Educational Research Association, Chicago, April.

Smylie, M. A., Brownlee-Conyers, J., & Crowson, R. L. (1992). *Teachers' responses to participatory decision making: The nexus between work redesign and the classroom.* Paper presented at the annual meeting of the American Educational Research Association, San Francisco, April.

7

Miami

AFTER THE HYPE

LeRae Phillips

Probably more than any other school district in the country, the Dade County Public Schools (DCPS) have consciously developed and courted the image of an educational change maker. However, more than seven years of reforms, recession-driven financial crisis, an increasingly skeptical press, and internal fatigue caused by the difficulty of implementing changes have forced the realization that the renewal process is far from complete.

A *Miami Herald* account of the district's site-based management efforts cited waning optimism and little student performance improvement (Grant, 1991). Even superintendent Octavio Visiedo sounded vaguely distant. "There were a lot of people who believed that this was the answer to education reform. I never believed that," he said. "It is a strategy in the arsenal of tools."

However, what has been called the Miami renaissance continues in the DCPS, which serve the city and its suburbs. Reforms continue because the extraordinary demographic changes still require response and because, despite the difficulties, the people still widely believe that the reforms are headed in the right direction.

Reforms have persisted through five superintendencies. Nonetheless, the district has remained remarkably stable. Its administrators are largely career veterans of the district. Its teachers' union has had substantially the same leadership since the 1960s. School board membership has also been stable, and board support for reforms has been nearly universal, even though it frequently splits on other issues.

The school district's stable elements have allowed it to produce change without having things fly apart at the same time. Labor relations and the labor contract are among the most stable elements around which long-term change can be structured. Change has been produced by a series of new programs, most of which were negotiated and jointly led by the Dade County Public Schools and the United Teachers of Dade (UTD).

A HISTORY OF CHANGE IN MIAMI

Images of Miami have always been widely exported. In a 1920s sepia tone, a housing developer seated in a fan-backed chair peers out confidently; in his white suit, he resembles a Southern Gatsby. The wealthy tourists of the 1950s smiled out on flickering television screens to proclaim Miami the sun and fun capital of the world. By the 1980s, black and white had given way to pastels and Technicolor, a "Miami Vice" multiethnic world of seductive style and violence. And in the 1990s, worldwide changes are raising political hopes of democratization, while a recession here is distancing the American dream.

Miami's schools also have a national image. The district has become synonymous with large-scale reforms in urban school districts. It has a breakthrough labor contract and a highly productive political relationship between district and union. School-based management and budgeting systems let schools allocate hundreds of thousands of dollars to uses of their own choosing. And in temporary quarters throughout the city, teams of teachers and administrators are planning new schools, called Saturn Schools, from blank yellow pads to reality.

How did the reform movement begin in Miami? In the early 1980s, the schools faced what one report called "a formidable challenge" (Dade County Public Schools, n.d.). The schools were experiencing serious overcrowding, low student achievement scores, and high dropout rates. A teacher shortage presented additional challenges to an already overburdened school system. "The methods then in place for dealing with these problems didn't seem to be working" (St. John, 1989). Changing the district's image was seen as instrumental to solving Dade's severe teacher shortage.

Historical Turning Points

Miami schools are accustomed to change. They grew rapidly during boom times and languished as the tides of fortune ebbed. But even the explosive past could not prepare the schools for this generation. In the 1970s, an economic slowdown and the end of the baby boom coincided, and between 1975 and 1983, Dade school enrollment declined by 23,000 students. Simultaneously, the composition of the student population was changing rapidly as waves of largely Latin American immigrants reached the city (Greater Miami Chamber of Commerce, 1990, p. 5). In 1960, 5 percent of Dade County's population was Latino; in 1990, 49 percent was. A new wave of growth is now under way. District projections call for continued enrollment increases up to 329,000 by the turn of the century.

Dade County is now the nation's fourth largest school system, with 297,411 students and 38,322 full-time employees, including over 16,000 teachers in 284 schools. The schools have become increasingly pluralistic and are now truly multiracial and multiethnic. One high school has 60 nationalities represented among its students. Nearly half the students are Hispanic. About 20 percent are white non-Hispanic and about 33 percent are African-Americans.

The Miami-Dade school system is seeking to graft teacher professionalism onto a complex bureaucratic and hierarchical structure, a structure that is in flux. In 1986 a Bureau of Professionalism was created to coordinate the School Based Management/Shared Decision Making (SBM/SDM) project and other labor relations initiatives. This bureau was collapsed in 1991 in the wake of significant central office cutbacks. Now the district is attempting to carry out reform through its traditional structures rather than create new ones.

National Attention and Reports

Public attention to the condition of public education in Miami helped create the climate for reform. Board member Michael Krop cites *A Nation at Risk* (National Commission on Excellence in Education, 1983) as gaining the board's attention. The union's chronicle cites the 1986 Carnegie Forum report. An American Federation of Teachers (AFT) task force, chaired by UTD executive vice president Pat Tornillo, wrote a third report. Similar themes were sounded: Public education was sufficiently troubled that business as usual would not suffice; organizational restructuring was required, with more autonomy and responsibility given to individual schools and heavy involvement required of teachers.

LABOR-MANAGEMENT RELATIONS

Miami's labor relations history is atypical. Although it has undergone the progression from perceived radicalism to partnership, its passage from one ethos to another has not been marked by the high levels of union-management conflict that characterize most other school districts. The phrase "a working relationship" appears in the union's account of the first contract negotiated under the Florida collective bargaining law of 1975 (Dade County Public Schools, n.d.). Indeed, one of the district's hallmarks has been a stable relationship between the district office and the teachers' union. Joint committees and collaboration on educational issues have been part of the labor-management scene since the beginning. Close organizational relationships are enhanced by long-standing personal ones.

The UTD has its roots in the Dade County Classroom Teachers Association (CTA). Founded in 1930, more than 90 percent of the district's teachers were members by the end of the decade.

In 1962, a Carol City Junior High School English teacher and counselor, Pat Tornillo, ran for the presidency on a platform that included merging the separate black and white teacher organizations. Tornillo, who was thought to be militant and antiadministration, won by 72 votes, the narrowest margin in the association's history. The following year, Tornillo became executive secretary. He has led the union ever since.

The 1960s was also a decade in which the teachers' organization established an identity and existence separate from the school district. Words such as "militant," "confrontational," and "intransigent" were used to describe the 1965 negotiations between the CTA professional practices committee and the school board (United Teachers of Dade, n.d.). A former school board member, now a state senator, described that confrontation as "the day teachers got off their knees, stopped begging, and started bargaining" (United Teachers of Dade, n.d.).

The year 1968, universally recognized as a pivotal one for labor-management relations, saw the district's first and only teacher walkout and its first negotiated contract. It was not until 1974, however, that the Florida legislature passed the Public Employee Relations Act, a bill Tornillo helped draft.

In 1974, the CTA dissolved its association with the National Education Association, merged with the Dade Federation of Teachers, and affiliated with the American Federation of Teachers as Local 1974. And it adopted its current name—the United Teachers of Dade.

Many of the relationships between union and management are personal as well as organizational. Former assistant superintendent Gerald Dreyfuss, who coordinated school-based management sites for the district, was a director of the union in the 1960s. Karen Dreyfuss, a director of the Dade-Monroe Teacher Education Center, is a long-standing union activist. Former superintendent Joseph Fernandez walked the picket lines as a teacher in 1968. Former superintendent

Paul Bell officiated at the wedding of a union staff member. As former associate superintendent Frank Petruzielo says, "I know Tornillo's people like I know my family. I've been dealing with them for 12 years. There's been a lot of water that's gone under the bridge."

The stability of leadership in Miami allows reform ideas to incubate long before they are hatched. Collaboration among long-standing leaders has allowed ideas to be remembered, to be developed, and to reemerge when the time is right.

After the release of *A Nation at Risk* in 1983, Tornillo and superintendent Leonard Britton began to meet regularly to discuss issues related to the professionalization movement. According to Tornillo, "What gave it continuity was that Leonard and I agreed that we were going to put into the collective bargaining contract the professionalization of teaching task force and the (necessary) flexibility that was going to give us, in terms of exploring a whole variety of different avenues. . . . Once that was done, it became part of the contract and we began to get legitimacy . . . and it didn't matter that Leonard left and Joe [Fernandez] came in because Joe was part of that whole movement, in terms of professionalization, and he embraced it totally" (Provenzo, 1989, p. 15).

The Changing Nature of the Contract

Miami has a fat contract — 252 pages of text in the 1988 agreement. However, some of the restrictive work-rule language found in other contracts is absent. Class size, for example, is not set according to an absolute maximum. Rather, the contract calls for a procedure using student enrollment to drive the resource allocation formula.

The contract specifies five instructional periods for secondary teachers (Dade County Public Schools and the United Teachers of Dade, 1988, p. 79). But hours of employment and length of the school day are not contractually specified, although school starting and dismissal times are established by the board.

The procedures and the substance of the evaluation system are specified in the contract. But so, too, is the establishment of a joint labor-management committee to make evaluation terminology consistent with the professionalization of teaching (Dade County Public Schools and the United Teachers of Dade, 1988, p. 30).

In contrast to other districts, the Miami contract is a working document, full of flex and change, rather than a trophy case of past victories whose preservation is a point of honor. Administrators and union leaders consciously ignore the contract admonition that "employee involvement and collective bargaining are quite different processes and as far as possible kept on separate tracks" (Rosow & Zager, 1989, p. 53). The reforms being made both add to the contract and deviate from it. Site-based management schools here, as elsewhere, can seek contract waivers, and more than a hundred such waivers have been granted. However, the waivers themselves are noted in the contract, put into an interim document, and later incorporated into the contract itself. The various reform committees also produce changes to the contract that are then incorporated.

This flexible use of the contract seems not to engender the resistance that might be expected. Administrators appear not to fear incidental broadening of bargaining scope or creating a possible pitfall for subsequent litigation.

As bargaining has come to concern itself more with reform issues, the process of reaching agreement has also changed. The district and the UTD develop proposals using joint committees that meet continually. "Each year now, we go back in and clean up the article on professionalization. We tune it, we modify it and put in new initiatives that have evolved in the course of the year," Petruzielo said.

The process of reform through contract also follows the rule of noncoerciveness. "We don't box people in, we test-pilot ideas before there is widespread dissemination," said Petruzielo. The contract not only allows for and documents change, but also sets the course for future change and keeps that course visible to teachers and the public.

The Role of Lead Steward

The union has created the position of lead steward to match the district's reorganization around lead principals who coordinate and facilitate the high school feeder pattern of schools. The stewards help coordinate "the feeder pattern councils along with the system's new lead principals" (Staff, 1989). Lead stewards receive a $2,000 annual stipend from the union and are expected to complete a certification program developed by the University of Miami.

PROFESSIONALIZATION THROUGH SBM/SDM

Professionalization of Teaching is the umbrella for reform in Miami-Dade. Its goals include decentralization through school-based planning, budgeting, and management; collegial control of the profession; expansion of professional development opportunities; educator responsibility; and paperwork reduction. As a system priority, professionalization goals and procedures have been widely documented in the contract, board rules, and the district's strategic plan.

The keystone of professionalization is Miami-Dade's boldly conceived School-Based Management/Shared Decision Making (SBM/SDM) program. School-based decision making is not mere decentralization. It affects the roles of teachers, principals, district administrators, and the union. Now implemented in over 160 schools, SBM/SDM began in 1986 with the selection of 33 pilot schools and a budget of $148,000 in a site-based management grant from the Florida Department of Education. School-based management was intended to focus all the system's resources, including budgetary authority, at the school level, where the resources could be applied directly to improve student learning.

Except for training support, SBM schools do not receive extra money. "Cost neutrality" is used as an underlying principle, so that the effects of SBM can be attributed to the processing and priority ranking of resources rather than to additional funding.

Infrastructure for SBM

In preparing for SBM, two Professional Issues Review Committees (PIRCs) were set up to clarify and gain consensus on the goals of SBM/SDM, develop models and sample proposals, and review a bibliography of literature assembled by the Bureau of Staff Development. One PIRC consisted of SBM principals, the other of UTD representatives.

Site-Based Budget System. The way for site-based management was paved with the Site-Based Budget System (SBBS), a modification of a software system developed in the 1970s. Financial discretion is substantial, amounting to as much as $1 million per school. Site-based management of nearly all salaries lets schools add and delete positions, including teachers, administrators, classroom aides, and community aides, according to school-determined needs. Some funds previously allocated through area offices, such as those for security and cafeteria monitors, are now allocated directly to SBM schools. Dollars saved during the year in the substitute teacher accounts may be converted to discretionary funds.

Waivers. Schools may request waivers to labor contract provisions, school board rules, or Florida Department of Education rules. Each waiver request is signed by the school principal, the UTD steward, and the SBM chairperson. As schools' programs change, waivers may be added or deleted at any time of the year. The policy of the Professionalization of Teaching Task Force, a joint labor-management committee, has been to approve waivers as long as schools can show a relationship between the proposed waiver and student outcomes. In each case, that school's plan, rather than practices at other schools, serves as the basis for the decision.

Implementation of SBM/SDM

Three groups of SBM schools have been developed, one each year starting in 1987–88. Teams from the 33 original pilot schools received training grants of about $6,200 and were encouraged to seek additional resources. Ideas for the decision-making process and reform were gathered from a large intellectual community: universities, district personnel and staff development facilities, businesses, and educational literature.

Shared Decision-Making Councils. Each school designed its own decision-making body, defined its membership and functions, and gave it a name. Some are called *cadres* or *cabinets* and others have been given school-specific names. The decision-making bodies are typically composed of teacher representatives, principals, and UTD stewards. Teachers on the councils may represent grade levels, departments, teams, or special assignment groups. Other administrators, nonteaching staff, parents, students, or community and business representatives may be included on either an ad hoc or a permanent basis.

Standing committees with designated functions are part of the decision-making structure in several schools. Typically, there are three subcommittees — budget, curriculum, and personnel. Ad hoc committees are formed for specific issues.

The "quality circles" approach was the most common method of committee or group functioning. But however schools organized their governance, teacher empowerment is a constant theme. As one teacher said, "When we say site-based management . . . we're talking about total control over what happens at this school."

School size appeared to influence group decision making; small was considered better. At larger schools, the communication system became more complex, and decision making was sometimes painfully slow. Still, big schools reported good progress in overcoming the effects of size. Overlapping with the size issue is that of the high school departmental structure and the special interests, categorical funding, subject-specific credentials, and community traditions associated with secondary schools.

Finally, school decisions were heavily influenced by a perception of crisis or great external pressure. For example, Little River Elementary rapidly took to site decision making after it was threatened with closure and reorganization by the superintendent. Those schools with pressing social, academic, or resource needs seem to have moved more quickly and more fully into reforms that help children.

Individual School Programs.   Specific school programs varied in response to perceived needs. By teaming up the speech teacher with the special-education teacher, Bunche Park Elementary was able to provide a more coherent program for its students who had special needs in both language development and learning.

Chapman Elementary established transitional classes for kindergarten and grade 1 students who were not quite ready for grade-level work. Smaller classes of 24 students, assisted by aides, were provided to give students a good start while preventing stigmatization. The successful program was extended to grades 2 and 3. Whole-language instruction was the main focus of change and staff development efforts at Coconut Grove Elementary. Language arts instruction was reorganized into two-hour blocks of time for literature-based instruction.

The "exploratory wheel" program at Myrtle Grove Elementary provided second and third graders with enrichment activities on a rotation basis and reduced class size for part of the day. Support staff — librarian, counselor, lab assistants, aides, and an hourly teacher — direct the lab activities for half the students; the teacher-student ratio is then 1:15 for reading instruction in the classrooms.

Henry Filer Junior High School adopted the middle school "house" concept. Grade levels were housed in separate wings of the school, teams of teachers worked with their shared groups of students, and an additional class period was established to give teacher teams common planning time.

Spanish teachers at Miami Palmetto Senior High School gave up their conference periods to reorganize their student load into smaller classes. Since beginning site-based management, the school has implemented a series of year-long programs to address the needs of students who are the most likely to drop out. Community service is the focus of two of the school's reforms.

Little River — Back from the Endangered List.   The thirty-third pilot school, Little River Elementary, achieved admission to the project after a hurried, but unanimous, decision to apply. The faculty had been outraged by negative newspaper publicity about their school and seized the opportunity to "make an impact" once they were informed about the project. Like running to catch a train, the school sped directly into student-centered reforms and measures to remedy the lack of materials and poor condition of the physical plant.

Little River's program included science and computer labs and a three-level kindergarten program designed to give all children a good start. Junior kindergarten was conceived as an early intervention program. By implementing a different curriculum for junior kindergarten, and working with parents from the beginning, the school has been able to avoid the label of "retention" or "failure" for the children who move from junior kindergarten to the more structured regular kindergarten the following year.

The school took on a major curricular project of integrating language arts, not only among the language processes of reading, writing, and oral language, but with all other curricular subject areas, such as social studies, math, science, and computer technology. Support for the project was provided by two resource teachers who offered staff development, worked in classrooms, and provided resources. Also as a part of the original proposal, the school organized the Parent Teacher Center, where varied materials and extended hours provide many opportunities for parents to work with their own children in a comfortable setting provided by the school and to check out materials for home use. "Early bird" and after-school programs were added to the school's successful, child-centered reforms.

The staff soon applied site-based management and shared decision-making practices to areas outside the original proposal. They recruited Creole-speaking aides, teachers, and a counselor to meet the needs of a rapidly shifting student population. When the opportunity arose to develop a schoolwide Chapter 1 program, a committee worked out a plan to double-staff K–2 classes, yielding a teacher-student ratio of 1 : 20. They also created six community liaison positions, one per grade level, to increase communication between school and home.

EVALUATIONS OF SCHOOL-BASED MANAGEMENT

Three years after the first school-based management pilot schools started, the district released data from an internal assessment (Collins & Hanson, 1991). The *Miami Herald* called the results "mixed" (Grant, 1991).

Student achievement did not improve significantly over the period of the pilot program based on either the Stanford Achievement Test or the Florida Student Assessment (competency) Test. However, relative to all DCPS secondary students, those in SBM schools had lower drop-out and suspension rates.

Although aggregate data from 900 teachers obscure the differences among individual sites, the findings clearly indicate program success in the areas common to all SBM/SDM schools—professionalization and shared decision making. Perceptions of teacher collegiality increased. Teachers were highly involved in the project, felt that it addressed important issues, said that it affected a substantial portion of school activities, and retained their belief that it has the potential to improve school operations (Collins & Hanson, 1991).

Most principals liked school-based management, but few of them (17 percent) said that it made their jobs easier. Over 90 percent indicated that the project had resulted in broader staff participation and had potential for improving most school operations. But participation takes time; overall they rated the program more effective than efficient.

Teacher participation in hiring was called the "most successful and widely supported" of the nontraditional teacher roles. Funded nontraditional teacher roles, involving administrative or other leadership duties, also were generally considered successful. Teachers assumed by far the most active roles in their councils (Strusinski, 1991).

A CONTEXT OF MULTIPLE REFORMS

The SBM/SDM project both operated in a context of concurrent reforms and influenced other reforms. For example, almost immediately after the selection of the first pilot schools, the Partners in Education (PIE) program was established, followed by the Satellite Learning Centers project, both of which incorporated school-based management. Additional reforms, including the Saturn School project and the Dade Academy for Teaching Arts (DATA), have furthered innovation and professionalization in Miami-Dade.

PIE Program

The Partners in Education program is a joint effort of the Urban League of Greater Miami, DCPS, UTD, and the Miami-Dade College/ Wolfson Foundation. Twelve Liberty City schools in a single high school feeder pattern were designated for the program because of academic need and a high dropout rate among the disadvantaged students in that area. The schools did not enter the program voluntarily; they were asked to write SBM/SDM proposals using guidelines similar to those applied to the pilot schools.

Improving student achievement, measured by test scores, is the primary goal. Shared decision making and parent involvement were also incorporated into each proposal. Activities devised by the schools include community-based study halls, a buddy system for students, typing classes to build reading skills, a Black Student Opportunity (scholarship) Program, and Saturday School.

Satellite Learning Centers

Schools in the workplace, called Satellite Learning Centers, have been developed to serve the children of employees of cooperating companies or groups of businesses or institutions. To participate in this program, a company provides the facilities and overhead costs for the satellite school. The school district provides the teachers, materials, and educational program.

The first satellite school in Dade was developed in 1987 with American Bankers Insurance Group (ABIG), one of the area's largest employers. The first class, a kindergarten, was a natural extension of the company's child-care and preschool program, which had been in operation for three years. Two additional satellite schools were started the following year, and the ABIG school expanded to first and second grades. The district continues to accept proposals and to plan for further satellite schools. However, the program has not grown because businesses seem unwilling to provide space on their property to house schools.

Nonetheless, the satellite school concept appears popular. Parents like the convenience, security, and peace of mind it affords. Children entering kindergarten benefit from the continuity of setting and classmates. Teachers enjoy their autonomy in the small school setting while maintaining ties to a neighboring school.

Dade Academy for the Teaching Arts

Dade Academy for the Teaching Arts (DATA) is a joint union-district program designed to enhance teaching as a profession and to afford a true professional status for teachers. Each year 80 high school teachers, called *externs*, are released from their classrooms for nine weeks of intensive professional development. They participate in seminars focused on current issues and research in mathematics, science, language arts, social studies, exceptional children, and developments in their subject areas. At least half an extern's time is spent conducting an individual research project.

The core curriculum gives teachers access to the current research on topics such as critical thinking, cognition, technology, gender issues, motivation, and societal factors affecting learning. The individual projects let them pursue their professional interests and disseminate the results; the allocation of time for such a project underscores the commitment to teacher autonomy and respect for professional and academic ability. Collegial interaction is fostered by housing the program at a single site—Miami Beach Senior High. Plans are under way for an elementary DATA program, but DATA faces serious cutbacks or possible closure in the 1992 budget crisis.

Saturn School Project

Faced with a need for 49 new schools over a five- to seven-year period, the district saw an opportunity to experiment with highly innovative programs built from concept to reality. In establishing Saturn Schools, former superintendent Joseph Fernandez asked for creative proposals: "We think there are a lot of other models out there that we haven't even thought of yet" (Olson, 1989). The first accepted proposals came from within the district, but requests have gone out soliciting ideas nationwide.

District applicant teams of one principal and one teacher were enlisted to write proposals that were required to include the school's philosophy or mission; programs for improved education; plans for shared decision making, staff development, and professionalism; selection and organization of staff; organization of students; and parent-community involvement. Proposals put forth by district teams and accepted in December 1989 included plans for an ungraded school, a school emphasizing community work and field trips, a school involving teacher research, a school emphasizing bilingual and multicultural studies, and a university school (Bradley, 1989).

Comprehensive training was planned for the district teams that would head up the first schools. The training encompassed orientation to the district's professionalization efforts and philosophy; presentations, review, and discussion of research on restructuring and school-based management/shared decision making; analyses of school data for the proposed sites; and budgeting and other topics of importance for opening a new school.

The Saturn program continues. South Pointe Elementary School in Miami Beach opened in 1991, a joint venture of the school district and Minneapolis-based Education Alternatives, Inc. The school is based on the child-centered Tesseract program pioneered in Minnesota.

South Pointe is designed around an unusually low teacher-student ratio: 25 students for a teacher and aide. Private foundations are being asked for $1.4 million to make up the difference between the school's normal public allocation and that which it requires. At South Pointe, as in other experiments, the object is to create examples of urban education that work.

The Overlap of Professionalization Reforms

SBM/SDM, PIE, and Saturn Schools have much in common. In addition to defining their governance, these schools all design and initiate their own reforms. Professionalization, teacher participation, peer evaluation, and the lead teacher position have been developed under all three. Decisions about supplementary programs, including schoolwide Chapter 1 programs, are subsumed under the governing councils of these schools. Yet differences in focus among SBM/SDM, PIE, and Saturn Schools are evident. For example, SBM/SDM schools, where participation was voluntary, seem more proactive and inventive than PIE schools, which, in effect, were ordered into the program.

Saturn Schools are different because of their newness — the focus is on creation rather than change. Much attention is therefore given to plant specifications, purchasing, and hiring functions. The school mission is created by a small group of leaders, then conveyed to the teaching staff in the process of recruitment and hiring. As new personnel are hired, they help shape the school program; site-based management is thus always seen as the refining of initial plans.

WHAT HAVE WE LEARNED FROM MIAMI-DADE?

As teachers in Miami-Dade take on new roles, their view of education expands to include the whole school, and they begin to act on behalf of that whole. A broader perspective begins with teacher participation in interviewing, hiring, budgeting, scheduling, and evaluating that far exceeds conventional school committee work. Each of these activities was previously the exclusive purview of the administration. Even in establishing shared decision making, teachers delineate the range and purpose of the decisions they consider and the decision-making process they use.

About Teachers' Roles

We were struck by the extent to which teacher decisions served the interest of the school rather than that of individuals. Teachers often voted to accept larger class loads or to give up a prerogative to achieve a school goal. Repeatedly, we heard such statements as, "It's brought us closer together. We realized we're not just dealing with our own personal needs or our classes. We're dealing with the total school." Through the experiences of peer evaluation, hiring, or making decisions together, teachers have become more committed to and more support- ive of one another. United by a common purpose, ethnically diverse groups of teachers have become working teams. Taking risks together, making mistakes, and trying again have contributed to collective com- mitment.

The decisions teachers made often involved trade-offs within a constant budget. Several schools used their assistant principal alloca- tions either to have lead teachers perform the duties or to provide other instructional services, aides, or materials. Similarly, student loads were often shifted around to provide better programs. In some cases, teachers agreed to teach more classes to reduce the number of students per class. In other cases, as noted earlier, teachers accepted larger student loads to let other classes, such as those for at-risk children, carry smaller loads. Such trade-offs were the subject of much serious deliberation, but they were common and generally accepted as necessary.

Through their interactions, teachers are reshaping the quality of communication in their schools. SBM/SDM schools have made consider- able efforts to keep their formal lines of communication open. Most have open cadre or council meetings. All teachers belong to a repre- sented group or quality circle and are potentially involved in generating proposals. A number of schools publish agendas before meetings, solicit suggestions for agenda items, and publish minutes immediately after. Informal complaining has decreased. The number of grievances has declined, and the topics of grievances are changing. Now teachers place a grievance when principals fail to use the schools' joint decision- making mechanism. Teachers are interacting with more of their peers about matters of more substance.

Teachers have become recognized as generators and seekers of ideas, as thinkers. As council members, they determine what type of in-service sessions to conduct for their school and which speakers to invite. Teachers, especially union stewards and council chairpersons who network through regular meetings, exchange ideas with people at other schools. Individually, many Dade teachers have pursued professional growth by attending conferences, pursuing research interests through DATA, presenting staff development programs, speaking in or out of the district, and researching and writing proposals for SBM schools or Saturn Schools.

In many schools, faculty meetings do not look the same as they did before. Teachers set the agenda, manage the meetings, and present proposals to be discussed and voted on. The group process training undergone by many councils and staffs brings greater efficiency and focus to meetings.

Teachers who serve as union stewards are generally pleased with the changes in their roles. Other teachers now come to them for information on the union point of view rather than to initiate grievances or voice complaints. Administrators, too, see stewards as resources rather than bearers of bad news. The stewards tend to see themselves as facilitators of communication and teacher involvement. Teachers seem to be taking more care selecting colleagues to represent them. As the status of the steward position increases, more elections are contested.

The newly created lead teacher roles have been uniquely defined by their school programs. Some lead teachers have responsibility for instructional leadership and management of an interdisciplinary team or a department. Some replace assistant principals, handling discipline and/or teacher supervision on a full-time or part-time basis. Some are released for one or more class periods; still others teach full time and provide additional services beyond the school day. In a satellite school, a lead teacher is, in effect, both teacher and principal.

Teachers also have begun to evaluate their peers. They have profited from observing others, learned from the suggestions of teaching colleagues, and found that they respected other teachers as evaluators more than they respected administrators in that role.

The new distribution of authority means that teachers have faced and made difficult hiring decisions. Not only did they learn about and develop skills in interviewing and ranking candidates, but many found that in the process of hiring someone, they had made a commitment to work with and help that person succeed once he or she was hired.

About Principals' Roles

Many school districts provide few incentives for principals to embrace expanded decisional roles for teachers. As Frank Petruzielo noted, "Nobody has advanced nationally a reason for them to buy in."

Miami-Dade has attempted to use both status and compensation to create an incentive for principal participation and engagement. Both secondary and elementary principals were reclassified into the district's executive compensation system at a level higher than all but a score of district administrators. Only assistant superintendents and above earn higher salaries than principals. This change was intended to signal that reform was focused on the schools and that it was no longer necessary to join the central office to advance a career.

The district has also made efforts to use and interpret school-based management as a way to provide flexibility and autonomy to *schools* as opposed to *teachers*. As a result, in SBM schools, the role of the principal has changed even more dramatically than the role of the teachers. The principal is seen as key to restructuring by management, labor, teachers, and the principals themselves. The descriptions we heard of SBM principals fit fairly neatly into three models: the prepared principal, the resistant principal, and the changed principal.

New principals, coming out of the Principal's Internship Program, are prepared for SBM schools. They know what to expect of their staffs and what is expected of them, and they are ready to begin.

Schools that have overtly resistant principals are not apt to have chosen SBM. These individuals are unwilling to give up power and they work actively to block the shared decision-making process.

Many veteran principals experienced major changes in their own roles and in their views about leadership when they entered SBM/SDM. Those who were established at a school went through the uncomfortable process of having their policies and practices inspected and reviewed by teachers. Those who had developed an authoritarian leadership style found that their staffs expected them to change—and some were able to change. Importantly, principals have emerged as advocates for the continuation of SBM/SDM (Daniels, 1990).

About Home-School Interaction

Parent involvement has increased in ways that are meaningful to the school communities involved. Parents in economically advantaged areas have pressed for a greater voice through involvement with the governing cabinet; parents in at-risk areas have most often been involved in activities focused on meeting family needs for nutrition, clothing, social services, work, and transportation. But it was the suddenness, the spontaneity, the "snowballing" effect of increased parent involvement in SBM schools that was most striking. As one school relates: "We started noticing more parents come in the minute we went SBM. . . . We used to have maybe five of the parents show up, and that's not much for a school of 1,200. The . . . year we went SBM, we noticed we had over a thousand parents in the cafeteria. And each year since then, it's been increasing, increasing, increasing."

About Measures of Success

Miami-Dade is seeking to professionalize teaching and invent new and better ways of schooling children. Site-based management offers potential in that search. School personnel say that it is working and point to many changes in the behavior of teachers, parents, and students. Teachers give their own time for peer observation, governance, and interaction with parents. They speak of unity, pride, and confidence. Parents communicate directly with school personnel, support program changes, and attend classes. More students attend classes beyond the school day and on Saturday and take pride in their school and their work.

About Risk, Trust, and Moving Forward

The UTD and the district have supported risk taking. "We need to get over this feeling that we can't do something because we're taking a risk," said UTD executive vice president Pat Tornillo. "I think the biggest risk we face is maintaining the status quo." Similarly, G. Holmes Braddock, vice chairman of the school board, related the board's position: "Our whole board has taken the attitude that education needs some restructuring. And if you think it needs that, then you can't not take risks." And former superintendent Paul Bell remarked, "I think that unless those two elements, trust and willingness to take risk, exist . . . there is a serious question of what you can really achieve" (Olson, 1989).

The message about risk and trust was received by administrators and teachers at SBM schools, where risk has come to mean potential for success without the fear of failure. Shared consequences and the responsibility to try something else are part of the system.

Dade teachers are on a path from which they see no turning back. Continued commitment to professionalization is clearly stated in the 1989–94 strategic plan for DCPS, but the momentum for professionalization is carried by the commitment of the people involved and the idea of professionalization itself. The idea has spread far beyond the influence of one person. Professionalization, according to union leader Pat Tornillo, is "an idea that, once launched, there's no way to stop" (Olson, 1987).

NOTE ON FIELD INVESTIGATION

Byron King gathered preliminary data by mail and phone. King, Julia Koppich, and Charles Kerchner conducted interviews and visited schools in spring 1990. Interviews were held with superintendent Paul Bell, other central office personnel, union leaders, and school board members. A telephone interview was conducted with union executive director Pat Tornillo. LeRae Phillips conducted several follow-up interviews.

REFERENCES

Bradley, A. (1989). Dade County chooses local designs in its competition for "Saturn Schools." *Education Week*, 13 December, p. 1.

Collins, R. A., & Hanson, M. K. (1991). *Summative evaluation report, school-based management/shared decision-making project 1987–88 through 1989–90*. Dade County Public Schools.

Dade County Public Schools (n.d.). *21st century labor relations: A study of the Dade County public school system*. Dade County Public Schools.

Dade County Public Schools and the United Teachers of Dade. (1988). *Contract between the Dade County public schools and the United Teachers of Dade, July 1, 1988–June 30, 1991*.

Daniels, C. T. (1990). A principal's view: Giving up my traditional ship. *The School Administrator, 47*(8), 20–24.

Grant, C. L. (1991). 3 years later, teachers mixed on "experiment." *Miami Herald*, 17 January, p. 1B.

Greater Miami Chamber of Commerce (1990). *Summit 2000*. Miami: Author.

National Commission on Excellence in Education (1983). *A nation at risk: The imperative for educational reform, a report to the secretary of education* (226006 ed.). Washington, DC: U.S. Department of Education.

Olson, L. (1987). The sky's the limit: Dade ventures self-governance. *Education Week*, 2 December, p. 1.

Olson, L. (1989). Dade County will solicit ideas nationwide for design, structuring of 49 new schools. *Education Week*, 13 December, p. 1.

Provenzo, E. F., Jr. (1989). School-based management and shared decision-making in the Dade County public schools. In J. M. Rosow & R. Zager (Eds.), *Allies in education reform: How teachers, unions and administrators can join forces for better schools*. San Francisco: Jossey-Bass.

Rosow, J. M., & Zager, R. (Eds.). (1989). *Allies in education reform: How teachers, unions and administrators can join forces for better schools*. San Francisco: Jossey-Bass.

St. John, D. (1989) A unique labor-management partnership has made Dade County Public Schools a model in educational reform. *Labor-Management Cooperation Brief*, no. 16. Washington, D.C.: U.S. Department of Labor, Bureau of Labor-Management Relations and Cooperative Programs.

Staff. (1989). *UTD Today* (October), p. 10.

Strusinski, M. (1991). *Shared decision-making in school-based management: Characteristics of those who become its leaders.* Miami: Dade County Public Schools.

United Teachers of Dade. (n.d.). *CTA/UDT: A thumbnail history.* Miami: United Teachers of Dade.

8

Rochester

THE ROCKY ROAD TO REFORM

Julia E. Koppich

Before 1987, Rochester, New York, was known principally as the home of Kodak, Xerox, and Bausch and Lomb, a solid if not stolid manufacturing city astride the Genesee River. But all that changed with a headline: "Rochester Teachers to Make $70,000 a Year." A labor contract that produced a 40 percent raise for all teachers and a nation-leading top salary had made Rochester famous for school reform. The reforms, the salary increases, and the magnetism of its leaders spotlighted Rochester's schools. They also raised expectations of rapid and visible changes.

Although all the indicators point in the right direction, Rochester, like the rest of the country, is finding that real change is hard and takes a long time. The community has grown impatient. When the union attempted to explain the difficulty of reform, it was met with the rejoinder, "Yeah, but you took the money real fast." By the time we visited, the death of reform had been announced in some quarters. The obituary, however, is premature.

IN THE SPOTLIGHT

Since 1987, the school reform efforts, and the new labor-management configuration nested within them, have been held up to the light of public scrutiny. Educators, politicians, business and civic leaders, and concerned citizens watched as the new union-district partnership in Rochester launched an armada of education reforms. Innovations included a teacher career ladder, called the Career in Teaching (CIT) Program; Home-Base Guidance, designed to give each middle school student a caring "home base" teacher; and School-Based Planning,

Rochester's version of site-based decision making. Key to Rochester's reform efforts was the strong, collegial relationship forged between the president of the teachers' union and the district's superintendent.

By fall 1991, however, the word within educational policy circles was that reform in Rochester was unraveling. Attempts to achieve a successive collective bargaining agreement had met with shattering resistance.

First, teachers rejected a contract recommended to them by their union leadership. Teachers ratified a second tentative agreement by 97 percent, but the school board unanimously turned thumbs down. Finally, in May 1991, nearly a year after the expiration of the previous contract, teachers and the district approved a new pact. But the national rumor mill said that reform in Rochester was no more. School change efforts and union-management harmony in Rochester would soon be a thing of the recent, and forgettable, past.

Rochester's reform labor relations represents what happens when visionary beginnings meet organizational and political reality. Rochester's leaders have been among the most articulate in the country, and the changes they are attempting to make among the boldest. No other district, for example, has publicly tackled the question of teacher accountability for student success or failure. Tackling difficult problems is not the same as solving them, however. Rochester's story illustrates the difficulty in maintaining political support for heroic ideas about progress against the clamor for short-term, measurable results and continued political differences about the goals and programs of reform. Rochester dove into the national mainstream of education, came up gasping, went down again, but seems not to have drowned. Yet long-term prospects for institutional reform in Rochester public schools remain uncertain.

SETTING THE SCENE: GREATER ROCHESTER

Rochester's 245,140 citizens reflect the multicultural complexion of the nation's cities. Slightly more than two-thirds of the city's residents (75 percent) are white, one-quarter (25 percent) are black, and 5 percent are Hispanic. They inhabit an area whose proximity to several waterways, including Lake Ontario, the Genesee River, and the Erie Canal, has made possible the development and support of a solid base of industry and commerce. Kodak employs 40,000 people. Xerox and Bausch and Lomb are headquartered there, as is the flagship of the Gannett newspapers.

Rochester also prides itself on being an education and cultural center. The University of Rochester, with four campuses housing eight undergraduate and graduate divisions and more than 150 degree programs, anchors the academic community.

All, however, is not picture-postcard perfect. Rochester is a struggling, largely minority, inner city surrounded by a more prosperous suburban metropolitan area. The complex array of child-related social issues that have become disturbingly ubiquitous on the nation's urban landscape is much in evidence. The city's core industries face increasingly stiff foreign competition, which has sensitized them to the need for dramatic changes. These companies are concerned that students emerging from Rochester's schools are ill equipped for productive employment in modern American industry.

ROCHESTER CITY SCHOOLS

Rochester City Schools enrolled 32,700 students in 1990–91, making it the third largest school district in New York state after New York City and Buffalo. Student enrollment in Rochester declined slightly between 1985 and 1989, but by 1990 it had begun to inch slowly upward again. The percentage of white students enrolled in Rochester public schools, however, has declined steadily during the last 15 years.

Rochester is essentially an inner-city school district with an inverse relationship between the student population and that of the municipality. Although 75 percent of Rochester city residents are white, nearly 75 percent of Rochester public school students are minority. More than half of the students are black, and nearly one-seventh are Hispanic. In a city wrapped in progressive commerce and civic boosterism, family poverty is a repeated theme within the public schools. Nearly three-quarters of the school district's students come from low-income families. Nearly half live in single-parent, often female-headed households — the family configuration most at risk for poverty (Hodgkinson, 1989).

The school district employs 500 administrators, 2,600 teachers, and 2,200 classified staff. Rochester's 5 : 1 ratio of teachers to administrators makes the district rather top-heavy and is a source of tension between the teachers' union and district officials. More than 75 percent of Rochester's public school teachers are white. The majority live in the suburbs, a fact not lost on Rochester's minority resident community.

Financial Issues

Like many school districts throughout the nation, Rochester is coping with declining revenues. Rochester, like most districts in New York, depends on state finances for the majority (54 percent) of its operating revenue—$234 million in 1990–91. After a decade of large state budget increases for education (double digits were not uncommon), Rochester began to feel the results of economic recession. In 1991, New York Governor Mario Cuomo reduced the state's education budget by $900 million. Rochester lost $18 million in state aid. The district lost an additional $2.3 million in federal magnet school money.

Yet, even in economic bad times, the effect of reform was present. In spring 1991, amid the glare of television lights, superintendent Peter McWalters recommended budget cuts that would leave reform programs intact. He acted early, before the governor's budget was final, and developed his budget plan as a preemptive strike.

Although people in Rochester are understandably concerned about declining fiscal resources, the schools' expenditures are relatively high. Rochester's per-pupil expenditure in 1990–91 was $7,226, more than 45 percent higher than the national average of $4,896.

The school district is fiscally dependent on Rochester's city government. The board of education must submit the district budget to the city council for approval at the same time the mayor presents the city's budget to the council. City officials have authority to change the district's revenue allocations. However, a predetermined revenue allocation formula was developed in 1972 and subsequently modified in 1985 and 1990. As long as the district's budget remains within these set boundaries, the city is unlikely to tamper with the revenue allocations.

THE IMPETUS FOR REFORM

Beginning in 1985, Rochester took stock of its students' academic achievement. The district did not like what it saw. More than one-quarter (28.5 percent) of the students left the school system before the twelfth grade. Nearly half (42 percent) of seventh, eighth, and ninth graders were failing at least one core subject. Of children entering kindergarten, 80 percent were one year or more behind developmental norms. One in five students in grades 7 through 12 was suspended from school for infractions of discipline rules.

By the mid-1980s, the nation's education reform movement was in full swing. The National Commission on Excellence in Education's report, *A Nation at Risk*, had captured headlines in 1983. In 1985, the Carnegie Foundation for the Advancement of Teaching released *Teachers for the Twenty-first Century*, offering a new vision of schools and teaching.

But the story of Rochester's reforms can best be understood by first introducing its major players — the superintendent, the teacher union president, and the school board.

Peter McWalters, Superintendent

Peter McWalters was an uncommon district superintendent. He was younger, more outspoken, more teacher oriented, and less experienced administratively than most of his colleagues. He was also firmly committed to change.

McWalters's philosophy about children and education is exemplified by the mission statement he proposed and the school board adopted: "Ours will be a district marked by strong achievement that is not predictable by a student's circumstances or background." He reduces education to the moment of learning: "The only critical moment in the whole institution [school] is the one between the teacher and the kids. The whole system is really a series of investments to get the very best creative, prepared, empowered, authorized energy [in the classroom], and get everything else the hell out of the way."

McWalters describes himself as a "teacher on leave." He first came to Rochester in 1970. As a classroom teacher, he was active in the Rochester Teachers Association (RTA). During the 1980 Rochester teachers' strike, McWalters walked a picket line in front of the district central office.

In the early 1980s, McWalters was placed in charge of the district's budget department by then-superintendent Laval Wilson. Wilson left Rochester in 1985 to take up the reins as superintendent in Boston. McWalters was appointed interim superintendent while a national search was conducted to locate Wilson's permanent successor. But McWalters himself surfaced as the most promising candidate. He was appointed superintendent later that year.

Since leaving teaching for administration, McWalters's professional career has kept him in the district central office. He was never a building principal, which is a source of considerable consternation to current district administrators. "He doesn't understand what we do because he's never been one of us," they lament.

McWalters describes reform as being about a "new unionism." He describes the goal of his relationship with RTA president Adam Urbanski as "professionalism through unionism." To change schools, McWalters believes that the teachers' union must work as a partner with the district from the beginning. "I need the union with me as I go down that road [of reform]," he says, "or I'm going to keep bumping into them every time I want to change something."

McWalters left Rochester in January 1992 to become chief state school officer in Rhode Island.

Adam Urbanski, Union President

Adam Urbanski has been president of the Rochester Teachers Association, an affiliate of the American Federation of Teachers, since 1981. A Polish immigrant and former junior/senior high school teacher with a doctorate in American social history from the University of Rochester, Adam Urbanski is articulate, quotable, and passionate about his work. A poster from the Polish trade union Solidarity hangs on Urbanski's office wall as a constant reminder that "all things are possible."

Urbanski is also unconventional. He unabashedly proclaims that "unions as they used to be [are] a mismatch with the times." He adds, "Change is inevitable. Only growth is optional, and all institutions, including the union, must change or atrophy."

Urbanski's 1981 election followed a troubled year. The RTA had led teachers out on a nine-day strike. In addition, the district hired a new superintendent, Laval Wilson, who arrived in Rochester after a stormy tenure in Berkeley, California. Wilson's term in Berkeley had been marked by his authoritarian, top-down management style. And "he didn't change on the flight east," one observer remarked. Wilson was not keen on strategies that involved the union in significant school district decisions. Not until McWalters became superintendent did the RTA leader glimpse the possibility of education reform.

"We had a choice," says Urbanski, "between buttressing what *is* versus substituting what *isn't*. However one viewed the [pre-reform] circumstances — politically, pragmatically, or educationally — it was clear we needed a change in kind, not just a change in degree. We had reached the point where not taking risks was a greater risk than taking risks." Urbanski gravely jokes, "You'd have to be a lot smarter than McWalters and me to come up with something worse than what we were trying to change."

Urbanski is realistic about the difficulties of fundamentally altering

Rochester's education system. He points to three primary obstacles to reform. Money he describes as a "weak third." Second is impatience with the pace of change. The community wants quick results and becomes frustrated when test scores do not immediately climb. "But the greatest threat [to reform]," he says, "is that deep down inside, teachers, just like the general public, hold suspect any school that doesn't resemble the school they remember. I see teachers who actually have signs on their doors that say, 'Knowledge dispensed. Bring your own container.' This in spite of the fact that we know you cannot 'learn' someone. They have to do the learning" (Towler, 1989).

But the RTA president seems unruffled by union members who do not support his agenda. "It's their union as much as mine," he says. He just continues to urge reform, to encourage members to rethink unexamined positions, and to be prepared to think and rethink them again. "We're like bumper cars," he says. "They bump into a wall and then turn away in another direction." To make the reform happen, he claims, "you cannot be wedded to any position you take."

The School Board

Rochester City Schools is governed by a seven-member board elected to four-year terms in city-wide, partisan elections. Each member receives $15,000 per year as compensation for board service; the board president earns $17,500. Six of the seven are virtually full-time board members. They maintain offices in school district headquarters and are there every day.

As this is written, the board is composed of three black male members, three white female members, and one male Hispanic. No white male — the classic "urban elite" — sits on Rochester's school board. Most of the current members have served on the board for more than a decade; all are Democrats. Five were parent activists in the 1970s; one has a background as a community advocate; and one, the newest and youngest board member, is employed in management at Kodak.

Board votes often split along race and gender lines. Board members seem to have formed relatively permanent voting blocks apparently anchored in different perceptions of the role and function of school. The three female board members want schools to nurture and to reach out to students and to the community. The three black members strive for a visible, structured curriculum as an open display of what is going on in the schools. The Hispanic member, often the swing vote on the board, carves his position down the middle.

PRECURSOR TO REFORM:
A CALL TO ACTION

"There is a crisis in our community. We are failing our young people," began *A Call to Action*, a 1986 report issued by the Rochester chapter of the National Urban League, an antipoverty organization focusing on social problems in the black community. The report likened the "waste of young lives" to a national tragedy, purposely juxtaposing it with the then-recent *Challenger* space shuttle disaster.

The report painted a stark picture of Rochester's youth. High absentee rates among students at all grade levels, unacceptably high dropout rates, low academic performance, and large numbers of suspensions for unacceptable behavior, compounded by high rates of poverty and limited chances of productive employment, all sketched a bleak future.

A Call to Action had its genesis in January 1985, when the Urban League of Rochester convened a group of prominent citizens to consider how the league might celebrate its twentieth anniversary. The Community-wide Initiative to Improve Rochester's Public Schools was the result of these conversations. The initiative generated two task force reports, which were collected into *A Call to Action*.

One task force, cosponsored by Rochester's Urban League and the Center for Educational Development (CED), a local clearinghouse for educational support and action, issued five principal recommendations to the schools: (1) maintain better contact with homes by giving parents "one dialogue partner — the homeroom teacher" (Rochester Urban League, 1986, p. 7); (2) make students more responsible for their own learning; (3) develop closer alliances with local social services agencies; (4) encourage the professionalization of teaching by establishing career advancement paths within teaching and internship programs for new teachers; and (5) expand opportunities for prekindergarten education.

The second task force, a joint effort of the Industrial Management Council and the Rochester Chamber of Commerce, focused on identifying positive ways in which business could help Rochester's youth. The task force set itself four major tasks: job placement, marketing public education, expanding staff training and development, and providing management consulting (Rochester Urban League, 1986, p. 30).

Many of the recommendations from these two reports became significant features of Rochester's reform agenda.

THE 1987 CONTRACT

The contract that brought Rochester to media prominence was signed on 15 October, 1987. Rochester's school board split, voting by a slim 4–3 majority in favor of the agreement. Teachers overwhelmingly approved it. The preamble to the contract, which emphasized joint union-district responsibility for fulfilling the educational needs of the school system and the legitimate expectations of the community, high-lighted shifting labor relations in Rochester and previewed the direction of educational change (City School District of Rochester, 1987).

Although the 1987 collective bargaining agreement contained a number of significant features, it was money, specifically teachers' sala-ries, that attracted the most publicity. In the first year of the contract, Rochester teachers would receive a $4,500 across-the-board salary in-crease. By year two of the agreement, half of Rochester's teachers would be earning at least $45,000 a year. In all, Rochester teachers would enjoy a 40 percent salary increase over the life of the three-year contract. The restructured salary schedule provided the possi-bility for teachers to earn an annual salary of nearly $70,000. The new accord made Rochester's teachers the highest paid urban instructors in the nation (Carnegie Foundation for the Advancement of Teaching, 1988).

Although Rochester's new contract encompassed 55 topics in 109 pages, much of the accord was in the form of an "agreement to agree" (Urbanski, 1988). Nonetheless, the contract also sketched the outlines of the Career in Teaching Program, School-Based Planning, and Home-Base Guidance.

Career in Teaching Program

The Career in Teaching Program restructured the salary schedule and began to reconfigure teachers' professional responsibilities. A four-tier career ladder would take the place of the conventional compensa-tion structure in which teachers advanced in salary on the basis of years of experience and college credits earned. The goal of the program was to make it possible for teachers to assume enhanced professional respon-sibility and enjoy greater professional discretion without leaving teach-ing for administration.

Level 1 of the career ladder is the *intern teacher* for individuals who are new to teaching or new to the Rochester school district. Level 2 is the *resident teacher* for individuals who have completed an intern-ship but are not yet permanently certified. Level 3 is the *professional teacher*, classroom instructors who are permanently certified and tenured. Level 4 is the *lead teacher*, professional educators who are selected through a competitive peer process to assume defined instructional leadership roles. These roles include mentors who assist and support intern teachers, demonstration teachers who offer specialized staff development services, adjunct instructors who work in cooperation with local college or university teacher preparation programs, and integrated curriculum designers who assist school sites in developing multicultural curriculum.

Lead teachers also serve as specialists in the intervention component of Rochester's Peer Assistance and Review (PAR). Patterned after the intern/intervention program developed in Toledo, Ohio, in the early 1980s, Rochester's intervention program is designed to assist tenured teachers whose performance is unacceptable.

Lead teachers are eligible to earn from 5 to 15 percent above their annual salaries as stipends for expanded professional responsibilities. By the 1990–91 school year, 90 Rochester teachers had been selected to occupy the lead teacher category.

The Career in Teaching Program is directed by a ten-member panel, five members appointed by the superintendent and five by the RTA. The chair rotates each year between teachers and administrators. Responsibilities of the panel include delineating roles and responsibilities of each of the four career levels, selecting lead teachers, and redesigning the performance appraisal system for professional teachers.

School-Based Planning

A single sentence in the 1987 contract triggered movement of significant educational decisions to individual schools: "The Board and the Superintendent and the Association agree to cooperatively participate in the development of school-based planning at each school location." The specifics of site planning were developed by a joint union-district committee convened after the contract was ratified. All schools participate.

School-based planning teams were first established in fall 1988. Composed of teachers (who form the majority of the team), administrators, parents, and (in high schools) students, school-based planning teams are decision-making bodies. By contract, the principal chairs the team. Decisions are made by consensus.

In effect, school-based planning moves collective bargaining to the school site. Each school team negotiates with the district to set targets for student performance and to secure the resources necessary to achieve the school's targets. The planning process, as outlined in the program's official guidelines, encompasses five stages: assessment, goal setting, implementation, monitoring and evaluation, and accountability. School-based planning teams are empowered to decide "anything that directly or indirectly relates to instruction and student performance" (Rochester City School District, 1988a). Schools are scheduled to be granted broad budget authority.

Teams are encouraged "to request waivers from the policies, procedures, and contractual language that constrain them from accepting greater responsibility for decisions about how best to educate their students" (Rochester City School District, 1988c). The burden of proof is on the central office — and the union when a contract provision is concerned — to find a compelling reason *not* to approve the waiver. Guidelines state, "Central office administrators will be expected to assist school-based planning teams by supporting their requests for waivers and working to remove barriers that impede them from accomplishing their goals" (Rochester City School District, 1988a).

Time is among the most precious commodities in ventures such as school-based planning. By contract, teachers' 1990 work year was extended from 185 days to 190 days to provide additional time for school planning and professional development.

Schools have met with varying degrees of success in their efforts to implement school-based planning. At some schools, teachers have been reluctant to assume additional responsibilities. In some instances, principals have bridled at what they perceive to be a diminution of their authority.

School-based planning is creating predictable role tensions in Rochester. Teachers previously established leadership by knowing and enforcing the contract. In school-based planning, teachers establish and maintain authority by displaying professional knowledge and expertise (Rochester City School District, 1988c).

Administrators used to establish authority by developing rules and regulations. Now, says the superintendent, "I'm saying, 'Sorry, now your authority is your competence, not your position. I am holding you accountable for your capacity to build consensus, to engage [teachers] as peers.'" Some principals, says McWalters, have adapted well to the new system. Others have not.

The superintendent reserves his greatest frustration for the district central office. "We have a meeting to decentralize and the staff leaves and turns decentralization into a directive. I'm having trouble getting central office to stop acting like central office."

Home-Base Guidance

Home Base Guidance was initiated in fall 1988 in Rochester's middle schools. Another "agreement to agree," the details of Home-Base Guidance emerged as the program was implemented rather than being a subject of explicit contractual agreement.

Each home-base teacher is assigned approximately 20 students and serves as these students' advisor throughout their middle school careers. The home-base teacher "provides a consistent focal point in each student's day" (Rochester City School District, 1988b). Twenty minutes are set aside each day for home-base students and teachers to work together.

Home-base teachers meet with students and parents at the beginning of each school year, maintain ongoing communication with the home, monitor cognitive growth and student behavior, serve as a resource to help students solve academic and social problems, refer students for additional services as appropriate, encourage participation in extracurricular activities, and promote attendance. Gaining teachers' acceptance for Home Base Guidance has been difficult. Although teachers generally agree that students have a range of needs beyond the academic, many teachers are reluctant to assume the responsibilities entailed in helping to meet these needs. The comment frequently heard is, "I'm not a social worker." (For a teacher perspective, see Murray, 1992.)

INITIAL REACTIONS TO REFORM

Not everyone was pleased with Rochester's 1987 contract. Adam Urbanski keeps a homemade greeting card he received from a teacher shortly after the accord was ratified. Constructed of faded-green, rough-hewn paper, the front of the card depicts the cover of the teachers' contract. To the inside of the card is taped a screw.

School administrators were neither early nor ardent champions of the district's reforms. Many continue to resist, and the Association of School Administrators of Rochester (ASAR), affiliated with the School Administrators Association of New York State, vocally denounces district reform efforts.

The current president of ASAR, Richard Stear, longs for the good old days before 1987 reform initiatives. "Everyone knew his role then," says Stear. "Principals [need] to reassert their educational leadership."

ASAR tried. In 1988, the organization filed suit against the RTA and the school district, alleging that the peer review program represented "a threat to the very heart of administrative functions." It did — and that was the point, said McWalters. ASAR lost the suit.

ASAR's views have not received a sympathetic ear from the superintendent. Peter McWalters has made it clear, said one RTA official, that "administrators were going to be on the train or under it." District legal counsel Adam Kaufman pokes fun at Stear and his organization by quoting a line from the film *Lion in Winter*: "Henry, this is the twelfth century."

THE ROLE OF THE BUSINESS COMMUNITY

Rochester BrainPower, designed to engage the local business community in improving the public schools, was born as the district's school reform efforts were launched. Spearheaded initially by Kay Whitmore, president of Kodak, and David Kearns, then chief executive officer of the Xerox Corporation, BrainPower has since been joined by managers from other companies.

Each year, on a rotating basis, one of the participating companies loans an executive to BrainPower to serve as that year's director. These individuals take their jobs seriously. Says Howard Mills, 1990–91 executive director of Rochester BrainPower, "I have never done anything as important in my life as this" — rather powerful words from a man whose career has included serving as program manager for the *Apollo* lunar landing and as manager of engineering facilities for Xerox worldwide.

BrainPower identifies five areas of business assistance to the schools and district. Each area is directly traceable to the Urban League's *Call to Action*. Rochester BrainPower (1) creates job opportunities by providing career counseling and job placement to Rochester students as inducements for improved academic performance; (2) develops school-business partnerships; (3) enhances professional development opportunities by opening corporate workshops to school personnel and providing funds to Rochester's Teacher Center; (4) makes corporate consulting resources available, offering sessions on organizational dynamics as well as personnel and budgeting operations to Rochester's central office staff; and (5) with the Advertising Council of Rochester, markets public education in Rochester.

Despite BrainPower's positive contributions and continued involvement with the district, there remains a nagging sense that the Rochester business community does not quite "get it." Corporate leaders assert the need for a new kind of work force, capable of handling high technology and competent to work in reorganized industries. Yet there is little "on-the-ground" realization of just how drastic, and how complicated, the changes in schooling need to be.

THE SECOND REFORM CONTRACT

It was in the negotiations for the 1990–92 contract that Rochester came to terms with differing expectations for reform and the difficulty of continuing to secure political and civic commitment. The agreement expanded Home-Base Guidance to the high schools, strengthened School-Based Planning, and enhanced the Career in Teaching Program. The preamble to the pact extended the notion of mutual district-union obligations that go beyond collective bargaining and included an explicit statement of extended professional expectations for teachers.

Eventually a second reformist labor contract was ratified, but the process of reaching it illustrates the challenges of using labor relations as a vehicle for reform. There were actually three "second contracts." The first one was rejected by teachers in September 1990. The second version, approved by teachers, was rejected by Rochester's school board in January 1991. Finally, a contract acceptable to both the board and teachers was approved in May 1991. The central issue was accountability.

The Issue of Accountability

The contract negotiated in 1987 expired 30 June, 1990. Talks were initiated prior to that date, and the union and the district decided that accountability would be the centerpiece of the new contract. The collective bargaining agreement, in other words, would be used as the vehicle for determining who is accountable to whom and for what, what students should know and be able to do, how student progress should be measured, and what incentives were reasonable to promote enhanced student achievement.

It all started with rational planning. To lay a foundation for the contractual agreement, the superintendent and union president jointly hosted a series of forums for parents, teachers, and Rochester school administrators. They also jointly appointed a Task Force on Shared Accountability for Improved Student Learning to make recommendations to the district and union bargaining teams. The task force report recommended that achievement be gauged on the basis of "authentic assessment" measures of what students know and are able to do. The report further recommended a set of requisite conditions, including smaller school units, reduced class sizes, and extended instructional time for students who require it.

Individual teacher accountability would be based on a Professional Code of Practice, based on criteria articulated by the National Board for Professional Teaching Standards. A new teacher evaluation system emphasizing peer review and assessment based on a structured professional portfolio would be developed, and salary increases could be withheld from teachers required to participate in the intervention component of the Career in Teaching Program.

The First Second Contract

Tentative agreement on a new contract between the union and the district was reached in September 1990. The contract included accountability provisions patterned after task force recommendations. Salary advancement would be determined by a Professional Practice Review Committee (PPRC) made up of two teachers selected by the union and an administrator chosen by the district. Teachers would submit to the PPRC professional portfolios, which might include supervisors' evaluations, examples of student work, results of peer reviews, and evidence of professional growth and community involvement.

The PPRC would have the responsibility to "affirm a rating" at one of three levels, each of which was attached to differential salary increases: (1) "meets or exceeds high professional standards," an 11 percent raise; (2) "must improve to meet high professional standards," a 4.2 percent raise; or (3) "unsatisfactory," no salary increase.

The school board was scheduled to vote on the contract before teachers voted. Prior to board action, details of the proposed pact were leaked. William Johnson, president of Rochester's Urban League, proclaimed that teachers had been "paid in advance" in the first contract in anticipation of substantial reform. The evidence of change, said Johnson, was insufficient to warrant additional salary increases. Other vocal community members urged the board to reject the agreement as too costly. The board approved the pact on a split 4–3 vote.

The RTA executive board unanimously approved the tentative agreement and recommended it to the union's policymaking body, the Representative Assembly. The 150-member assembly overwhelmingly endorsed the proposed contract and urged teachers to ratify it.

But before teachers had an opportunity to vote on the contract, the superintendent was quoted in the press as saying that teachers would need to work hard to reach the "excellent" category and that he expected very few to be assigned that ranking initially. Board members were quoted as saying they expected a "normal bell curve," with most teachers in the second, "must improve," pay category. By the time teachers met on 24 September, 1990 to vote on the contract, the controversial professional accountability section had been labeled "pay for performance."

Finally—and unfortunately—union officials organized the contract ratification meeting in such a way that teachers were allowed to cast their ballots before union officials could explain the agreement. By a vote of 849 to 774, Rochester teachers rejected the contract recommended to them by their union leadership. A thousand teachers chose not to vote at all. For the first time in New York labor relations history, a school board had voted to approve a contract and teachers had rejected it.

Rochester teachers' repudiation of the contract struck a blow to RTA president Urbanski. He considered resigning, but more than 500 letters of support arrived at his office, urging him to stay on. Urbanski did not characterize the teachers' defeat of the September 1990 contract as a rejection of reform. Neither did he take the contract vote lightly. About the contract, the RTA leader says simply, "I was wrong."

The Second Second Contract

For a month following rejection of the September 1990 agreement, the superintendent and school board demanded that the RTA president take the defeated pact back to his members for a second vote. Urbanski refused. Finally, the parties returned to the bargaining table. Linda Darling-Hammond of Columbia University and Lee Schulman from Stanford University were brought in to frame the accountability and evaluation issues.

In December 1990, as the district and the union renewed negotiations on a new contract, Rochester's school board extended the superintendent's contract by three years. According to the board, this action was designed to send the message, "reform isn't going away."

At least one board member remained critical of the superintendent. Ben Douglas, who voted in favor of renewing the superintendent's contract, nevertheless wrote an editorial that ran in Rochester's *Democrat and Chronicle*. Douglas wrote, "City school superintendent Peter McWalters talks a lot about 'accountability' in the schools. But now that his contract has been renewed the community needs some serious discussion of his own accountability both for the day-to-day management of the schools and the agenda of reform" (Douglas, 1991).

Another proposed contract was achieved in January 1991. Merit pay was gone, and in its place appeared a modified professional accountability plan, one described by district counsel Kaufman as "more user friendly." The Career in Teaching Program incorporated "remediation," including "full or partial salary withhold[ing] during the period of remediation." Teachers, who would earn approximately 9 percent more for each year of the two-year pact, ratified the contract by a 97 percent margin.

By this time, public knowledge of the New York State budget crisis was widespread. Gannett newspaper editorials urged the board to reject the contract. In the center of a 13 January editorial titled "Say 'No' to This Contract," the newspaper printed the names and home telephone numbers of the seven school board members and urged community members to follow the newspaper's lead. The board unanimously rejected the contract.

The Third Second Contract

The parties did not return directly to the bargaining table. In a curious turn of events, the four male board members paid a visit to union president Urbanski in early February 1991. The meeting was unofficial, off-the-record, and conversational. The three female board members were not invited to the meeting and were angry when they discovered their colleagues' activity, attributing it to "the old boys being at it again." What was accomplished by the meeting? Says board member Frank Willis, "Adam helped us understand we could settle this thing."

Despite agreement that a settlement was within reach, both sides knew that contract rejections had damaged their credibility. The union and the district jointly sought the assistance of a neutral third party, the New York State Public Employment Relations Board (PERB), which formally declared an impasse in Rochester negotiations. On 26 February, 1991, PERB appointed a tripartite fact-finding panel, which made the following recommendations: (1) that the union and the school district create a task force to develop a new teacher performance appraisal system, (2) that "opportunities be created for parent/community input into the discussion and development of performance appraisal design criteria," and (3) that teachers receive a 7 percent salary increase (New York State Public Employment Relations Board, 1990).

Once more, the parties returned to the bargaining table, now under a news blackout imposed by PERB. Finally, a new contract emerged. Approved unanimously by the school board and overwhelmingly by teachers, the 1990-92 accord incorporated most of the fact finders' recommendations. Teachers' salaries were increased by approximately 7 percent for each year of the contract, a new accountability task force was established under the auspices of the CIT panel, and the CIT panel was empowered to withhold raises for teachers who are rated "unsatisfactory." Despite false starts and setbacks, the new contract, say McWalters and Urbanski, "protects the [reform] agenda."

THE CHALLENGE OF RISING EXPECTATIONS

The good news is that education reform in Rochester is being swept along on a tide of rising expectations. The bad news is that rising expectations grow impatient of fulfillment.

When the 1987 teachers' contract was first publicly announced, a leader of Rochester's legislative delegation who had helped win additional state funds for the district's education reform programs said, "The [union and the district] are really going to have to demonstrate results." Added a colleague, "And the sooner the better" (Towler, 1989).

In the same vein, shortly after the 1987 contract was ratified, Rochester's *Democrat and Chronicle* (Staff, 1987) wrote, in what might have been construed as a warning, a threat, or a challenge, "The education reformers have promised improvements all along. Now they had better deliver."

When tests scores in the early elementary grades posted a slight improvement in 1988, Peter McWalters and Adam Urbanski wished aloud that it had not happened and cautioned against attributing these small increases to just-initiated reform efforts (Wilson-Glover, 1988). And Rochester journalist Desmond Stone (1988), in a report to the Center for Educational Development, warned, "There's evidence that the Rochester community does not fully grasp the immensity of the task it has set for itself. What is implicit in changing the way we educate our children is a wholesale top-to-bottom reordering of society's priorities." Stone's warning went relatively unheeded.

By 1990, the third year of the contract, nearly half of the Rochester citizens polled about school reform reported that they wanted more — and faster — evidence of educational improvement (Reid, 1990). The Urban League's Bill Johnson said that it was time to "call the question" on reform. Peter McWalters laments, "Everybody's asking, 'How's it going? Is it over yet?'" — as if reform should be "finished."

Contract rejections and community reaction to the proposed pacts have had a sobering effect on Rochester reformers. The school board in particular has been affected. Says board member Archie Curry, "We made the expectations too high, we did not explain that change takes time, we did not celebrate our successes. We did not talk enough about reform *after* the contract."

"When teachers rejected the [September 1990] contract, a crack appeared in the wall," says board member Rachael Hedding. "We had the public with us only superficially. Our only real power base was public opinion, [but] we did not solidify parental support."

Other board members worry that Rochester is trying too hard to be all things to all people. Board member Mike Fernandez says, "The laundry list [of all possible reforms] could become our strategic agenda."

Rochester remains in many ways a captive of its own publicity.

THE CHANGING SHAPE OF LABOR RELATIONS

Conflict over the second contract did not mean labor relations war in Rochester. Board president Kathy Spoto says, "The only way we're going to effect the kind of change we want to put in place is through collective bargaining. The contract is part of our strategic education plan. It [the contract] is an investment which moves the [reform] agenda forward."

The collective bargaining agreement, say union and district officials, is designed to serve as evidence that the community can expect teachers to engage in serious discussions about the teaching profession *specifically as it relates to student achievement*. "The contract," says RTA president Urbanski, "should be the floor, not the ceiling, for what teachers should be willing to do for students."

The union and the district are dealing consciously and publicly with "big-ticket" items and consequential ideas — accountability, student outcomes, and the definition of competent teaching. They have assumed joint custody of reform and turned the tables on the conventional wisdom of issue ownership. "Much of the change," says Urbanski, "is in who is saying these things, not in what is being said. [It's in] who owns what piece [of the reform agenda]." That the teachers' union actively pursues an outcome-oriented accountability system as the focus of its collective bargaining agreement is evidence of change.

Labor relations in Rochester is no longer a zero-sum game with victors and vanquished. The collectively bargained contract has become the principal vehicle for education reform. Labor-management cooperation is the strategy of choice to maintain the momentum for change. "We don't play the same game anymore," says the union's Urbanski.

UNANSWERED QUESTIONS, UNRESOLVED ISSUES

By conventional objective measures, Rochester has made gains since the onset of reform efforts. In October 1990, superintendent McWalters announced that more elementary students are being promoted to the next grade, fewer elementary students are enrolled in special-education classes, and elementary students' performance in reading and mathematics is up. More eighth graders are passing their English, mathematics, science, and social studies classes. In addition, more students are enrolled in New York State Regents courses, more students (and increased numbers of minority students) are taking the Scholastic Aptitude Test (SAT), fewer students are receiving long-term suspensions, and more home contacts are being made by school staffs.

Yet Rochester remains a district simultaneously full of promise and problems. Unanswered questions focus principally on issues of leadership and support. What would happen if Urbanski or McWalters left? We will find out. In January 1992, Peter McWalters left his position as superintendent in Rochester to assume new duties as chief state school officer in Rhode Island. Manuel Rivera, a Rochester school district "insider," was appointed superintendent. Time and political circumstances will write the next chapter of labor relations in Rochester.

Will parents stay committed? Some Rochester parents are now saying, "You are experimenting on our kids. Just give us what the white kids in the suburbs get." How long the community will wait for reform results remains an open question.

Circling around community concerns is the issue of teacher salaries. Teachers have received regular, and hefty, salary increases. Yet little money has been sequestered for program advances. The purposes for which school district money is allocated have become a "big-ticket" item in Rochester politics.

Can more change bubble up from the bottom? Reform in Rochester has been "top down," albeit with heavy union involvement. Change efforts have "bubbled up" only minimally from the schools and classrooms. Union and district officials have placed many of their hopes for school-initiated innovation in the school-based planning process. At present, school-based planning, with its emphasis on student outcomes, looks good on paper but seems shaky in operation. Few schools are making substantial changes. It simply is not clear that teachers (or administrators) have the same appetite for risk and tolerance for ambiguity as do their leaders.

Then there is the issue of business support. School board members acknowledge that business has "backed away" from intense involvement with the district. McWalters says, "When we were twisting in the wind, no one [in the business community] spoke up for us." Board president Spoto suggests that business leaders are not using their considerable clout to leverage dollars for schools, but instead are lobbying to keep their taxes down.

None of these issues has an easy resolution. What is clear is that Rochester City Schools has, for the present, weathered some severe storms with its reform agenda and collegial labor-management relations intact. Yet, say the cautious Peter McWalters and Adam Urbanski, "Those who wanted [Rochester] to fail or [to] be a shining point of light will just have to wait a little longer."

NOTE ON FIELD INVESTIGATION

Julia Koppich, Byron King, and Charles Kerchner conducted interviews in Rochester in April 1990 with union officers, administrators, and school board members. Three schools were visited, and interviews were held with approximately 20 teachers. Kerchner and Koppich returned to Rochester in 1991 in the wake of the contract negotiations cycle. Several persons were reinterviewed, and interviews were held with all board members.

REFERENCES

Carnegie Foundation for the Advancement of Teaching. (1988). *The condition of teaching: A state-by-state analysis, 1988.* Carnegie Foundation.

City School District of Rochester, NY, and the Rochester Teachers Association (NYSUT-AFT-AFL/CIO). (1987). *Contractual agreement between the city school district of Rochester, New York, and the Rochester Teachers Association (NYSUT-AFT-AFL/CIO), July 1, 1987–June 30, 1990.*

Douglas, B. (1991). *Rochester Democrat and Chronicle,* 14 January.

Hodgkinson, H. (1989). *The same client: The demographics of education and the service delivery system.* Washington, DC: Institute for Educational Leadership.

Murray, C. (1992). Rochester's reforms: The teacher's perspective. *Educational Policy,* 6(1), 55–71.

New York State Public Employment Relations Board (PERB). (1990). *Factfinding report and recommendations in the matter of impasse between Rochester Teachers Association and Rochester City School District.*

Reid, S. (1990). 48% want good students now. *Rochester Democrat and Chronicle*, 23 August.

Rochester City School District. (1988a). *Guidelines for school-based planning 1988–89.*

Rochester City School District (1988b). *The home base guidance program in Rochester city school district middle schools.*

Rochester City School District. (1988c). *Questions and answers about school-based planning 1988–89.*

Rochester Urban League. (1986). *A call to action.* Rochester: Rochester Urban League.

Staff. (1987). Now the hard part, earning the $45,000. *Rochester Democrat and Chronicle*, 23 August.

Staff. (1988). Why Al Shanker wants a revolution in the classroom. *Rochester Democrat and Chronicle*, 17 January.

Stone, D. (1988). *Continued commitment: The call to action three years later.* Rochester: Center for Educational Development.

Towler, M. A. (1989). Great expectations: Reforming the schools. *Rochester Times-Union*, 21 September.

Urbanski, A. (1988). The Rochester contract: A status report. *Educational Leadership* (November), 50.

Wilson-Glover, R. (1988). Elementary scores give new hope for district. *Rochester Times-Union*, 25 October.

9

Toledo and Poway

PRACTICING PEER REVIEW

James J. Gallagher
Perry Lanier
Charles Taylor Kerchner

Setting and enforcing standards is one of the hallmarks of professional work. Among students of professionalism and sociologists of teaching, movement toward peer review is thought to be among the most powerful agents of occupational self-determination. We agree. However, within labor relations, peer review remains highly controversial because it violates the core assumptions of the industrial organization under which management is responsible for assigning workers' duties and evaluating their performance. For a union and a management to embrace peer review requires a clear departure from established norms. But as Rochester's union president Adam Urbanski puts it, "peer review is only controversial where it hasn't been tried."

Unlike most other innovations in education, the origins of peer review can be pinpointed. In 1981, the Toledo (Ohio) Public Schools (TPS) and the Toledo Federation of Teachers (TFT) reached a contractual agreement containing one sentence that pledged the parties to begin a program of teacher evaluation. The idea of a teacher union evaluating members of its own bargaining unit was so controversial at the time that TFT president Dal Lawrence waited several months before telling a shocked American Federation of Teachers (AFT) executive council what he had done.

In Toledo, peer review is applied in two situations: to novice teachers during their probationary period, and to veteran teachers whose performance has deteriorated to the point that dismissal proceedings are imminent. Peer review has persevered in Toledo, and the idea has been transplanted to other districts. Although only a few school districts and unions have developed full-fledged peer evaluation systems, a much larger number have instituted programs of formative assistance for new teachers and veteran teachers who are having difficulty (see Gallagher and Lanier's technical report on peer review listed in the Appendix).

Perhaps the most inventive of the transplants has been undertaken in Poway, California, a suburban community just north of San Diego. Poway modified the Toledo plan for novice and malperforming teachers and then added an alternative evaluation program for tenured teachers wishing to opt out of the annual teach-a-lesson-for-the-principal routine.

TOLEDO: AT THE SOURCE

Toledo, Ohio, is in the heart of the industrial union Rust Belt. A city of more than 300,000, it lies on the southwestern shore of Lake Erie bordering Michigan. Toledo is an hour away from Detroit and is similarly sensitive to auto industry fortunes. Over half of Toledo's labor force is production workers, with government workers the second largest group. Toledo's neighborhoods are mostly blue-collar racial and ethnic enclaves.

With 40,000 students in 1989–90, Toledo is the fourth largest district in Ohio. The students reflect the population diversity of the area: 57 percent are white, 37 percent African-American, 5 percent Hispanic, and 1 percent Native American and Asian. Approximately a third of the students are eligible for Chapter I services.

They are taught by 2,283 aging teachers. As enrollment has declined (down 4,000 students over the last six years), the average length of service among teachers has increased to its current level well beyond 15 years. Within this context of decline, the schools and the TFT have forged an alliance that is implementing peer review and other transformative practices.

The Challenge of Teacher Evaluation

The present alliance of the TFT and the TPS administration was unplanned. After ten years, the accomplishments of the alliance are impressive, and although it has never been fully accepted by school administrators, the alliance has encountered and withstood both political and financial turbulence.

Since 1973, the TFT had regularly included a beginning teacher/intern evaluation program plan in its bargaining proposals. The district regularly refused to consider it until the 1981 negotiations, when James Duggan, a new attorney for the school district, challenged the union with a proposal: "We'll look at an intern program, if you'll look at an intervention program for seriously ineffective teachers with tenure." Somewhat stunned by the amendment, the TFT agreed to the dual evaluation plan for beginning teachers and for very ineffective experienced teachers.

The intern/intervention program went beyond policy setting; it involved joint operating *responsibility* for and *cooperation* between teachers and administrators. The union-management agreement on peer evaluation has been sufficiently accepted by the teachers that threats to eliminate funding for the program in 1991 nearly brought on a strike. This initial agreement has served as the foundation for allied ventures into a career ladder program for teachers, a support system for mathematics and science teachers, and an urban student-centered, teacher-directed project.

Lawrence and Lehrer: The Inventors.   Dal Lawrence, as a high school history teacher, was elected the first TFT president in 1967. He has been president ever since. He describes himself as "stubborn . . . [someone who] suffers fools badly." He understands the historic significance of teachers judging their own work.

Lawrence has not only established himself as a local leader and spokesperson for teachers, but has also become an influential representative at the state and national levels of the AFT. He currently serves as vice president of the Toledo area AFL-CIO. He pressed for the legal sanctioning of peer review in Ohio, and in 1990 the legislature amended the state's collective bargaining statute to specify that engaging in peer review did not violate a union's responsibility to represent and defend its members (Ohio Revised Code, 1990). He has also actively spread the peer review idea, answering literally thousands of requests for information about the process, and dispatching himself and other teachers to explain the program in other districts.

William Lehrer, assistant superintendent for school management and teacher personnel, is the school administrator on whom the alliance depends most. As president of the Toledo Association of Administrative Personnel (TAAP) during the 1970s, he opposed the intern evaluation plan when TFT first brought it to the bargaining table because it was perceived to take power away from principals. Later, as assistant superintendent, Lehrer was instrumental in developing the 1981 agreement.

Lehrer's ability to keep classroom teaching and learning at the forefront of thought and action is notable. He has encouraged proposals to improve practice regardless of whether the union or management came up with the idea.

However, the ideas that prompted the alliance and guide its development still reside primarily with Lawrence and Lehrer. The district has had four superintendents in the last decade. None could fairly be called parents of the new labor relations. Indeed, the union now faces a backlash from the administrators' association and some board members who intend to "reestablish strong principal control" (Staff, 1991b).

Leading Up to the Agreement. Between 1967 and 1981, and through strikes in 1970 and 1978, the TFT negotiated enough job protection into its agreements that Lawrence, and supporters following his lead, embarked on negotiations for teacher participation in a wide range of educational activities. Meanwhile, as Toledo industry declined, the tax base failed to generate enough funds to operate as planned. Two schools closed, a bond levy failed, and wealthier parents began putting their children into private or parochial schools.

In 1978, the school board hired a new superintendent from outside the system who sought a constructive rather than an adversarial relationship with the TFT. This approach encouraged a cooperative spirit that contributed to the 1981 teacher evaluation agreement; then, in 1982, this joint TPS-TFT effort helped pass a large bond levy supported by 70 percent of the voters. Shortly thereafter Lawrence stated, "Now the system is on its way back to sound health" (Staff, 1984, p. 28).

Since 1981, the contract has embodied "two different conceptions of teaching work" (Darling-Hammond, 1984, p. 125). First, it offers strong job-control protections in its labor-versus-management role. Second, it assumes the exercise of both professional rights and responsibilities based on expertise. This latter view stems from Lawrence's goal to "use collective bargaining as a means for establishing a profession for classroom teachers."

Friction with Administrators. In the arena of gains and assurances for teachers, the TFT has been impressive. The union gained the right to appoint teachers to serve on all committees related to curriculum, testing, and staff development and to have department chairs and building-level teacher representatives elected rather than appointed. But the federation faces a challenge from administrators and their organization.

Initially, administrators opposed peer evaluation because it intruded on traditional managerial work. But more recently, TFT forays into professionalism have generated acrimony between the teachers' union and the TAAP. As the teachers have extended their activity at school sites, they have come to consider many central office positions, such as curriculum supervisors, superfluous. Predictably, TAAP opposes that stance because cutting those positions would reduce TAAP membership by about 20 percent. A current TAAP plan (Staff, 1991b) would end the intern program and reduce the strong role of building site representatives in school decision making.

Two Teacher Evaluation Programs

The Intern/Intervention Evaluation Program is really two distinct programs. The intern program applies to all teachers during their first two years in the district, and the intervention program helps teachers whose performance has been judged by their colleagues and supervisors to be unsatisfactory. The program, which currently costs about $400,000 for teachers supervising 160 interns, is incorporated in the district budget. In any school budget, this amount is a substantial commitment; in hard times it is extraordinary.

The Intern Program.   Since 1981, all teachers new to the district must participate in the intern program for two years, regardless of prior experience, unless exempted by the joint management-union Intern Board of Review. It takes six votes to carry an action on the board, which is composed of four district and five union appointees. But there has never been a "party-line" 5–4 vote. During the ten years since its inception, 1,141 teachers, or 40 percent of the teachers now employed in the district, have completed the intern program. Seventy-three of them (6.4 percent) resigned, were not renewed, or were terminated. In the five years before the internship program began, when new teacher evaluation was done by administrators, *only one new teacher was terminated* (Lawrence, 1985).

The intern program hinges on the work of a cadre of *consulting teachers*. Consulting teachers are experienced faculty selected by the board of review after an application and screening process. They are released from all teaching duties for three years; at the end of that time, they return to their regular classroom assignments. Faculty are forbidden to apply for administrative jobs while serving as consulting teachers.

The number of consulting teachers varies each year depending on the number of interns. Each consultant supervises up to ten interns.

During an intern's first year in the program, the responsibility for supervision, evaluation, and goal setting is the province of the consulting teacher; the principal has the responsibility to inform the consulting teacher of the intern's conformance to district and school policies pertaining to such matters as attendance and discipline. Although the consulting teacher must inform the principal of the intern's progress, the consultant has final responsibility for recommending to the board of review continued employment of the interns under his or her jurisdiction. The board of review makes the final determination for recommending the future employment of each intern to the superintendent.

Interns and consulting teachers work together through a continuous process of mutual goal setting, based on detailed observations in the intern's classes and follow-up conferences. Working as a team, the two analyze the intern's work with his or her classes and set practical goals for improvement during the first two years of employment.

Guidelines given to all new teachers are published jointly by the union and the district (Toledo Public Schools and Toledo Federation of Teachers, 1991). They include the following "Important Notice to All Intern Teachers":

> This will be a cooperative effort. Mutual goals will be established based on your strengths and weaknesses. Your input will be invited and your consultant stands ready to assist you throughout this school year. It is clearly the criteria of the intern program that the performance standards must be met or exceeded. You will be evaluated on your progress in December and March. Your consultant will recommend to a joint union-management review panel the future status of your employment with the Toledo Public Schools. *In the event it is necessary to recommend non-renewal or termination, the Toledo Federation of Teachers will not process a grievance contesting the non-renewal or termination* [emphasis added]. (Toledo Public Schools and Toledo Federation of Teachers, 1991, p. vii)

These guidelines clearly place the union in the business of defending good teaching rather than protecting the employment rights of any one teacher.

The Intervention Program. The intervention program component focuses on experienced teachers whose teaching performance is unacceptable—"the local legends," as one teacher called them. The intention of the program is clear:

> The Intervention Program in the Toledo Public Schools is a cooperative effort between the federation and the administration designed to

assist non-probationary teachers who have been identified as performing in a way so unsatisfactory that improvement or termination
is imperative. (Toledo Public Schools and Toledo Federation of
Teachers, 1991, p. 35)

In the ten years since the program was initiated, 35 teachers have been
placed in the intervention program. In 12 cases, teachers improved
enough to continue; 23 teachers were dismissed or left the district voluntarily.

The identification process that ultimately places a teacher in the
intervention program has been designed to prevent abuse by either the
district or the federation. It contains a set of checks and balances under
which both the principal and the union building representative must
concur that a teacher should be assigned to intervention. Refusal by
either union or management means that the teacher in question will
not be placed in the program.

When a teacher is placed in intervention and assigned a consultant
teacher, an intervention plan is drawn up that includes the purpose of
the intervention, the role of the consultant in the process, the kinds of
help that may be offered, and the length of the intervention. However,
because each intervention is unique, no standard methods for raising teacher performance have been adopted. The consulting teacher is
free to use a variety of methods to help teachers raise performance to
a level they consider satisfactory (Toledo Public Schools and Toledo
Federation of Teachers, 1991, p. 38). However, the consulting teacher
must report twice yearly to the board of review to justify actions taken
and to appraise progress made. Thus, although the consulting teacher
is free to use whatever means seem appropriate, the Intern Board of
Review stimulates the consulting teacher to think deeply and critically
about the needs of the person in intervention and to act creatively to
bring about his or her improvement.

The interventions used with teachers have been as varied as the
teachers' needs. One "burned out" teacher simply asked for a nonteaching position with the district's grounds maintenance staff. After negotiations with the two unions, the transfer was made and both the teacher
and district officials are pleased. Other teachers resigned rather than
face dismissal proceedings; five were dismissed. Twelve teachers successfully improved their work and have returned to the classroom. But
the important matter is that in ten years, 35 poor teachers have either
left the district or improved as a result of the cooperative work between
the district and the federation. This program signals a major change
from the traditional protective stance of unions to a position in which

the union works with the administration to improve or remove the least effective members of the teaching force.

POWAY: THE WESTWARD MIGRATION

Peer review migrated to Poway, California, along with about 100,000 inhabitants who, in the last three decades, turned ranch land and orchards into a suburban belt northeast of San Diego. In Poway, the initial attraction of peer review was less a question of ideological redefinition than a solution to a long-standing practical problem — how to establish and maintain a distinct organizational and academic culture when the district had to hire and socialize more than 100 teachers every year.

As the district grew from 12,000 to more than 26,000 students between 1975 and 1990, it realized that without institutionalizing teacher socialization, the instructional focus on which the district prided itself would change. There were more new teachers than principals could socialize, so the district initiated a teacher development and training program in 1982.

Three years later Don Raczka, a middle school math teacher and past president of the Poway Federation of Teachers (PFT), suggested a teacher assistance plan in his application to be a mentor teacher. The mentor teacher program, part of California's school reform legislation, allows a school district to designate 5 percent of its teachers as "mentors," release them part time from the classroom, and provide them $4,000 in extra compensation. Raczka had read about Toledo's peer review program and thought that it could be brought to southern California. Toledo teacher Terry Wyatt and assistant superintendent Lehrer came to Poway to explain their program.

By 1985, when Raczka had begun directing the professional assistance program, the district and the union had been negotiating under the California collective bargaining statute for a decade. Relationships between the school district and the PFT were best described as antagonistic. Never during that time had they achieved a contract agreement before school opened in the fall, and in several years they barely finished negotiating a contract before it was due to expire.

September school openings were traditionally marked by teacher demonstrations and sometimes boycotts of school-opening in-service education activities. In Raczka's words, concerted action just short of a strike became "the foreplay to an agreement." Picketing the school central office became an annual ritual, and sometimes these demonstrations extended to picketing school board members' homes, a tactic that infuriated superintendent Robert Reeves.

For his part, Reeves was looking for ways to undercut the union. Long a believer in "situational leadership," Reeves sought to apply the work of Hersey and Blanchard (Hersey, 1985) to the schools. A framed copy of their four-celled leadership scheme hangs in the boardroom just outside the superintendent's office. "I just want to move these guys from telling to participating." Reeves freely shared the idea that if "real teachers" were given the opportunity to voice concerns and involve themselves in the district, the union troublemakers would recede into irrelevance. Reeves sounded more like a union buster than a collaborator.

Yet out of this situation has come what is arguably the country's most fully developed peer review program, a vastly improved labor relations climate marked by two expeditiously negotiated settlements with substantial salary increases, and a stronger union. Because this chapter concentrates on peer review, it gives scant attention to the contract negotiations and interpersonal dynamics between district and union leadership, but it is important to realize that all three moved forward at the same time.

Professional Assistance and the Trust Agreement

The Poway Professional Assistance Project (PPAP) has three structural components, each negotiated with the district in the form of an educational policy trust agreement (Koppich & Kerchner, 1990). These trust agreements rest outside the contract but within the agreements between union and school district.

Poway was one of a dozen California locations involved in the trust agreement project originally advocated by Charles Kerchner and Douglas Mitchell (Kerchner & Mitchell, 1988) and directed by Julia Koppich. A separate agreement allowed the PFT and the district to discuss educational policies, such as peer review, away from contract negotiations, where a frosty labor relations climate meant little chance of reaching creative agreements. The trust agreement also allowed Raczka, Reeves, and PFT president William Crawford to solve problems that each of them cared deeply about without feeling that they had given something up in the solution. Finally, the trust agreement process allowed union and management to target substantial resources (more than $100,000 a year) for the benefit of teachers and teaching in the district rather than for the personal benefit of any employee. The trust agreement project continued for five years with the generous support of the Stuart Foundations. Since the project's formal close, the agreement is continuing in the form of workshops and publications. Poway has continued to use trust agreements to create joint labor-management operations for its staff development and its mentor teacher program, its superintendent's forum with elected representatives from each school, and its non-adversarial problem solving program.

The Novice Teacher Program. PPAP began with the novice teacher program, which was implemented in the 1987–88 school year. The Poway program, like Toledo's, assigns novices to a teacher consultant who provides both formative assistance and a substantive recommendation prior to a decision about contract renewal. In California, all new teachers are hired as probationary employees under one-year contracts. Tenure, or continuing employment status, is granted after the second year. A 1982 change in the law shortened the probationary period from three years to two and made early intervention and evaluation necessary. "We can't wait five years to find out whether someone can teach," said one teacher consultant.

The program in Poway started with the designation of three teacher consultants — Christine Evans, Charlotte Kutzner, and Veleta Rollins. Into their care and judgment came 37 new teachers out of the 125 hired that year. (In the beginning only elementary and some junior high school teachers were involved. Now the project involves virtually all new teachers.) Principals volunteered to be part of the program, and they still have that option, although all 26 volunteered in 1992–93.

Evans, Kutzner, and Rollins were released from classroom assignments full time, and Raczka was released part time to act as director. Teacher consultants serve three-year terms (with some exceptions), after which they are expected to return to the classroom. As in Toledo, the object is to avoid the suggestion that becoming a teacher consultant is a route to school administration.

The project is governed by a board of union-appointed teachers and superintendent-designated administrators. During the first year these members were PFT president Crawford, fifth-grade teacher Terri McNaul, primary teacher Sondra Kapp, assistant superintendent for personnel Tom Robinson, and assistant superintendent of instruction Romeo Camozzi. The board hears consulting teacher reports and makes recommendations about continued employment to the superintendent and the school board. Four votes are necessary to carry recommendations, but to date the board has operated entirely by consensus.

In the first five years, 297 teachers were part of the program.

Fourteen first-year teachers were released, and seven were released during or at the end of their second year. In no case was a governing board recommendation overturned by the school board.

The program was principally supported by $100,000 from the California Lottery that union and management had contractually agreed would be set aside for "joint projects of special value."

Negotiating funds to "hold in trust" for new educational programs was one of the driving ideas behind the educational policy trust agreement concept, and it is exemplified in Poway's sequestering of lottery money (Kerchner & Mitchell, 1988).

Survival Skills for New Teachers.   Interaction between consultants and novice teachers began with simple survival assistance — something the consultants had not anticipated. Consultants helped teachers set up rooms, plan lessons, and establish discipline. Consultants taught model lessons in novice teacher classrooms, and in some cases took over the class so that the newly hired teacher could spend a day visiting with an experienced master teacher in his or her area of concentration. Early, formative, nonjudgmental assistance established the consultants as people who could help. One case became known as the story of the nails.

One hapless new teacher was assigned to teach in a brand new portable classroom, a setting bare of any teaching equipment or supplies. The teacher walked into a room bereft of books, construction paper, tape, and pencils. No one had thought to provide them. The teacher received her first lesson in the pedagogy of procurement.

But the room did include several large roll-up wall maps, which were found lying on the floor. The small metal hooks that hold maps to the tops of blackboards had been on back order for several months, so when school started, the maps were still on the floor, unused and unusable. The consulting teacher took direct action. She returned with a hammer and a fist full of 16-penny nails, which were expertly pounded through the wallboard and into the studs. Maps were hung and the lessons began.

When the story of the nails was repeated at a governing board meeting several months later, it caused a great outcry and substantial recrimination in the purchasing department that lack of basic supplies had been allowed to interfere with teaching. But, of course, the point is that without the consulting teacher, the problem would likely have continued, and the central administration would have been unaware of it.

More Support. PPAP for new teachers changed not only who was conducting evaluations but what happened with a teacher during the first critical year. Administrative evaluations in Poway, as in most schools around the country, had been based on an hour or two of classroom observation and whatever individual attention a principal could spare. PPAP involved at least 40 hours of interaction between a novice and a consulting teacher, and if a new teacher appeared to be in difficulty, more than 90 hours of consulting time was not unusual. New teachers were able to call consultants at any time, and consultants soon found that evenings and weekends were spent on the phone.

Interviews with new teachers found that "supportive" was the word most frequently used to describe the relationship (Lux & Wagner, 1991). Other evaluations have also been positive (Moore, 1988, 1989). Two teachers commented:

> *Teacher one:* My first year has gone well enough for me to want to come back. It's the only career in which someone with no experience has maximum responsibility overnight. In most careers there is a gradual earning of responsibility.
> *Teacher two:* I would have felt abandoned without it. (Lux & Wagner, 1991, p. 12)

Listening to the PPAP Governing Board

Meetings of the governing board followed a clinical case model. Consulting teachers presented the evaluation of each teacher, and the review board probed and queried. In the ensuing conversations, the review board functioned not simply as a body that rendered decisions about continuing employment, but as an organizational subunit that triggered administrative action, redefined the role of the union, and sharpened and amplified the definition of good teaching in Poway. The following examples show the governing board's varying functions.

Prodding an Underachiever. The conference began with a case of a first-year teacher who was having difficulty. The consultant presented a summary recommendation on the district's standard evaluation form: a decision on second-year employment should be delayed. Several more visits were necessary. The consultant presented her worksheet showing the various times she had visited the classroom. The teacher in question was enthusiastic and popular with the students. But the teacher showed very little interest in preparing for class. Lessons were haphazard and demonstrated little of the craftsmanship emblematic of good teaching. The teacher had made improvement following a correctional conference at which both the consulting teacher and the principal were present. But the supervising teacher and the principal were both concerned that the teacher would not continue to develop without the pressure of external evaluation. The board voted continued vigilance.

From Wine to Vinegar.   The conference continued with cases of stellar young teachers who were performing at expected levels, and a routine was established in which consulting teachers would present a case, administrators would check off teachers as not needing additional scrutiny, and file folders would be closed upon recitation of the magic words "meets district standards."

This scenario was repeated several times until, as the case folder was being shut, one teacher added, "meets district standards . . . but something about this teacher bothers me." Heads rose from their paperwork as the consultant teacher said, "This (24-year-old) teacher is like fine white wine that has begun to go to vinegar. She teaches like someone over 60."

A remarkable discussion followed. The district's evaluation form, modeled after a Madeline Hunter lesson plan, did not mention joy, enthusiasm, or engagement in teaching. The Hunter method of teaching had been the district standard, widely taught in in-service education courses; the presentation of lessons with all the appropriate steps had been the basis for classroom observations, originally by principals and then by the consulting teachers. The district's evaluation form did not consider situational adaptivity or receptivity to new ideas, but all agreed that these qualities were what made good teaching.

Redefining Good Teaching.   In effect, the criteria for being a good teacher in Poway changed that afternoon. The review panel recognized the artistic dimension of teaching. Within the next year, consulting teachers were to coin a new phrase, "in, through, and beyond Madeline Hunter." New teachers were expected to have basic craft skills in lesson presentation, but they were also expected to develop their classrooms as interesting places of inquiry and learning—not merely to repeat the rote of lesson forms, however well prepared and executed they might be.

The change in teaching criteria was illustrated by another case later in the afternoon. This novice teacher was enthusiastic and hard-working, but had difficulty controlling a classroom. In this situation the existing district criteria could have allowed the review panel to recommend dismissal. But the panel believed that this young novice was potentially a great teacher who needed help developing basic classroom routines. The teacher was continued and assisted.

New Roles for Teachers and Administrators

Through witnessing the review board in action, we could see substantial deviations from expected roles among unionists and administrators. Administrators, initially wary of teachers as evaluators, came to trust their judgments. In one case, a principal had recommended a novice for a first-year teaching award based on a single observation of the teacher's classroom and the normal kinds of principal-teacher interactions. The consulting teacher disagreed, and carefully presented evidence of repeated interactions with the teacher. The district administrators agreed with the teacher.

In another situation, Crawford, the union president, remarked of a candidate, "I'm a little worried that she is not taking an interest in the staff development courses *we* offer." "We," in this case, is the district, which offers noncredit, voluntary, and unpaid training and development classes. The idea of a union leader suggesting participation in uncompensated activities as a mark of good teaching cuts against the industrial expectations.

Back at the Bargaining Table

As the three consulting teachers started to work in September 1987, contract negotiations were at a standstill. Even though PPAP was operating and the review board was meeting, the teachers and the district had no formal agreement and no labor contract. The usual round of demonstrations was planned. As one of its usual negotiating pressure tactics, the union ordered teachers not to attend back-to-school programs scheduled by the district. But in 1987, the union excluded new teachers from the job action. The union realized that new teachers, who were about to be evaluated by other teachers, would be put in a difficult psychological position if they were asked to choose between the union and the school district that had just hired them. It was the first of many events in which PPAP was to have an overflow effect on the conduct of negotiations. As was the case in other trust agreement sites, relationships begun outside contract negotiations spilled over into that process.

The union and the district finally reached agreement on the 1987 contract in April 1988, just about the time when negotiations were to begin afresh for salaries. During the following two years, superintendent Reeves and union president Crawford embarked on an experiment to change the way contracts were negotiated. Using an external consultant, the district and union reached a two-year (1990–92) contract before school began in September 1989. As they were jointly to report, "This is a feat that had not been accomplished in the history of negotiations for the last 13 years. The attitude and trust level established in our early days with the PPAP certainly helped to make that [contract] decision easier" (Koppich & Kerchner, 1990, p. 34).

Poway's Intervention Program

During the 1990–91 school year, PPAP was expanded to include an intervention program for permanent teachers found to be "in serious professional jeopardy" (Koppich & Kerchner, 1990, p. 33). A tenured teacher who receives an unsatisfactory rating by the administration may request assistance, and a second unsatisfactory rating requires intervention.

The program is structurally similar to Toledo's, but the teacher consultant serves outside the formal evaluation process. Any reports made to the school board may be placed in the teacher's personnel file and are thus usable in dismissal proceedings.

One teacher was being considered for this program in September 1992. Teachers who had been rated as unsatisfactory prior to the program's initiation cannot be subjected to mandatory intervention.

The Alternative Evaluation Program

Also during the 1990–91 school year, the district and union instituted an alternative to conventional teacher evaluation. The program is open to teachers with five years of experience and site administrator approval. (Some teachers who transferred to different schools, and thus had new principals, were denied approval.) This program is also operated by a joint union-management governing board. As with the other programs, a trust agreement memorandum between union and management established the program.

Alternative evaluation begins with a teacher-made goal statement for professional growth. At a conference held early in the fall, teacher and principal meet, discuss, and agree on acceptable goals. They also decide on alternative means of evaluation. These may include portfolios, peer coaching, classroom action research, participation in structured staff development, a collaborative group of teachers that self-evaluates, or a modification of the standard observation system (Poway Unified School District, 1991, p. 3). In practice, most teachers developed individual or group projects that allowed them to alter their curriculum or teaching methods. For example:

Goal: Study instruction of editing skills . . . present results. *Evaluation:* Collaborative team.

Goal: Attend Socratic Seminar and integrate strategy into advanced placement English. *Evaluation:* Peer and principal evaluation.

Goal: Attend class on fairy tales and art and implement strategy in a painting course. *Evaluation:* Portfolio of student work plus administrator evaluation. (Poway Unified School District, 1992a)

Early in the fall, teachers who elect to participate meet with their principal and reach agreement on goals and evaluation criteria. Administrators and teachers have two evaluation conferences during the year, and all teachers who have elected the alternative method meet twice a year to discuss their projects and the system's operations. The administrator conducts a summary year-end evaluation.

In its second year of operation, 225 of the 615 teachers due for evaluation chose the alternative evaluation over the conventional system that rested on two principal observations of lesson presentation. Analysis of an evaluative survey conducted by the district revealed four reactions to the alternative system.

First, almost everyone likes it. Teachers thought it was more professionally valuable than traditional evaluations (4.7 on a 5-point scale) as did administrators (4.1) (Poway Unified School District, 1992b). However, only about 35 percent of the teachers chose the alternative. In the words of one principal, "Teachers' perception is that it is too much work. We need to challenge that perspective and value growth" (Poway Unified School District, 1992b, p. 37).

Second, the new system forms an important critique of the old one: "personal growth versus a puppet show," wrote one teacher, commenting on years of preparing lessons to present to visiting principals (Poway Unified School District, 1992b, p. 5). Teacher comments showed how the alternative allows evaluation of their whole job rather than a single lesson, and it creates the opportunity for dialogue about educational philosophy and values:

With the traditional type of system, the administrator came in and didn't really know what came before or after the lesson or what philosophy it was based on. At least with my goal, the administration knew what I was doing and why and how and when it was being implemented throughout the year. (Poway Unified School District, 1992b, p. 1)

Several teachers commented that the alternative motivated them to be creative where the old observation system reinforced their use of standard lesson presentations. For example: "I was happy to focus my time and energy into something new and exciting. Now I use my classroom computer and network program during most of the day" (Poway Unified School District, 1992b, p. 4).

Third, the new system takes more time. Teachers who elected it put more of themselves into the program, and they appeared to have done so willingly. Their major cautionary remarks were directed toward not letting the paperwork associated with the project get out of hand. Teachers commented that because their evaluations were explicitly connected to projects they had chosen, they "could devote more energy" to them (Poway Unified School District, 1992b, p. 21).

Fourth, the goals varied enormously. Some were quite substantive, but others seemed insignificant, activities that would be expected of any competent teacher. Both teachers and administrators mentioned the need to screen projects better. Many seemed "fluffy" and not focused directly on student achievement, one administrator commented (Poway Unified School District, 1992b, p. 36).

AFTER THE FLOOD

Both the Toledo and Poway stories have unsettled endings. In 1991 the Toledo Federation of Teachers went to the mat with the district over elimination of the peer review program and the other jointly operated programs. The issue was ostensibly money (a levy election had failed). But board members and the administrators' union judged that the teachers' union had become too powerful. TFT president Lawrence became the object of personal attack (Staff, 1991a, 1991b).

The contract dispute went to a hearing before the employment relations board fact finder, who recommended that the programs continue (State Employment Relations Board, 1991, p. 31). They have, and a levy election dulled financial peril. Lawrence survived an election challenge within the union.

In Poway, relations between the district and union continue to expand, and discussions are taking place about teachers running their own staff development. In spite of California's $10 billion budget crisis, the school board continued the program for 1992–93 even in the face of $3 million in program cuts, much to the pleasure of the superintendent and the union president.

NOTE ON FIELD INVESTIGATION

The field investigation of Toledo's labor relations was undertaken by James J. Gallagher and Perry Lanier of Michigan State University. Their field visits took place between May 1991 and April 1992. Their case study, which covers peer review and other aspects of labor-management relations, may be ordered through Project V•I•S•I•O•N (see Appendix).

Charles Kerchner made five visits to Poway during the Educational Policy Trust Project (1987–91), and the Poway section was written from field notes and subsequent telephone interviews.

REFERENCES

Darling-Hammond, L. (1983). Teacher evaluation in the organizational context: A review of the literature. *Bureau of Educational Research*, 53(3), 285–328.

Hersey, P. (1985). *The situational leader*. San Diego: University Association.

Kerchner, C. T., & Mitchell, D. (1988). *The changing idea of a teachers' union*. New York: Falmer Press.

Koppich, J., & Kerchner, C. (1990). *Educational policy trust agreements: Connecting labor relations and school reform, annual report*. Berkeley: Policy Analysis for California Education.

Lawrence, D. (1985). The Toledo plan for peer evaluation and assistance. *Education and Urban Society*, 17(3), 347–54.

Lux, Y., & Wagner, L. (1991). *California new teacher project sub-study: A case analysis of the Poway professional development program*. Sacramento: California State Department of Education.

Moore, B. (1988). *Poway professional assistance program: Research and evaluation, first annual report*. Poway Unified School District.

Moore, B. (1989). *Poway professional assistance program: Research and evaluation, second annual report*. Poway Unified School District.

Ohio Revised Code (1990) Section 4117.01.

Poway Federation of Teachers and Poway Unified School District (1991). *Agreement: Permanent teachers intervention program*.

Poway Unified School District. (1991). *Alternative evaluation program*.

Poway Unified School District. (1992a). *Alternative evaluation participants for 1991–1992*.

Poway Unified School District. (1992b). *Results of alternative evaluation survey, 1991–1992.*

Poway Unified School District and Poway Federation of Teachers. (1990). *Trust agreement, alternative evaluation program.*

Staff (1984). Teacher excellence: Teachers take charge. Dal Lawrence discusses the Toledo plan. *American Educator*, 22–29.

Staff. (1991a). Board turns to the right. *Toledo Federation of Teachers News Focus*, Spring, p. 1.

Staff. (1991b). TAAP has a plan for you. *Toledo Federation of Teachers News Focus*, Spring, p. 6.

State Employment Relations Board. (1991). *Impasse findings and report* (No. 90-MED-11-1158).

Toledo Public Schools and Toledo Federation of Teachers. (1991). *The Toledo plan: Intern intervention, evaluation.* Toledo, OH: Toledo Public Schools, Toledo Federation of Teachers.

10

Chicago

A RESTLESS SEA OF SOCIAL FORCES

William Ayers

When we began this study, we thought of labor relations changes as being brought about by the joint action of the union and management. The previous cases more or less followed this pattern. Union and management either stepped off in a reform agenda together, or one led and the other followed.

However, we soon found that not all changes in labor relations are the creatures of reform efforts originating within public school systems. Increasingly, we began to take notice of reform efforts originating outside the institution. When those reform efforts are successful, the school district becomes the object rather than the agent of reform. Power, influence, oversight, and criticism reside outside the existing public school system, and they plot revolutions. The system and all its existing relationships are brought into question, particularly patterns of labor relations.

Teacher unions appear as part of the problem to the eyes of citizen and civic reform groups plotting external takeovers. Labor-management conflict is seen as just another example that the existing system does not work, and unions are tarred with the same brush of intransigence and self-protection that is used to paint school administrators.

External takeovers, even incomplete ones that balkanize rather than solidify authority, pose massive problems for teacher unions, and it is too early in the process to know how the unions will respond to external takeovers and whether they will prosper. However, it would be naive not to expect the process of external pressure on school districts, particularly those in the nation's most troubled cities, to intensify.

Our studies included three cases of external takeover, each quite different. In Chelsea, Massachusetts, operation of the public schools was turned over to Boston University (BU). As Mark Nichols reports (see Appendix), the Chelsea Federation of Teachers was virtually swept aside in the takeover. It was clearly not part of the reform design, its sources of influence were badly dented, and aspects of its contract were voided. The success of Boston University in carrying out reforms appears equally problematic. BU, no less than the previous school administration, is fiscally dependent on the state of Massachusetts. Private fiscal angels failed to land in the tiny school district, and Chelsea finds itself trying to preserve basic operations rather than engage in fundamental reforms.

In Colorado, Governor Roy Romer applied a little-used 1913 statute to intervene in a labor dispute between the Denver Public Schools and the Denver Classroom Teachers Association. He literally wrote the 1991 labor contract, which effectively restructured the schools in ways that neither the school district nor the union would have chosen. Michael Murphy's analysis of reform in Denver (see Appendix) shows that collective bargaining can become a point of entry for external forces, not simply a site where external pressures are reflected. The Denver case also illustrates that changing a contract may not change the mindset of labor and management or their relationship with each other. But the new Denver contract has initiated a cycle of change and unleashed a sea of social forces that have yet to be calmed.

And then there is Chicago, where reforms represent the most radical structural and social changes within U.S. public education in the last 70 years. This chapter focuses on the labor relations implications of these changes.

SCHOOL REFORM: CHICAGO'S *PERESTROIKA*

On 12 December, 1988, Governor James Thompson signed the Chicago School Reform Act, creating strong Local School Councils composed of parents, teachers, citizens, and principals at each schoolhouse. Power was to shift from a large central office to each school site, and a bureaucratic, command-oriented system was to yield to a decentralized and democratic model. The traditional pyramid-shaped organizational structure was to be inverted.

In a sense, school reform is Chicago's *perestroika*. As in Europe, a command-style central authority has collapsed practically of its own weight, and a radical democracy is proposed as a solution to years of stagnation and backwardness. A previously insulated and impenetrable central office accustomed to unquestioning obedience has lost its authority, bringing down to human size those who were once omnipotent.

In Chicago, the Chicago Teachers Union (CTU) was seen as omnipotent even though its leaders would deny the influence ascribed to it. During the 1960s and 1970s, the CTU's influence in Chicago school politics became the prototype for developing interest-group theories of politics (Peterson, 1976). To some, the CTU represented "union rule" of the political system (Grimshaw, 1979) and the creation of a private government beyond the reach of ballots or citizen voice. Political scientist Norton Long characterized it as "legitimating a degree of callous selfishness that surpassed that of the managerial elite of reform [government] and even the rapacity of the [Chicago political] machine" (Grimshaw, 1979, p. xiii).

The CTU is clearly massive. Of the 32,000 Chicago Public Schools (CPS) employees eligible to join the CTU, some 30,500 are members (95 percent of teachers, 98 percent of aides). Ninety-six percent of the 45,600 CPS employees are represented by bargaining agents. Eighteen other unions (teamsters, engineers, custodians, shade makers, glaziers, and so on) are represented in the system in 21 separate contracts. Principals are not; they have an effective and active association but were denied the right to unionize under Illinois law.

The Worst Schools in America

Although Chicago encountered many catalysts to reform, the pivotal event may have been a visit from William Bennett, Ronald Reagan's flamboyant Secretary of Education. Bennett flew from Washington to Chicago in late 1987 and proclaimed at an airport press conference that Chicago's public schools—the country's third largest district with 440,000 students—were "the worst in America." His comments made the national news, and that single superlative became a headline around the country. In Chicago the reaction to Bennett's performance was decidedly mixed. Practically everyone noted that his rhetorical excess came in the midst of a massive federal retreat from support for schools and children, and the wholesale abandonment of poor, urban youth in particular. (Chicago's students are 61 percent African-American, 25 percent Hispanic, 12 percent white. Sixty-eight percent of the students are from families with annual incomes below $13,000.)

Still, the notion that Chicago schools were the worst touched a nerve, and the phrase stuck; within months a lengthy *Chicago Tribune* series on the state of the schools began. The *Tribune* series was eventually edited, published as a book, and distributed widely throughout the city (Staff, 1988). No one really cared to debate whether the schools were better or worse than the schools in Detroit, say, or New York, or whether they were just awful or truly terrible. No one cared to point out the ways in which Chicago was merely a case among cases, a typical failing urban system. It was enough to know that the schools were failing Chicago's children massively, and that fact was well established and deeply felt by late 1987.

THE CTU: A FOUNDATION OF TEACHER UNIONISM

The Chicago Teachers' Federation (CTF) was formed in 1897, 16 years earlier than the American Federation of Teachers (AFT), with which it is affiliated. At its origin, the CTF vowed to fight for better conditions and wages and to resist being "treated like clerks." Its history is intertwined with the struggle for social change in America (Herrick, 1971; Murphy, 1990). Jane Addams and the settlement house movement influenced the thought of teachers early in the century, as did the philosophy of John Dewey. More recently, the union was a leader in welcoming women and people of color into leadership positions. But real power — clout in Chicago terms — was created at the onset of collective bargaining.

The Beginnings of Clout

In September 1965, the board of education authorized elections to determine which teachers' organization would be the sole collective bargaining agent in Chicago, and in May 1966 the CTU won the right to represent elementary and high school teachers, assistant principals, and truant officers. In November 1966, bargaining began on the first CTU contract, a contract won in January 1967 after the threat of a strike and the intervention of Mayor Richard J. Daley (father of the present mayor and sometimes called the "real Mayor Daley"). That first contract won a substantial pay raise, a nondiscriminatory policy, an increase in teachers' aides in high schools, and leaves for study and travel, among other things.

In April 1969 the CTU went out on strike for the first time. The two-day strike was the result of contract violations: the threat to lay off 7,000 teachers and increase class size and teaching load. The settlement included an agreement to limit class size to 30 students in primary grades, 33 in intermediate, and 35 in high school based on students in each class rather than the old method of looking at student-teacher ratio overall.

A Pattern of Coercive Deficiency

The pattern was being established. The union would threaten a strike or pull its members out, politicians — specifically the mayor — would come into the process, money would be found as the legislature was brought into line, and life returned to normal. The CTU was developing a reputation for redistributing power and authority in the schools and stood as a model of big-city union clout through its ability to garner political influence and to use the strike as a lever to extract money. By the 1970s strikes appeared partly as a way of short-term budget balancing: wages unpaid during the strike saved money in one fiscal year and pushed the deficit into the next

Strikes occurred repeatedly over the next several years: 1971, 4 days; 1973, 12 days; 1975, 11 days; 1980, 10 days; 1983, 15 days; 1984, 10 days; 1985, 2 days; 1987, 19 days. Teachers' actions over these years were geared toward wages and benefits, working conditions, some educational issues, and even the right to a contract. The January 1980 strike was in reaction to three consecutive payless paydays and the board's scuttling of the contract. Once again the mayor's office played a pivotal role in negotiations and in saving the contract.

Union Discussions about Reform

In 1985 the CTU published "Perspectives from the Classroom," a booklet on educational reform in response to the rising tide of educational reform reports. Intense debate on reform revealed a range of opinions within the CTU on issues from merit pay to vouchers, school organization to teacher accountability. School-based management was a sticky issue within the union, but it had appeal as a voluntary process for those schools that were ready for it.

John Kotsakis, assistant to the president of the CTU on educational issues and thought to be the intellectual leader of the union, took the lead on reform. Kotsakis was a leader in the union's founding in 1965, a member of the left faction pushing for collective bargaining and the use of the strike weapon. Kotsakis's office walls exhibit oil paintings he created years ago depicting heroic labor struggles with black and white workers fighting side by side in the style of socialist realism. Kotsakis is sophisticated, bright, witty, and entirely devoted to the union cause.

According to Kotsakis, the CTU has been in serious transition since 1985. Union members had become thoroughly disenchanted with the lack of success in the schools, the funding of schools, and the lack of quality instructional programs. He describes teachers as disaffected by the long-standing "unwillingness of the central administration to effectuate any kind of long-lasting and significant change in the classrooms and the instructional process." For example, during the early 1980s, the superintendent instituted a "continuous progress mastery-learning program" based on the venerable behavior-modification approach to learning. The program infuriated many teachers with its massive record-keeping (hundreds of skills had to be entered on key-punched cards in order to register success), and its teacher-proof process that not only de-skilled teaching but appeared to kill off student interest in reading and writing. Continuous learning was not successful in teaching kids to read, but it did promote talk of educational reform among union members.

But the union was less than prepared for the kind of reform that resulted. Kotsakis believed that a nonlegislative reform, in the style of Rochester or Miami, would have been preferable. However, he claims that the superintendent and board sought to reestablish a stronger central administration in the mid-1980s.

THE 1987 STRIKE AS CATALYST

In September 1987, the CTU failed to reach a contract agreement with the district, and its members went out on their ninth walkout in 18 years. The sense of a permanent state of "negotiated conflict" between the teachers and the school board had become part of the political landscape, punctuated each August by loud demands and dramatic posturing, followed by a miraculous last-minute solution or a relatively brief strike. This time would be different. The strike dragged on through September, a record 19 school days. Forty-one thousand employees were idled for a cumulative 570,000 days—the longest public employee strike in Illinois history. And instead of a temporarily satisfactory solution and a return to business as usual, the strike contributed to a strong and growing view that Chicago was saddled with a failing school system, now spinning completely out of control.

"Parents don't blame us for the '87 strike," said CTU president Jacqui Vaughn, but the union looked whipped to many observers when it accepted a meager 4 percent wage increase after losing nearly a month's pay. And they were not the only losers. The superintendent and the board proved decisively that they were incapable of leading or managing the schools, and they too appeared weak and beaten. The contention had been real, the bitterness palpable, and the fallout would be lasting.

The most significant difference between this strike and every other strike was the powerful role of "outsiders," specifically parents, business leaders, and community organizations. The strike became the catalyst for people to express their rage and frustration with the full range of school problems. For the parents the strike was not the real issue but merely the precipitating event for a heightened level of struggle. Their goal was never a contract settlement between the board and the union.

Parents and community activists raised the broader issue of the quality of Chicago schools and the related concern of making schools accountable to the people they were supposed to serve. New organizations emerged. Reformers organized "freedom schools" throughout the south and west sides, serving some 30,000 youngsters in September. Rallies were held at Pershing Road, the State of Illinois Building, and even union headquarters. As the strike wore on, demonstrations grew in size and intensity, and a broad range of forces was galvanized into a working reform coalition.

Enter a Different Mayor

Mayor Harold Washington — popular, populist, and black — called a meeting for the week following the strike. Over 1,000 people converged on the meeting (organizers had planned for a few hundred), demanding a strong voice in reforming the schools. The mayor created a 54-member Parents Community Council as a part of the Education Summit. Coretta McFerren, a south-side activist with children and grandchildren in the public schools and an organizer of the "freedom schools" during the strike, regularly convened meetings with a cheery greeting: "Welcome to the revolution!"

More than rhetoric connected these school reformers to the activism of previous decades. As parents fought their way to the center of the school reform movement, they staked claim to a rich history of African-American parents struggling for a decent education for their children: "When we were bound in slavery our forefathers fought to learn to read," argued Mrs. McFerren. "Reading was a subversive activity. When they kept us out of the good schools, trapped in overcrowded boxes, our parents fought to break out of those segregated ghettos. They were beaten and arrested. Now it is our time. We've got to seize control of our schools to prevent the destruction of our children's minds."

What Mrs. McFerren and other leaders had in mind was adapting the unfinished business of community control of schools to the late 1980s. "People say we don't have the skill, the intelligence to run the schools," Mrs. McFerren argued. "I have the intelligence to see what they're doing to me and my babies. And I can't do worse."

A Convergence of Reform Pressures

Besides the strike, several other ingredients were present in 1987 and 1988 that made a new version of community control suddenly realizable. First, there was widespread agreement that the schools were in crisis, and there was a broad, general understanding of the problems. Second, several major players in Chicago school politics were weak or inactive. The CTU, for example, was remarkably isolated, partly as a result of the strike but also because the Illinois Federation of Teachers, with which the CTU is affiliated, had endorsed the Republican governor, James Thompson, thereby alienating the powerful Democratic legislative leadership. The superintendent was without a constituency or a base of support and, along with his board of education, was unable to answer the mounting criticism of the system in a straightforward way. And, following the death of Harold Washington in November 1987, the mayor's office was without direction or leadership.

The fourth catalyst was two school research and advocacy groups. Designs for Change (Designs) and the Chicago Panel on Public School Policy and Finance (the Panel) had by 1987 created a credible and readable body of research that drew a devastating picture of Chicago schools. In 1985, Designs and the Panel released studies that together undermined the credibility of the system's top administrators (Designs for Change, 1985; Hess & Lauber, 1985).

Fifth, business leaders in Chicago were poised to take an active, progressive role in reform. Business concern and involvement with the schools had gone through a rather typical evolution over the previous decade: "adopt-a-school" programs, commissioned studies, advice, management training for administrators, and so on. After years of effort, nothing of substance had changed, and business leaders increasingly turned to Designs and the Panel for answers and increasingly aligned themselves with parent and community activists. Business and business people, of course, play multiple roles. While business in general supported the school reforms, Chicago banks and financial institutions had long participated in, and profited from, the school district's deficit financing that perpetuated the old system.

The political history of the reform effort cannot be recounted in full here (Hess, 1991). Suffice it to say that action eventually moved to the state legislature, where a grassroots lobbying campaign resulted in the Chicago School Reform Act.

THE CTU ON THE DEFENSIVE

The reforms placed the CTU on the defensive. It participated in the Summit and in the legislative process although somewhat reluctantly. It was an active participant in the final legislative settlement . . . It was not the reform the union would have chosen, but as Alfred Hess (1991) notes, "it is unfair to imply that the CTU was opposed to school reform in Chicago" (p. 71). Public perception of the union as "insiders" meant that the problems of the system were laid at its feet, and the solutions being crafted were largely conceived as relying on groups that had previously been excluded. McFerren, a leading "outsider" (now an "insider"), said, "The schools and the teachers have tried to ruin our children; we need to control the schools so they won't do any more damage."

The CTU thought of the reformers as everything from opportunists to concerned outsiders lacking the expertise to effectively improve the system. Kotsakis characterized the mayor's Education Summit that developed the reform plans as degenerating into "a food fight in the school cafeteria."

The CTU pushed a site-based management concept dominated by teachers in partnership with administrators (and in consultation with parents). This approach was completely unacceptable to the reformers, some of whom wanted no teachers on the local teams at all. Others argued for equal representation of parents and teachers on councils, but this proposal had no support from the CTU, which was focused on site-based management, nor from militant parent groups. The legislated compromise (six parents, two teachers, two community representatives) failed to build a real sense of partnership, mutual trust, and collective gain.

Local School Councils. These Local School Councils (LSCs) have the real power in Chicago schools. Beyond appointing the principal to a four-year performance contract, each LSC is required to develop and approve a school improvement plan that details how the school intends to raise student achievement, reduce truancy, and provide an adequate education for its youngsters. And each LSC has the power of the purse, including much greater flexibility over spending and the right to approve or modify the school budget.

Chicago's reform marks the end of lifetime tenure for principals, a practice that had become a long-standing system of patronage and abuse. It ends special system-wide eligibility requirements that had controlled the number of candidates for school leadership. Simultaneously, reform increases the authority of principals to hire and fire teachers, as well as to oversee the engineering and food service staff. Principals can hire teachers directly and can refuse transfers from other schools in the district, and the process of dismissal has been streamlined.

Teachers, besides holding two seats on each LSC, are mandated to create Professional Personnel Advisory Committees (PPACs) at each school. PPACs are intended to be vehicles for teachers' professional judgment concerning curriculum, teaching, and assessment. They are advisory to the principal and the LSC.

WE WON! NOW WHAT DO WE DO?

In the celebration following the passage of the Chicago School Reform Act, one longtime community activist enthusiastically exclaimed, "We won! Now what do we do?" His face shifted in mid-sentence from euphoria to concern.

Organizational implementation of externally introduced change is difficult and awkward. The school system, and particularly its central bureaucracy, was designed to carry out legislative mandates. The years since World War II had produced hundreds of categorical or targeted programs, and school bureaucracies responded by establishing bureaus and sub-bureaus to implement and monitor these programs. Despite the legislative intent of "serving" a particular group of children, the effect was to further centralize control of resources and rules. With the Chicago School Reform Act, the central office was being asked to design a radical shift in power and influence away from itself, in effect to engineer its own demise.

Rather than go out of business, which is typical of successful legislative reform groups, Chicago reformers reenergized and grew to implement reforms. A new superintendent, Ted Kimbrough, was hired, and the central office was downsized, but its functions were relatively unchanged. As one administrator put it, "rather than having us do less, we're doing all the old things with fewer people."

What of the Teachers?

Partly because it concentrated on governance, the reform movement failed to effectively fire the imaginations or energies of significant numbers of teachers. The law has no provision for teacher education or development, and many teachers find the idea of parent-led councils ironic at best, evil at worst. Although teachers recently expressed a positive attitude toward reform (about 60 percent felt that the reform is improving their schools), 57 percent said that it has not changed the way they teach. And more troubling, about 68 percent said that students' attitudes and habits reduce chances for success (Consortium on Chicago School Research, 1992).

CTU president Jacqui Vaughn tells teachers that they "can use parents to be your most effective allies," and that "having parents in the schools has worked to our advantage." But Vaughn's notion of partnership is framed mostly around the acquisition of resources. Parents will see that schools need books, paint, and equipment, that class sizes are too large, and they will advocate for more resources. However, teachers in Chicago, as elsewhere, have not historically viewed parents as partners in the education of children. To a lesser degree, perhaps, than with administrators, parental involvement is perceived as parental intrusion.

The CTU Quest Initiative

The CTU is struggling to maintain many of the gains of the past 25 years even as it moves in the direction of a more professional union. Two initiatives are under way. The first is an internship program for new teachers coordinated through the Golden Apple Foundation, the deans of the area education schools, and the CTU. The hope is that within five years Chicago teachers will enter the profession in a more planned, organized, and thoughtful way.

The second initiative is the creation of the Quest Center for school improvement and restructuring. The center will be a place where teams of school people can study, plan, access information and resources, and develop strategies for change. The center operates under the principle that teachers must take a leadership role in changing traditional teacher-centered instructional processes into ones that embrace a child-centered, holistic climate for learning. It is hoped that this approach will stimulate active learning, social interaction, and cultural diversity in the school context. The center will accommodate 10 to 20 selected school teams a year. The MacArthur Foundation has funded the center for three years with $1.5 million, the largest grant ever given to a union effort.

The Quest Center represents the most visible attempt to promote teacher-led educational change; it is also a counterpower within the union, a force for a new approach to union activity. Yet no one inside the CTU talks about it in these terms. Quest is part of the union, but it is separate, with its own board and staff. Quest aims to sponsor several demonstration projects for school restructuring in its first year and to become a model for serious and sustained teacher-led change. Quest will support waivers for innovative projects and hopes to inspire "break-the-mold" initiatives.

Quest is led by Debbie Walsh, a Chicago native who worked for years developing innovative projects at the national AFT office; she has hired three staffers, each a CTU in-the-trenches veteran. John Kotsakis splits his time between CTU and Quest duties.

Reform Chicago style has been strong on governance, but the point, of course, is to bring about improvement in classrooms, changes in the lives of teachers and children. That is the ongoing challenge. The conditions for change now exist in Chicago's schools, but that does not make change inevitable. With some power in the hands of local schools, it now depends on what people do. Without compelling, visible alternatives, decision makers are uncertain, and the obstacles to change remain strong and deep: inertia, routine, self-interest.

Teachers Outside the Union

One potentially important new development was the formation in 1988 of the Teachers' Task Force. The task force is composed of Chicago teachers and advocacy groups concerned with the role of teachers in school reform. It believes that long-term capacity building for school reform will be realized through strong Professional Personnel Advisory Committees at each school, with teachers who are leaders and decision makers in curriculum and instruction. The teacher leadership envisioned, according to task force staff person Ann Porter, is "not just a shift in traditional power, but rather true democracy at work through the appropriate use of the power of the teacher in curriculum and instruction in relationship with the principal and the LSC." Porter argues that this vision is the intent of the reform law.

The task force is led by young and militant teachers who find the CTU's initial ambiguous position on reform troubling. Kotsakis says that the union does not communicate with or endorse the Teachers'

Task Force. It is not, he says, a "vehicle for any significant achievement," but rather a way for reformers to create "some kind of entity that is in competition with the union." If the task force is competing with the union, it is not doing so for electoral office. In the May 1992 elections, no one ran against Vaughn or the incumbents in the other top four offices.

However, the task force has created an independent, proreform presence outside the CTU. It publishes a newsletter called "Teaching Matters" that features articles on teacher successes, models of PPAC organizing, and curriculum ideas. It has sponsored several events, including a series of PPAC workshops, curriculum fairs, school exchanges and visits to innovative schools, and speeches and forums.

Negotiations with the Interim Board

The interim board of education, appointed by Mayor Daley as part of the reform act, negotiated the 1988 contract before the permanent board was elected. Those negotiations represented "a 180-degree turn" from the tradition of board-CTU negotiations, according to CTU president Vaughn. Prior to the interim board, the CTU and board negotiators had exchanged thick proposals, and "a grinding process of working through . . . minutia" went on for months. The interim board, on the other hand, got down to business and avoided posturing.

It also agreed to hold talks at CTU headquarters, an unprecedented act and a significant symbol. The board was short-lived, focused, and composed of reformers, and the process was more collegial and efficient than ever before. It produced a multiyear contract in June — another first.

Breakthrough or Giveaway?

Superintendent Kimbrough, hired by the interim board, had a much less sanguine view of the 1988 contract; he called it a giveaway. "You have to remember that one of the interim board's mandates was to negotiate a peaceful contract. They didn't have to live with its consequences. I do."

Among the contractual consequences is a supernumerary provision in the reform act that protects the jobs of virtually all tenured teachers. The law now guarantees a job within the system to supernumeraries in either a school or a central office position. Teachers who are not placed in one of these positions will continue to receive a salary. Teachers can no longer "bump" one another because of seniority. It is up to the principal to determine whether a teacher will be selected for a vacant staff position.

The supernumerary decision is considered by many to be a "budget buster" and an example of union selfishness. The closings of 17 schools in 1991 increased the supernumerary count to 520. Several hundred of these teachers were eventually placed in other schools or central office positions; the rest continue to draw salaries.

To Kimbrough, the contract also contains too many decisions about educational matters that ought to "either be a joint decision at the school or revert to administration." And the contract is silent about teacher responsibility. "Teachers don't have the right to fail the children they meet every day. Teachers need to place themselves in a framework where they get assistance if they are having trouble making it in the classroom."

THE 1991 NEGOTIATIONS AND FISCAL CRISIS

In the summer of 1991, superintendent Kimbrough faced a serious fiscal crisis at the same moment he was bargaining a new teacher contract. His theme was that school reform could not proceed without further resources, but the time-honored tactic of finding money in Springfield did not work. He threatened several school closings and eventually closed a handful of schools, saving a tiny percentage of the deficit. In this climate many people were discouraged about participating in their schools.

The fiscal crisis led to tense negotiations between the CTU and the board in the fall of 1991. The board asked the union for a range of givebacks, and a strike was called for December. The strike was averted through a frenzied weekend of negotiations led by Mayor Daley. It seemed like business as usual, but instead of the intervention causing resources to flow to meet teacher salary demands, teachers agreed to a settlement that deferred the 4 percent raise they had negotiated in 1987.

Teachers were bitterly disappointed, and at more than just the financial settlement. The tone of negotiations had once again become harsh. CTU vice president Thomas Reece said:

> It's the worst situation in the last ten years in terms of a complete lack of movement from the board of education. It's especially bad in contrast with the interim board's attitude, which was very positive and responsive.

Chicago schools opened on time in 1992, but with the old pattern reasserted: a threatened strike, frenzied around-the-clock negotiations in the mayor's office, money borrowed against the future, and the mayor commenting that the superintendent "is not working out." Kimbrough subsequently announced that he would not seek renewal of his contract.

CRITICAL DECISIONS IN THE 1990S

The district and union will face a number of crises in the early 1990s. Fiscal reform is one of them. Kimbrough is facing an enormous crisis in September 1992 when he is bound to replace the 4 percent raise denied teachers in 1991. As this chapter is written, the budget currently shows a $200 to $300 million deficit.

Kimbrough believes that the current financial structure dooms reform. Through a series of reform efforts that predate the 1988 act, the district is fiscally dependent on an external School Finance Authority, who some say is becoming the "real" school board. "Every year you go through a crisis, and during the crisis politics takes over. Prudent fiscal planning is impossible."

A second crisis revolves around the central office's ability to monitor and discipline local schools. There is vast disagreement about whether central office actions amount to recentralization in contradiction of the reform act or to carrying out the monitoring and control function prescribed by the act, which is to put failing schools in receivership, remove the LSCs and restaff them.

It is likely that the central office will attempt to close schools based on nonperformance, and the political and legal resolution of this effort will determine whether a central authority exists within the Chicago Public Schools. The crisis over central authority has profound implications for labor relations because the current system is built around negotiating and enforcing agreements with a strong central authority.

IMPLICATIONS FOR THE CTU

The Chicago reform has many implications for the CTU, union-board relations, and the future role of teachers and teachers' unions. Yet it is unclear whether the union is seriously wrestling with alternatives to the status quo.

If the system is decentralized in the manner many reformers (including leading advocacy and business groups) envision—an open question, since the contention over control continues to be fierce, with the central office holding many important advantages—the CTU will be thrust into untraveled and unknown terrain. Who would the union negotiate with? What centrally made contract would be binding? How would teachers bring a grievance, and against whom? How would the superintendent enforce compliance? A radically decentralized system would throw traditional union-board relations into chaos. Add to this the ongoing (and mounting) fiscal crisis and the weakened authority of the center to gather and deliver resources, and we see relations on the verge of a major shift. Even if the current reform fails, the result is not likely to be a return of centralized bureaucracy. The political steam is building around vouchers, contracting out, and privatization, not recentralization.

The CTU leadership has not openly grappled with the implications of this shift. It is plagued with doubts and faces many uncertainties. There are simply no ready-made models for doing big-city teachers' union work in a decentered system. Over the last generation, the CTU has translated member loyalty into political power because it could often outwrestle a large central bureaucracy. When power flees from the center, there is no known path to union organization.

One indication of at least an implicit grasp of the changed situation is the development of the Quest Center inside the union, yet following a different agenda. The CTU is bound to existing forms of representa-tion—lobbying, contract negotiation, and representation for all teach-ers. Because Quest exists outside of these obligations, it is free to vigor-ously pursue the changing role of those teachers who are rethinking and restructuring their schools. It offers what may well be the union's greatest hope of internally developed renewal.

Kotsakis spoke of the prospect of decentralized bargaining, indicat-ing that the idea had not been actively discussed within the union. He pointed out that the union staff had not really internalized the meaning of reform, had not begun to project possible scenarios for the future, and had not begun to operate in new ways. "Teachers at the local level know more about school reform than the union staff," he said, "and more about its operational requirements, such as how to create a bud-get." Kotsakis indicated that teachers are learning from one another at the building level, inventing practical responses to concrete problems, and soliciting training not from the board or the CTU, but from the old outsiders, like Designs and the Panel. These new approaches have created at the school site a counterpower to the CTU; after all, 1,200 teachers sit on governing boards (LSCs), and in the first election only half the union delegates who ran for LSC representative won seats.

The CTU is the classic "negotiated-conflict," trade-union type of teachers' union. According to Kotsakis, "we were probably the most industrial of the teachers unions." Change will be difficult and painful, and yet, from Kotsakis's point of view, necessary. "People are beginning to see clearly that their success is tied to the success of the school system," he says. "[But] our people are scared to death of change and what it might mean. . . . There is no clear vision of the future." Kotsakis worries about how to move ahead without leaving the membership or the old trade union types — conservative and change-resistant — behind. He says almost wistfully that there is no "rump group of radicals in the union thinking about how it might be organized," a role he played in the 1960s.

NOTE ON FIELD INVESTIGATION

William Ayers has lived with Chicago school reform for much of the last five years. Much of the historical progression derives from this experience. In addition, he carried out interviews with union leaders, principals, and LSC members. Charles Kerchner assisted with additional administration and union interviews conducted in March 1992.

REFERENCES

Consortium on Chicago School Research. (1992). *Charting Reform: The Teachers' Turn*. Chicago: Author.

Designs for Change. (1985). *The Bottom Line: Chicago's failing schools and how to save them*. Chicago: Author.

Grimshaw, W. (1979). *Union Rule in the Schools*. Lexington, MA: Lexington Books, D.C. Heath.

Herrick, M. J. (1971). *The Chicago schools: A social and political history*. Beverly Hills: Sage.

Hess, G. A., Jr. (1991). *School restructuring, Chicago style*. Newbury Park, CA: Corwin Press.

Hess, G. A., Jr., & Lauber, D. (1985). *Dropouts from the Chicago public schools*. Chicago Panel on Public School Policy and Finance.

Murphy, M. (1990). *Blackboard unions: The AFT and the NEA, 1900–1980*. Ithaca, NY: Cornell University Press.

Peterson, P. E. (1976). *School politics Chicago style*. Chicago: University of Chicago Press.

Staff. (1988). *Chicago schools: Worst in America?* Chicago: Chicago Tribune.

11

Getting Started

A PRIMER ON PROFESSIONAL UNIONISM

Julia E. Koppich

In the first chapter, we introduced the concept of professional union-ism. The chapters that followed described the districts in which we see the outlines of professional unionism beginning to emerge. In this concluding chapter, we briefly revisit the underlying principles of pro-fessional unionism. We then turn to an exploration of the essential preconditions that must be present or, more likely, conditions that unions and districts must create, as they begin down the road toward professional unionism.

THE OUTLINE OF PROFESSIONAL UNIONISM: A RECAP

Professional unionism represents a radical departure from the clas-sic industrial-style unionism that has characterized American education labor relations for nearly three decades. At its core, professional union-ism is anchored in three mutually reinforcing tenets: joint custody of reform, union-management collaboration, and concern for the public interest. Each of these principles of the emergent unionism breaks with tradition, giving a different cast and a new shape to the organizations that embrace them.

First, under the umbrella of professional unionism, union and management begin to assume joint custody of reform structures and procedures. Change efforts are not the personal province of the union or the district; risk and reward are equally shared. Rochester's account-ability system and Pittsburgh's instructional cabinets are at least as much "owned" by the union as by the district. Credit and blame for success or failure are mutually acknowledged and mutually accepted.

Second, although approaches may differ, collaboration becomes the new labor relations mantra. Some districts employ the "win-win" bargaining strategies developed by the Harvard Negotiation Project. Others use a more informal, less structured approach. But the result is the same. The "we-they" mentality that commonly characterizes industrial-style labor relations gives way to working, collegial union-management teams. Negotiations become a continuous set of ongoing problem solving sessions in which union leaders and administrators are able to lay their organizational cards on the table and work toward resolution of mutually identified education issues. As Rochester's Adam Urbanski notes, with characteristic frankness, "We don't play the same game anymore."

Collaboration for the union does not mean co-optation or capitulation. The union maintains its organizational identity. But it is able to make its points, assert itself, and gain a professional advantage for its members in ways other than ritual saber rattling or actual concerted action.

The manifestation of the third tenet of professional unionism is perhaps the most significant. As industrial unionism begins to give way to professional unionism, the union as an organization begins to develop and promote a new balance of rights and obligations. The commonwealth of the institution of education and the welfare of the school district become the union's concern.

Professional unions begin to link strength with professional responsibility. When Pittsburgh union leader Al Fondy says, "The union shares responsibility for assuring the effectiveness, stability, and long-term viability of the institution or enterprise in which its members are employed," he is widening the scope of the union's obligation to its members and to the entire school community.

"Representing the interests of members" is thus redefined. The new union seeks not only to secure a set of minimal work rule parameters for its members, but also to engage its members in conscious thought about ways in which their professional actions impact on their public responsibility.

Unions are initiating discussions around issues of quality: What is good teaching? What is a good education? In many instances, it is the union that is attempting to reestablish the public trust in education by redefining its interest as the public interest.

These three overarching principles—joint custody of reform, union-management collaboration, and a concern for the public interest—provide the framework for emerging professional unionism. We turn now to a consideration of the necessary precursors to this form of organization.

GETTING STARTED

We believe there are four essential preconditions requisite to a union and school district moving down the road toward professional unionism. These conditions are the essential precursors to change. The four, each of which will be described in turn, are:

1. Understanding that change is not an option.
2. Keeping the politics at bay.
3. Moving beyond anger.
4. Believing the necessity of an expanded professional role for teachers.

Understanding that Change Is Not an Option

Moving toward professional unionism involves the pain of unlearning old values and behaviors and the discomfort of working in ambiguous situations where the division of authority is unclear and solutions to problems are largely unknown. Only desperate people will do this. The people we watched were desperate to make public education work. Each of them knew that their schools were going to undergo large changes. Each of them had read the demographic, political, and social signals to mean that *their* schools would face radical change *whether or not they led them toward change.* If they did not lead, change would be thrust upon them from the outside.

The belief that change is inevitable is very liberating. It allows leaders to depart from seeing themselves as defenders of the status quo and defenders of their own status. They can come to believe that the existing organization of *their* schools, not just schools in general, is fundamentally flawed.

Even given the belief that change is inevitable, managers and union leaders differ widely in the size and speed of the steps they take. In Louisville, they created the phrase "little tries," and in many places the first steps in change were quite modest, but the view has always been that small changes empower people toward bigger risks. In Miami, they have attempted to create islands of radical experimentation, but much of the district is relatively unchanged.

Keeping the Politics at Bay

Professional unionism cannot grow in permanently contested terrain. Schools need a cushion for change, a zone of tolerance within which experimentation can occur. Unions and districts thus need to develop strategies that keep both internal and external politics at bay.

Paradoxically, flexibility, discovery, and experimentation in the schools and classrooms require stability at the top of the organization. Rapid turnover among school superintendents and other school executives, tension and split votes on the school board, and angry, vocal parent groups signal teachers and principals that they make changes at their own peril. In one school district, whose case is not related in this volume, teachers and administrators worked for several years to develop affective values in their schools. Characteristics of honesty and caring took a place in the curriculum. A model family life curriculum was put in place that combined discussions of values with those involving procreation. In the midst of these events, religious fundamentalists were elected to the school board, and a rump group of dissatisfied teachers sought to bring in a different union. Little happened on the reform agenda for several years.

If schools and teachers are to be given the flexibility to experiment, they also need the freedom to take risks and permission to fail without having their efforts publicly criticized or scrutinized. And they must be insulated from shifting political winds that pull them in one reform direction and then another.

The schools in our study that have taken the greatest leaps, engaged in the most far-reaching changes, are those that have been protected from politics. It is notable that many of the districts in this study have had superintendents whose tenure has been several times the 2.5 years that is now the average for urban school chiefs. Many have school boards whose membership is internally non-conflictual and whose turnover is not large. And all of them have stable teacher unions in terms of reform values and often in terms of leadership. Indeed, one of the values of unions as reform partners is that unions are relatively stable organizations.

However, this does not mean that educational reform is apolitical. Quite to the contrary. But the process of reform in schools and classrooms occurs best *during* what we have called a labor relations generation, when the battle over the appropriateness of rearranging work and decisions in schools along professional lines has already been fought (Kerchner & Mitchell, 1988). Under these conditions, the union and district consciously have tried to designate school reform as the object of common interest, the object of civic pride and general support. We should hasten to add that these conditions do not appear to hold in many communities, including many in our study.

How have the districts we have studied attempted to insulate schools from the distractions of politics? First, districts and unions together have worked to build community-wide coalitions in support of school change. Parents, business leaders, and often the media have been brought consciously into the change process early.

In Louisville, the superintendent forged a coalition with the business community. In San Diego, a blue-ribbon, largely elite community commission met and developed ideas about schools of the future. Cincinnati's business community, which maintained a working relationship with the teachers' union, powerfully intervened to restructure the schools following the general direction established by the union and district in two labor contracts. Pittsburgh used a goal-setting process with the community and the school board to set general directions. Rochester involved both the business community and the larger political community. In Miami the Dade County Chamber of Commerce was instrumental in cementing relations between schools and business.

As Hill (1989) and others have found, too, wide involvement creates a mandate for change that then partially insulates the change process from being picked apart. In each of the districts we studied, a community coalition was present at the beginning. And it was present as a partner, not as a sidelines player. That involvement leads to the second strategy designed to make reform "safe."

Districts must involve community actors in the substance rather than just the symbol of change. The business community in Rochester has not been simply a fiscally potent window dressing for reform efforts, but has participated, in the form of Rochester BrainPower, in substantive work of organizational change.

Involving outsiders in district operations is a difficult change for schools, long accustomed to relatively closed operations. Conceptually, opening the schools to continuing external influence appears as a contradiction with our major point about holding politics at bay. But direct participation within the framework of a reform agenda appears to strengthen rather than lessen the political coalition around the schools.

Historically, community involvement would appear to be at odds with the professionalization we see occurring. Professionalism has customarily been defined as worker hegemony over the client. However, ideas about profession are also changing. Those whom Schön (1983) describes as reflective practitioners no longer have a knowledge monopoly. From the perspective of client or recipient of services, I join "with the professional in making sense of my case, and in doing this I gain a sense of increased involvement and action" (p. 302).

Instrumental involvement in the fundamentals of reform is also an essential element in building parent support for change. While only a small number of parents can be involved in school district affairs as members of organized interest groups, virtually all parents can focus their concern on their children's particular schools. The schools we visited were increasingly comfortable with parents as partners in providing education for their children.

All of the districts in our study are engaged in site-based management to some degree. Parents are included on the school-based decision making teams. They are partners with teachers and administrators. The system, to be sure, is not perfect. Districts continue to experience difficulty involving parents in ongoing school-based meetings. And some site councils have found themselves drowning in the minutiae of governance. But the goal remains to keep people involved and informed, insiders rather than outsiders.

Community coalitions and substantive involvement by parents and community leaders, then, are two strategies designed to give the larger public a stake in reform and thus diminish the impulse to agitate politically against unclear or unexplained change. These strategies ameliorate the possibility of external political exigencies moving organizational change efforts off track. But what about internal politics: what steps have been taken to hold internal politics separate from reform?

First, strategies were developed in each district to block people who were not in favor of reform. Administrators who opposed change, for example, were reassigned or encouraged to resign. Miami, Pittsburg, Rochester, and several other cities experienced a higher-than-normal turnover rate among principals after wide-spread teacher involvement contracts were negotiated. By word and deed, superintendents discouraged those who would sabotage reform plans. In one district where several veteran high school principals were moved from their posts, the word flashed through the school grapevine that "the rocks of Gibraltar" had moved. In most cases, early participation in school site reforms was voluntary, and thus early opposition was blunted because the most vocal opponents were not being forced to participate.

Unions had a more difficult time restraining opponents, and union meetings in several cities were described as spirited. Because union officers are elected, they frequently had to put their positions and political skills on the line. They faced electoral challenges and generally won.

Finally, internal political actors figuratively made a pact to cease the public bickering. School board members developed new norms of public civility (even if in private disagreements were sometimes fierce).

Union-management public displays of hostility were kept to a minimum.

This last point, about quelling the publicly expressed antagonism, leads to the third precondition for professional unionism.

Moving Beyond Anger

Industrial-style unionism is organized around anger — workers' anger about the conditions under which they labor, which often manifests itself as antipathy for the employer. When this system is applied to education, administrators become the classic "they" to teachers' "we."

But if one lesson is to be taken from the experience of the districts we studied, it is that progress toward professional unionism cannot occur in an atmosphere of continual hostility. In part, the need to move beyond anger is linked to the first necessary precondition, creating a safe haven for reform. The public has little tolerance and less appetite for the continuation of what they often perceive to be petty internecine warfare. If school change has the prospect of being insulated from politics, then the parties must learn to deal with one another in a professional manner. Anger must give way to a willingness to work together, conflictual labor-management relations must be replaced by collaborative approaches to problem solving.

Replacing conflict with cooperation does not mean that the superintendent and union president must develop warm personal relations. Pointed verbal exchanges still occur along with public disagreements about issues. Most of the relationships we witnessed could be termed cordial but proper.

Moving beyond anger also does not mean that labor-management disagreement ends. But it does mean the fighting is no longer personalized. The union president and superintendent do not engage in name-calling and personal attacks. The union does not release flyers calling for the superintendent's resignation. The superintendent does not malign the union leadership in the press. Bickering remains in-house. And when trouble is aired in public, both union and management take pains to paint the issues as differences of principled positions, not differences of personalities.

Moreover, the two sides never stop talking with one another, no matter how stormy the seas become. They continue to seek peaceful ways to settle disagreements. Rochester is a case in point. Even at Rochester's lowest ebb, when recommended contract settlements had been rejected by the school board and by the teachers, Peter McWalters and Adam Urbanski kept the dialogue going.

Finally, while union and management continue to have areas of disagreement, battle lines are drawn over different issues. Educational concerns take center stage. Battles are waged over systems of accountability and peer review.

This new approach requires some changes in strategy, particularly for the union. Traditional troop rallying is no longer a viable tactic. The parties must be convinced—and must convince their respective constituents—that issues can be solved, even contracts settled, without the traditional saber rattling.

This new approach also means that the union must be in a strong position organizationally, and that the union leader must occupy a secure political position. Union members still want the union to be "their" organization, to represent them personally in their struggles with management. Thus, union leaders must tread a careful path between advocating grand strategies for reform and continuing to care about and work on individual teachers' problems. The example of Greece, New York's Richard Bennett is particularly instructive here.

Believing the Necessity of Teacher Professionalism

Finally, for professional unionism to begin to take root, management and union must believe in greatly expanded professional roles for teachers. Those who believe in a centralized web of controlling rules simply cannot do professional unionism.

At least one implication of this precondition for professional unionism is that school boards and superintendents must exercise leadership and send the right messages to district administrators. Much of the initial resistance to reform we encountered has been generated by administrators, particularly administrator associations. Site administrators, themselves held on short leashes by superintendents, rules and mandates, express fear that teachers are usurping what little running room they have left. As former Miami-Dade associate superintendent Frank Petruzielo put it, "No one has given them a reason to buy in." In Miami and elsewhere, districts have tried to provide a balance of carrots and sticks, but the transition from authoritarian to participative leadership is difficult.

Central office administrators have been among the most ardent foes of organizational change and are particularly difficult to move off dead center. Rochester superintendent Peter McWalters lamented, "I can't seem to get central office to stop acting like central office. I hold a meeting on decentralized decision making and they turn it into an edict."

Thus, it is incumbent on district leaders who desire to move down a path toward professional unionism to reorient administrative expectations about appropriate roles for themselves and for their teacher colleagues.

The admonition to believe in an expanded role for teachers applies equally to the union. Professional unions, and their teacher members, must be willing to assume roles that fly in the face of conventional unionism.

Teachers must assume an obligation to be active partners in the development of educational policy. They must be willing to tackle thorny issues of colleague competence and resource allocation. They must struggle to come to terms with the definition of good teaching and with important issues of quality — how to measure it, how to achieve it, and how to retain it.

The union as an organization must be prepared to "let go" of standardized and centralized work rules. Union structure often mirrors the bureaucratic organization of school districts. As such, unionization develops its own web or rules and procedures. Historically, these have focused on standardization across schools partly to avoid deviation by weak or ineffectual teachers or domination by strong principals. Deviation from standard rules was associated with favoritism and particularism.

One form of centralized rules is the collectively bargained contract. The contract typically establishes the parameters of teachers' relationships to their employer and to their profession. The union, through the collectively bargained contract, defines teachers' professional roles. Yet if professional unionism is to flower, one-size-fits-all contractual provisions cannot continue to be the sole written arbiters of professional conditions and obligations. Teachers must be afforded the freedom to exercise professional judgment in the spirit of what is best for students.

None of the districts in our study has abandoned collective bargaining or the contract. But nearly all have made provisions for school-based agreements that stray from the standardized collectively bargained agreement. Trust agreements and waivers, or similar extra-contract agreements, provide the flexibility that expanded professional roles for teaching, and serious engagement in organizing schools for teaching and learning, require.

DOES PROFESSIONAL UNIONISM MATTER?

Getting started on the road to professional unionism, then, requires teachers' unions and school district leaders to establish the text for change. The initial pages of that text revolve around a set of precursors to organizational reform: believing that change is required, not optional; developing strategies designed to hold both internal and external politics at bay; moving beyond anger to productive labor-management relations; and believing in the rightness of greatly expanded professional roles for teachers.

The thoughtful reader might reasonably ask at this point, "So what? Why does professional unionism — its development or disappearance — matter?"

We believe it matters because professional unionism is fundamentally about education reform. We do not think that it is possible to make much change in schools and schooling without it. This new unionism — flexible, responsive, and public spirited — offers the prospect of altering teaching work and thereby changing schools.

Professional unionism enables teachers to take positive action, to decouple from the bureaucracy, create flexible programs, and make significant changes for their students. In essence, professional unionism allows teachers to invent situations in which they can be responsive to their clients. In so doing, it also "ratchets up" the need for high quality professionals who are capable of employing expertise to solve educational problems. Expertise, linked to public responsibility, becomes a first principle of union organizing and educational reform.

Professional unionism encourages teachers to tackle issues of school productivity and effectiveness. It places the union in a position of helping to solve educational problems as it expands the charter of labor-management relations. Collaboration replaces conflict. Ownership of change is shared. Policy bargaining begins to replace a focus on self-interest and self-protection. Most significantly, perhaps, the public interest — what is good for students — come to the fore.

Professional unionism is not, we believe, a temporary or politically expedient tactic. It is not simply another variation on the cooperative labor-management relations theme. Rather, professional unionism is about a new way of doing business.

In the end, the development of professional unionism is about building the capacity of professionals within an organization to diagnose and solve complex problems and to change systems. It is also about building the capacity of the union to become the organization that speaks for teaching as well as for teachers.

Many teachers, administrators, scholars, and unionists have echoed the sentiment that creating a community of professionals is a prerequisite to reshaping American education. None said it better than John Kotsakis of the Chicago Teachers' Union who noted, "It is essential for us to understand that the union empowers teachers collectively in areas for which there is general consensus: salaries, benefits and so forth."

He continues, "There is another kind of empowerment that teachers need. That is the need to feel that what they do is important and makes a difference. In essence teachers have to feel they are part of a successful enterprise which is going somewhere and doing something. They have to experience success right where they work. . . . "

"Only they can be successful at what they do."

REFERENCES

Hill, P. T., Wise, A. E., & Shapiro, L. (1989). *Educational progress: Cities mobilize to improve their schools*. Santa Monica: RAND Center for the Study of the Teaching Profession.

Kerchner, C. T., & Mitchell, D. (1988). *The changing idea of a teachers' union*. New York: Falmer Press.

Schön, D. A. (1983). *The reflective practitioner*. New York: Basic Books.

Technical Publications

Project V•I•S•I•O•N has issued a series of technical and case studies on which this book is based. These include:

Anthony M. Cresswell, *Greece Central School District: Bridging the Brink*.
James Gallagher and Perry Lanier, *Toledo: Peer Review and Beyond*.
Susan T. Holderness, *Site-Based Management and Consensus Decision-Making in Albuquerque*.
Charles Taylor Kerchner, *Louisville: Professional Development Drives a Decade of School Reform*.
Charles Taylor Kerchner, *Pittsburgh: Reform in a Well Managed Public Bureaucracy*.
Charles Taylor Kerchner and Julia E. Koppich, *Professional Unions for 21st Century Schools*.
Charles Taylor Kerchner, Julia E. Koppich, and Byron King, *Smart Work & Smart Workers: The Complex Change from Bureaucratic to Professional Leadership in Public Education*.
Byron King, *Cincinnati: Betting on an Unfinished Season*.
Julia E. Koppich, *The Rocky Road to Reform in Rochester*.
Betty Malen, *Bellevue: Renewal and School Decision Making*.
Lani Martin, *Innovative Labor Relations Practices in U.S. Public Schools*.
Michael J. Murphy, *School Reform and Labor Relations — Denver Style*.
Mark Nichols, *Chelsea, Massachusetts: An Unequal Partnership*.
LeRae Phillips, Charles Taylor Kerchner, Byron King, and Julia E. Koppich, *Miami: After the Hype*.
Mark A. Smylie, *Glenview, Illinois: From Contract to Constitution*.
Mark A. Smylie and Ute Tuermer, *Hammond, Indiana: The Politics of Involvement v. The Politics of Confrontation*.

These and subsequent reports may be ordered from the project: Claremont Project V•I•S•I•O•N, Center for Educational Studies, The Claremont Graduate School, 150 E. Tenth Street, Claremont, CA 91711-6160. Telephone 910-621-8075.

About the Authors

Charles Taylor Kerchner is professor at The Claremont Graduate School in Southern California where he directs the program in educational leadership. He has studied teacher unionism for more than a decade, and is the coauthor of *The Changing Idea of a Teachers' Union* (Falmer Press, 1988) and numerous articles and book chapters.

Before coming to Claremont in 1976, Kerchner was on the faculty at Northwestern University, where he received his Ph.D., and was a member of the Illinois Board of Higher Education. He also served on the staff of the *St. Petersburg (Florida) Times* in a number of editorial and managerial positions. He holds a B.S. and an M.B.A. from the University of Illinois at Urbana.

Julia E. Koppich is deputy director of Policy Analysis for California Education at the University of California at Berkeley. She previously served in a staff position with the California legislature, worked as a classroom teacher, and was staff director for the American Federation of Teachers in San Francisco.

Koppich earned a bachelor's degree in political science at the University of California at Davis and an M.A. and Ph.D. in educational policy analysis at the University of California at Berkeley. Her research interests focus on the politics of education, public sector labor relations, and the politics of school reform. She is also a founding partner of Management Analysis and Planning Associates, an independent consulting firm specializing in organizational analysis and development.

* * *

William Ayers is associate professor of education at the University of Illinois at Chicago. He is author of *The Good Preschool Teacher* (Teachers College Press, 1989) and the forthcoming *To Teach: The Journey of a Teacher* (Teachers College Press), and coeditor of *Teacher Lore* (Longman, 1992). He served as assistant to the deputy mayor for education for one year (1989–90) and chaired an activist coalition, the Alliance for Better Chicago Schools, from 1989 to 1991.

Krista D. Caufman is a doctoral student in the Center for Politics and Policy at The Claremont Graduate School. She holds a bachelor's degree in economics from the Colorado College, where she was a Boettcher Scholar and winner of the Curren Award. Her research interests include educational reform, the intersection of law and policy, and the role of experts in a democracy. She is presently conducting a study of parent involvement in schools in Santa Ana, California.

Anthony M. Cresswell is professor of education at the State University of New York at Albany. He is the coauthor of *Teachers, Unions, and Collective Bargaining in Public Education* (McCutchan) and *Education and Collective Bargaining* (McCutchan). Cresswell is currently involved in international development work in education concentrating in Asia and Africa. He received his doctorate from Teachers College, Columbia University.

James J. Gallagher is professor of science education at Michigan State University and codirector of an NSF-funded project, "Using Assessment in the Service of Teaching and Learning in Middle School Mathematics and Science." He and Perry Lanier direct the MSU/AFT/Toledo Public Schools Support Teacher Program. Gallagher received his B.A. and M.A. at Colgate University, his M.S.T. at Antioch College, and his Ph.D. at Harvard University. His research interests include science teachers' thinking, the ecology of secondary school science teaching and learning, and the professional development of secondary science teachers.

Byron King is a mathematics teacher at O'Farrell Community School (grades 6 to 8) in the San Diego Unified School District. O'Farrell has no vice-principals or school counselors; those responsibilities are divided among the teachers. Based on this experience, King coauthored "Is Restructuring a Threat to Principals' Power?" for the *NASSP Bulletin*. King is in the Joint Doctoral Program in Education through The Claremont Graduate School and San Diego State University. His research is on the changing role of principals in the context of restructuring.

Perry Lanier is a senior researcher in the Institute for Research on Teaching at Michigan State University. His recent field research includes the General Mathematics Study and the Middle Grades Mathematics Study at SMU, Summer Math for Teachers Study at Mt. Holyoke, and the IRT/AFT Toledo Support Teachers Project. He also directs the Academy Learning Program, an alternative teacher education program at MSU, and is involved in the school/university partnership to create professional development schools.

LeRae Phillips has been involved in school reform for the past two decades as a facilitator and teacher in compensatory education and school improvement programs. Her current research focuses on the professional growth and change processes of experienced teachers in school and district contexts. She is a program facilitator in the Long Beach Unified School District, and a staff associate in the teacher education program of The Claremont Graduate School, where she is a doctoral student.

Mark A. Smylie is associate professor of education at the University of Illinois at Chicago and a former classroom teacher. He received his Ph.D. in Educational Leadership from Vanderbilt University and his M.Ed. and B.A. from Duke University. Smylie's research focuses on school organization and leadership, teacher learning and work redesign, and their relationships to the improvement of classroom instruction. He also studies organizational issues related to the development and implementation of coordinated children's services.

Index